THE
𝕃𝕒𝕨𝕤 concerning 𝔾𝕒𝕞𝕖.

Of *Hunting, Hawking, Fishing* and *Fowling,
&c.* And of Forefts, Chafes, Parks, Warrens, Deer, Doves, Dove-cotes, Conies:

And alfo of

Setting-dogs, Grey-hounds, Lurchers, Nets, Tunnels, Lowbels, Guns, and all Manner of Engines
and Inftruments mentioned in the feveral Statutes
to deftroy the *Game;* fhewing who are qualified
by Law to keep and ufe them, and the Punifh-
ments of thofe who keep them, not being qualified. Likewife the proper Seafons allowed by
Act of Parliament for Hunting, Fifhing and
Fowling.

Together with the Foreft Laws:

Shewing the Method of Chufing, and Oaths of the
refpective Officers; and the Authority, Power
and Duty of *Chief Juftice in* Eyre, *Clerks of the
Peace, Conftables, Forefters, Game-keepers, Juftices
of Peace, Keepers, Lords of Manors, Parkers,
Rangers, Regarders, Sheriffs, Stewards of Foreft
Courts, Stewards of Leets, Verderors, Wardens*
and *Woodwards.*

By *William Nelfon* of the *Middle-Temple,* Efq;

To which are now added,

Englifh Forms of *Convictions, Declarations, Indictments, Juftifications, Licences, Mittimus's, Pleas,
Warrants,* &c. Digefted under proper Titles, in
an Alphabetical Order.

𝕿𝖍𝖊 𝕾𝖎𝖗𝖙𝖍 𝕰𝖉𝖎𝖙𝖎𝖔𝖓, with all the Acts of Parliament and Cafes in Print, and alfo a large Col-
lection of Manufcript Cafes, down to the prefent
Time.

LONDON: Printed by *E. Richardfon* and *C. Lintot,* Law-
Printers to the King's moft Excellent Majefty; for *T.
Waller,* oppofite *Fetter-Lane, Fleet-Street,* 1762.

THE
PREFACE.

AS Ignorance of the Law excuseth no Man*, therefore it is absolutely necessary for every Person to be well acquainted with the Laws of ENGLAND concerning the Game; for there are scarce any Laws of this Kingdom that require to be more universally known; all Ranks from the Peer to the Peasant, not being exempted from Punishment for the Breach of them; on which Account the Revisor of this Edition has endeavoured to shew, what is accounted Game in the Eye of the Law, their Proceeds and Seasons of Hunting, &c.

* Ignorantia juris non excusat.

what

The PREFACE.

what are the proper Receptacles for the
Game; what Officers peculiarly belong
to such Receptacles; the Manner of
Choosing or Appointing them, their
Oaths and Duties in their respective
Posts, and how far their Power and
Authority extends; who shall be ac-
counted Offenders; to whom it belongs
to punish such Offenders, and how and
in what Manner to proceed against
and punish them, either in the Forest-
Courts or otherwise.

 In this Edition are contained the
Forms of Original Writs, Informations, Indictments, Convictions, Declarations, Pleas, Justifications, Warrants, Mittimus's, Commissions, De-
putations, Licences, Notices, and other
Precedents and Proceedings, *(relating*
to the Game in General) more than in
the former Editions, and the Statutes
(which are the Foundation of such Pro-
      ceedings)

The PREFACE.

ceedings) down to the Present Time
are immediately referred to before
each Precedent, which must make this
Edition still more useful and satis-
factory to the Reader.

And whereas several Obsolete
Words are made use of in the ensuing
Treatise, the Revisor of this Edition
has explained them in the following
Work, in proper Order, that the Reader
may the better understand the Forest
Laws, and the Nature of their Courts.
The Statute Law concerning the Game;
the Cases, Resolutions and Judgments
in the Assises, Iters, and Courts of Record at Westminster, down to the present Time, are here particularly and
carefully added; in short, the present
Laws of the Game are freely and
clearly Treated of in this little Tract,
and the whole System divided into several Titles, in an Alphabetical Order;

a most

The PREFACE.

a moſt approved Method for the ready
finding any Thing in a Book, whereby
the Reader may at once ſatisfy himſelf in his Inquiry without turning over
the voluminous Works in which the
Laws of this Nature promiſcuouſly
lie diſperſed.

THE

THE

INTRODUCTION.

BEFORE I treat of the feveral Laws relating to the Game, it may be neceffary to mention fomething of the Original and Growth of the grand Receptacles of the Game, which are the *Forefts in Great Britain.*

'To begin with the Time of the *Britons,* when their Princes and great Lords had no Occafion to fet apart Places for the Prefervation of Game and Beafts of Venary, (their Bruery, *i. e.* Thickets and uncultivated Lands, being fuch Nurferies and Shelter for them), it was the Intereft of both Princes and Lords rather to deftroy than preferve them.

a

During

During the Wars between the *Britons*
and *Saxons*, so many of the *Britons* were
killed, and so many fled from the conquering
Saxons, that the cultivated Lands were
more than sufficient to maintain the Con-
querors and the miserable *Britons* who
staid amongst them; for at that Time
there were no foreign Markets where
the *Saxons* traded with the Produce of
their Lands. When the *Saxons* found
themselves Masters of the *British* Lands
and People, the *Saxon* Captains, as Con-
querors, in Common Council agreed to
divide the Lands they had taken amongst
themselves, their Friends and Companions
in Conquest. The Woods, Wastes, and
Bruery Lands, that were not appropriated
to any particular Persons, remained to the
Chief Captain, who in Process of Time
assumed the Title of King, who, as Occasion
offered, granted Parcels of such Woods to
whom he thought fit.

Of

On this Succeſs of the *Saxons* in *Britain,* their hungry half-ſtarved Friends and Relations ſwarmed out of the *German* Hive, to ſuck the ſweets of our Iſland; Multitudes coming over Time after Time, more and more uſeleſs Woods were appropriated and improved; and as Improvements were made, the Game and Beaſts of Venary retired from thence for Shelter into the unfrequented Woods; whither the *Saxon* Kings, that took Delight in Hunting, went for their Diverſion, where was ſuch Plenty of Game, that there was no Occaſion for reſtraining Laws to preſerve them. Theſe Royal unimproved Woods are the Foreſts pointed at by Sir *Edward Coke* in his 4 *Inſt.* 319; who ſays, they are ſo ancient as no Record or Hiſtory doth make any Mention of any of their Beginnings.

Whilſt the ravenous Beaſts of Prey were ſo numerous in the Royal Woods, as to prevent the Increaſe of the Beaſts

of

of delicious Tafte for the Table, the Kings gave free Liberty to the Nobility and Gentry to hunt in their Woods; but in *Edgar's* Time, the Breed of ravenous Beafts being much leffened, he having an elegant Tafte prohibited Hunting his Deer, and appointed Officers to preferve all Game of the Table, in his Woods, who fo rigoroufly put in Execution their Orders, that the Nobility and Gentry were prevented of taking their Diverfions and their Tenants of their refpective Rights: At length this arbitrary Procedure of the Officers grew to fo great a Grievance, that Noblemen, Gentlemen and Farmers, made great Complaints for Want of a Law to afcertain the King's Prerogative and the People's Privilege in this Cafe; on which King *Canute*, through his innate Goodnefs and Juftice, in a Parliament holden at *Winchefter* in 1016, brought the Proceedings to a Certainty, that all Men might know what they fhould, and fhould not do, by publifhing Foreft Laws, therein fetting out the Bounds of his Forefts, and limiting the

the Power of the Foreſt Officers. *Man-wood* 401. 8o. ſays, they were firſt pen-ned in the *Daniſh* Language: but Lord *Coke* in his 4 *Inſt.* 320. ſays, *Canute* never publiſhed any Law for *England* in the *Daniſh* Tongue, and by the Tranſlation of them it may be fairly conjectured they were originally penned in *Saxon*, from the *Saxon* Words retained, and not by the Tranſlator turned into *Latin*; which ſhews he was neither Maſter of the *Saxon* Lan-guage or Character: For Inſtance, he miſtaking ƿ for a *Roman* P. makes *Pegan*, (and leaves it untranſlated, which is neither *Saxon* nor *Daniſh*,) inſtead of ꝥeᵹen a *Thane*, and *Leſſpegend* he puts inſtead of *Leſthegan*, again miſtaking the *Saxon* ƿ for a *Roman* P, &c.

The *Saxon* Kings and the *Daniſh* King *Canute* made no new Foreſts, but were contented with the Woods that were their own Demeſnes, and were never granted to, or poſſeſſed by the Subject; but the Kings of the *Norman* Race, not

being

being fatisfied with fixty-eight old Demefne Woods or Forefts, depopulated well-built Towns and Villages, to make to themfelves Places appropriated to their own Diverfion only.

William the Conqueror laid wafte thirty-fix Towns in *Hampfhire* to make a Foreft, which ftill retains the Name of the *New Foreft*; and his Foreft Officers, Mr. *Gurdon* fays in his Hiftory 113. exercifed fuch arbitrary Rule, as to abridge even the great Barons of the Privileges they enjoyed under the *Saxon* and *Danifh* Kings; not at all regarding the Liberties given to the Subject by *Canute's* Foreft Laws.

His Son *William Rufus* is recorded in Hiftory for the Severity of his Proceedings againft all that hunted in his Forefts; inflicting the Punifhment of Death upon fuch as killed a Stag or Buck in his Forefts, without any other Law than that of his own Will.

Henry

Henry I. and *Richard* I. were as arbitrary in this Cafe, as their Predeceffors, [following their Precedents] in punifhing Nobility and Gentry who hunted in the Royal Forefts, which was with the greateft Severity, *viz.* with the Lofs of *Eyes and Tefticles,* other Offences fineable at the Will of the King; fome were never to be pardoned, and no Perfon whatfoever was exempted from appearing at the Court of Juftice-Seat, upon a Summons of the Chief Juftice in *Eyre*; by which the People were grievoufly oppreffed by thofe perfonal Services they were bound to perform at thofe Courts in the Foreft.

In the Reign of King *John*, thefe and other Oppreffions, having exafperated the Barons, they took up Arms, and chofe *Robert Fitz-Walter* their General, and marched to *Northampton*, and by the Way of *Bedford* to *London*; from whence they fent Letters to the Earls, Barons and Knights

3   that

that adhered to the King, that if they would
not defert the perjured King, and join
with them in afferting their Liberties, they
would proceed againft them as publick
Enemies.

Thefe Threats drew from the King moft
of the Barons that had adhered to him,
which Defeftion left the King hopelefs,
and induced him to fend *William* Earl of
Pembroke and other faithful Meffengers
to let the confederated Barons know he
would grant them the Laws and Liberties
they defired : Upon which a Meeting of
King and Barons was agreed to be on the
fifteenth of *June* 1215, at *Running Mead*,
between *Stains* and *Windfor*, where a con-
ference began between the Barons that adhered to the King and the confederated
Barons, who were fo fuperior in Number
to the King's Barons, that he feemed to
make no Difficulty of granting the Laws
and Liberties demanded; which were
drawn up as the confederated Lords thought
fit, in two Charters, *viz.* The Great Charter,
                                              and

and the Charter of the Liberties and Cuſtoms of the Foreſt.

Henry III. in 1225, in the ninth Year of his Reign confirmed the Charter of Liberties and of the Foreſt under his Seal, and ſent one into each County of *England:* And this Charter was witneſſed by thirty-one Biſhops and Abbots, and by thirty-three Lay Barons ; in his fourth Parliament alſo Archbiſhop *Boniface* denounced a Curſe in *Weſtminſter-Hall,* in the Preſence of the King and ſeveral Biſhops and Noblemen, againſt thoſe who ſhould break this Charter ; and to add to the Solemnity, the Biſhops were apparelled in their *Pontificalibus,* and each held a lighted Taper in his Hand; and the Archbiſhop denounced the Excommunication in the following Words, *viz:*
" By the Authority of God the Father, the
" Son and the Holy Ghoſt, and of the Glo-
" rious Mother of God and perpetual Vir-
" gin *Mary,* and of the Bleſſed Apoſtles
" *Peter* and *Paul,* and of all the Apoſtles
" and Martyrs, of Bleſſed *Edward* King
" of *England,* and of all the Saints of Hea-
" ven,

" ven, we excommunicate, accurfe and
" from the Benefit of our Holy Mother the
" Church we fequefter all thofe, who hereaf-
" ter fhall violate, break, diminifh or change
" the free Cuftoms and Liberties granted
" in the *Charter of the Foreft*, by our Lord
" the King, to the Prelates, Earls, Barons,
" Knights, and other Freeholders of the
" Realm, and all who fecretly or openly by
" Deed, Word or Counfel fhall bring in
" Cuftoms, and keep them when brought
" in againft the faid Liberties, or any of
" them, and all thofe who fhall prefume to
" judge againft them; all and every which
" Perfons, that fhall willingly commit any
" of the Premiffes, let them know that
" they incur the aforefaid Sentence *ipfo*
" *facto*, and thofe who commit them igno-
" rantly ought to be admonifhed, and ex-
" cept they reform themfelves within fifteen
" Days after fuch Admonition, and make
" full Satisfaction for what they have done
" *at the Will of the Ordinary*, fhall be
" from thenceforth wrapped in the faid
" Sentence, to the perpetual Memorial of
                       " which

" which Thing we the aforefaid Prelates
" have put our Seals to thefe Prefents."
Thus the grievous Oppreffions, which the
Subjects of *England* then laboured under,
were remedied by this Charter, which the
Reader will fee under proper Heads in the
following TREATISE.

THE

THE

LAWS of ENGLAND

Concerning the

𝕲𝖆𝖒𝖊, &c.

ACtion, of Debt, &c. for *Pecuniary Pe-nalties* inflicted by the Game-Acts, may be brought in any Court of Record, by Stat. 8 *Geo.* 1. See Title 𝕲𝖆𝖒𝖊.

Action for killing of Game; upon Not Guilty, and Verdict for the Defendant, a new Trial was prayed, on Pretence that it was a Verdict against Evidence; for which the Plaintiff referred himself to the Notes of the Judge who tried the Cause. *Cur.* New Trials are not grantable in penal Actions. *Eafter* 4 *Geo.* 2. *Seymour, Qui tam,* and *Day, M. S. Rep.*

𝕬𝖌𝖎𝖋𝖋, Is derived from the *French* Word *Gifte, i. e.* a Bed or refting Place; whence to *Agift*, fignifies to take in and feed the Cattle of Strangers in the King's Foreft.

B.   The

The King's Demeſne Woods and Lands
muſt always be *agiſted* by his Foreſters, Verderors and Agiſtors. *Manwood* 3, 4.

Every Freeman by *Chart. Foreſtæ*, *Ar.* 9.
may *agiſt* his own Wood within the King's
Foreſt, at ſeaſonable Times; the Words of
the Act are ' at his Pleaſure', ſee **Swainmote**; but not with Goats or Sheep without
Licence. *Quia præbent exilium ferarum Foreſtæ*,
that is, *they ſo taint the Paſture where they feed,
that the Beaſts of the Foreſt will not depaſture
there; ſo that they do as it were baniſh them
from every Place where they are:* but he may
drive his Swine through the Demeſne Woods
for to *agiſt* them in his own; if the Swine lie
one Night within the Foreſt, no Treſpaſs; the
Agiſt of Swine is for the Pannage.

If a Man who dwelleth within the Foreſt,
and hath common in the Waſte, will take the
Beaſts of Strangers to *agiſt*, this is an Offence
fineable to the King. *Manwood* 6.

Agiſtment, Signifies the Herbage of Lands
or Woods, or the Money received, or due for
the ſame, and is of two Sorts, *i. e.* of the
Herbage of Woods, Lands, and Paſtures; and
of Woods alone, *viz.* of the Maſts of Trees,
properly called Pannage. *Manwood* 2.

Agiſtment is only for ſuch Beaſts as are Commonable, *Manwood* 3. but not for Geeſe, Goats
or Sheep.

Agiſtments muſt be inrolled in the Verderor's
Roll, which Roll muſt agree with the Agiſtor's
Account. *Ibid.* 4.

The

The Time of taking in *Agiftments* of all Manner of commonable Beafts, in the King's Demefne Woods and Lands, for Herbage only, doth begin fifteen Days before *Midfummer*, and ends on *Holy-Rood-Day*, 14th. *September* ; for Swine and Hogs to feed on the Maft, it begins on *Holy-Rood-Day*, and ends on the Feaft of St. *Martin*. *Ibid*. 7, 8. See the Table.

𝕬𝖌𝖎𝖘𝖙𝖔𝖗, Is an Officer that takes Beafts to depafture within the Foreft, and the Cattle which feed there are Levant and Couchant. He is conftituted by Letters Patent, and in Forefts where there is any Pannage (for where there are no Woods there are no *Agiftors*) there be four in Number. 4 *Inft*. 293.

He is to prefent Trefpaffes done by Cattle, *Manwood* 11.

The *Agiftors* alone are to receive the Money for Agiftments and Pannage. *Manwood* 5.

Every *Agiftor* in the King's Foreft muft bring before the Lord Chief Juftice in Eyre of the Foreft at the Juftice-Seat, a true and juft Account of what Money he hath received for any Agiftment or Pannage (*a*) of the King's Woods and Lands. *Ibid*. 4. and likewife the Profit of Rufhes, Fern, Gorfe, Sedge, &c. *Itin. Lanc. fol.* 8. *Manwood* 232.

If *Agiftors* fail of their Rolls and Accounts, they fhall be amerced and diftrained by their Lands to bring in the fame. *Ibid*. 333.

If he prefent any Thing which doth not belong to his Charge, the Prefentment is void

(*a*) The Time of Pannage begins on *Holy-Rood-Day*, and ends 40 Days after *Michaelmas*. *Manwood* 228, 230.

Ibid.

Ibid. 11. And therefore one *Finch* was fined 10 *l.* at the Juſtice-Seat for the Foreſt of *Windſor*, for making the *Agiſtors* preſent Things which did not belong to them. *W. Jones* 280. See *Table.*

Amerciament. See **Diſtreſs, Reeve.**

Appearance at the Chief Juſtice Seat.
Thoſe under the Age of Twelve, thoſe that are Sick or Blind, ſeventy Years of Age or upwards, thoſe employed in the Service of the King in any other Place, Archbiſhops, Biſhops, Earls and Barons, though they have Lands within the Foreſt, are not compellable to *appear* at the Time when the General Summons is made. *Manwood* 14.

But Archbiſhops, Biſhops, Earls, and other Noblemen, who claim any Liberties, Freedoms or Privileges within the Foreſt, muſt *appear* upon ſuch General Summons to claim the ſame : Otherwiſe ſuch Privileges, *&c.* will be ſeized into the King's Hands for Nonclaimer; but they need not *appear* in Perſon, but by Attorney. *Ibid. Vide* Table.

Apprentices. By Stat. 4 & 5 *W. & M.*
c. 23. ' If any inferior Tradeſman, *Apprentice*, or other diſſolute Perſon, neglecting his
' Trade and Employment, ſhall preſume to
' hunt, hawk, fiſh or fowl [unleſs in Com-
' pany with the Maſter of ſuch *Apprentice*,
' qualified by Law] ſhall be carried before a
' Juſtice of Peace, and being convicted before
' him upon Oath, ſhall forfeit not exceeding
' 20 *s.* nor under 5 *s.* to be aſcertained by the
' Juſtice, one Moiety to the Informer, and the
' other

' other to the Poor, &c. to be levied by Di-
' ftrefs and Sale, and for want of Diftrefs, fhall
' be committed to the Houfe of Correction not
' exceeding one Month, nor under Ten Days,
' there to be whipped and kept to hard Labour,
' and *may be fued and profecuted for wilful Tref-*
' *pafs in coming on other Perfon's Land ; and if*
' *found guilty, the Plaintiff fhall not only recover*
' *Damages, but his full Cofts of Suit.*'

Law Cafes.

It was held, that *Conviction* on the Stat. 4.
& 5 W. & M. c. 23. fhewing the Defendant
exiftens perfona diffoluta, &c. did hunt and kill
fo many Hares, &c. ought to be quafhed,
becaufe it did not fhew he was not qualified.
2 *Mod. Cafes* 40.

Note ; The Stat. 4 & 5 W. & M. c. 23.
makes an inferior Tradefman liable to *full
Cofts* for hunting in another's Ground, not-
withftanding his being *qualified* by an Eftate.
1 Ld *Raym.* 150. (*Vide* S. C. Tit. *Hunting.*
p.   .) Even tho' the *Jury give Damages* under 40 s. for this Statute, as to this Point of *inferior Tradefmen,* repeals the Stat. of 22 & 23
Car. 2. c. 9. which gives no more Cofts than
Damages, when the Jury give Damages under
40 s.

A. was convicted upon the Stat. of 4 & 5
W. & M. c. 23. for deftroying of Game, not
being a Perfon duly qualified. *A.* took feveral
Exceptions to the Conviction ; 1ft, That the
Information which was fet forth in the Convic-

tion

mon Perfon in the Regard of the Foreft, is bailable for the firft and fecond Offences, but not for the third : for in fuch Cafe his Body ſhall be imprifoned until he hath paid a Fine to the King, unlefs the Chief Juftice in Eyre will bail him as aforefaid ; and in both Cafes the Fine is arbitrary. *Manwood* 21, 22, 23. See *Table.*

Attachiamenta *de Spinis & Bofco.* A Privilege granted to the Officers of a Foreft, to take to their own Ufe, Thorns, Brufh and Windfall, within their own Precincts or Liberties.

Attachment. The Court of the *Attachments,* or the *Woodmote* Court, is one of the three Courts of the Foreft, and is to be kept before the Verderors every forty Days throughout the Year, and therefore is called the Forty-Day Court. At this Court the Forefters bring in the Attachments of Vert and Venifon, the Prefentment thereof, and the Verderors do receive the fame, and inroll them, but this Court can only Inquire, and not Convict : But it is to be obferved, that no Man ought to be attached by his Body for Vert or Venifon, unlefs he be taken in the very Fact within the Foreft, otherwife the *Attachment* muft be by his Goods. 4 *Inft.* 289. *Manwood* 23 to 32.

Badger. See **Fox.**

Bail. Trefpaffer in a Foreft committed to Prifon may be *bailed* upon giving fufficient Sureties to appear at the next Eyre ; if fuch *Bail* is refufed, he may in Term-Time move he Court of King's Bench for an *Habeas Cor-*
pus,

pus, which will be granted, or he may move the Court of Common Pleas or Exchequer (if privileged) or the Court of Chancery, either in or out of Term, and upon this Writ he may be *bailed* to appear at the next Eyre to be holden for the Foreſt. *Manwood* 34.

A Foreſter may detain a Man till he gets *Bail. Ibid.* 35. See *Table.*

Bailiff. (*Ballivus*) See **Conſtable.**

Barons. See **Appearance.**

Bedel, Is derived from a *Saxon* Word, ſignifying *to call or warn,* and is an Officer of the Foreſt, that doth warn all the Courts of the Foreſt, executes the Proceſs of the Foreſt, and makes all Proclamations as well within the Courts, as without. 4 *Inſt.* 313. *Manwood* 36.

Biſhop. See **Appearance.**

Boar, Is a Beaſt of the Foreſt, and is called the 1ſt Year a *Pig of the Sounder,* 2d, A *Hog,* 3d, A *Hog's Steer,* 4th, A *Boar,* and after a *Sanglier;* and in Seaſon from *Chriſtmas* till *Candlemas.* 4 *Inſt.* 316.

Boundary, Foreſts muſt be meered and bounded with Marks, Meers and *Boundaries,* which are Rivers, Highways, Hills, Churches, and ſuch like; and for want of ſuch *Boundaries,* great and remarkable Trees have been uſed for the ſame. And they are either known by Matter of Record, or by Preſcription; and though a Foreſt doth lie open, and not incloſed with Hedge, Ditch, Pale or Wall, yet in the Eye of the Law it hath as ſtrong an Incloſure by theſe Marks, Meers, and *Boundaries,* as if it were incloſed with a Wall. *Manwood* 37.

B 5. By

By Stat. 17 *Car* 1. *c.* 16. ' The Metes,
' Limits, Meers and *Boundaries* of all Forefts
' fhall be taken, adjudged and deemed to ex-
' tend no farther than they were commonly re-
' puted, known, *&c.* in the 20th of King
' *James.*'

It is abfolutely neceffary that every Officer
of the Parifh fhould know the *Boundaries, &c.*
For though by Stat. 21 *Ed.* 1. ' A Forefter,
' *&c.* fhall not be queftioned for killing a
' Trefpaffer who will not yield himfelf; yet
' in this Cafe the Limits of the Foreft are
' iffuable, becaufe the killing of the Offender
' within the Limits or without, makes it Fe-
' lony, or not. And alfo if a Man be pre-
' fented for killing a Beaft of the Foreft, if
' it was killed out of the Limits thereof, it
' may be no Offence againft the Foreft Laws.'
Manwood 40.

Bow-Bearer, An under Officer of the
Foreft, who is to make Inquifition of Trefpaffes done, either to Vert or Venifon, and
prefent the Offenders the next Court of Attachment.

Browfe, Are young Sprouts of Trees that
fhoot out early in the Spring.

Buck, Is the firft Beaft of Chafe, and is
called the firft Year a *Fawn,* fecond a *Pricket,*
third a *Sorel,* fourth *Sore,* fifth a *Buck of the
Head,* fixth a *Buck.* The Seafon begins at
Midfummer, and ends at *Holy-Rood-Day, viz.*
fourteenth of *September.*

An

An Indictment for chasing a *Buck* in the King's Forest with Wares.

Essex, *to wit.* THE *Jury for our Sovereign Lord the King upon their* Oath *present,. That* B. T. *late of* G. *in the County of* E. *Gentleman, the 30th Day of October in the seventh Year of the Reign, &c. the Forest of our said Lord the King, of* E. *in the said County of* E. *broke and entered, and one* Buck *to the Value of* 20 s. *then and there found, without Licence and Consent of the said Lord the King, with Grey-hounds hunted and chased, and the said* Buck *at* S. *within the Precincts of the Forest aforesaid, with Wares did hang and kill, and that Buck so hanged and killed unjustly took, and carried away, against the Peace of our Sovereign Lord the now King, his Crown and Dignity.*

A Warrant for a *Buck.*

To the Keeper of, *&c.*

UPON *Sight hereof, you are to kill and deliver to* R. C. *Esq; one fat* Buck *of this Season, for which this shall be your Warrant.*

Dated, *&c.* R: P.

Buckstalls, Are Toils to take Deer.

Certiorari. ' No *Certiorari* shall be al' lowed to remove any Conviction, or other ' Proceedings upon the *Stat.* 3 & 4 *W.* & *M.*

B 6 ' *c.* 10.

' *c.* 10. unlefs the Party, before the Allowance
' thereof, be bound to the Profecutor in 50*l.*
' with fuch Sureties as the Juftice fhall
' think fit, to pay in a Month after the Con-
' viction confirmed, or *Procedendo* granted, full
' Cofts and Damages to be afcertained upon his
' Oath, and at the fame time become alfo bound
' to the Juftice before whom fuch Conviction
' fhall be made, with fuch Sureties as the Juf-
' tice fhall approve of, in the Penalty of 60*l.*
' for each Offence, with Condition to profecute
' the *Certiorari* with Effect, and to pay fuch
' Juftice the Forfeitures due by the Conviction,
' to be diftributed as the faid Statute directs; or
' to render to the Juftice the Perfon convicted
' within one Month after the Conviction fhall
' be confirmed, or a *Procedendo* granted. And
' in Default thereof, the Juftice and all other
' Perfons whatfoever may proceed to execute
' fuch Conviction.' *Stat.* 3 & 4 *W.* & *M.*
c. 10. *f.* 6. 5 *Geo.* 1. *c.* 15. *f.* 1.

' And after delivering to the Juftice the Rule
' by which the Conviction fhall be confirmed,
' he may proceed, as if a *Procedendo* had been
' granted.' *Stat.* 5 *Geo.* 1. *c.* 15. *f.* 2. See the
Cafe of the King *v.* Whitlock, p. Tit.
Deer.

' *Certiorari* to remove a *Conviction* or other
' Proceedings before any Juftice of the Peace,
' or General or Quarter Seffions, to be applied
' for within Six Calendar Months, and upon
' Six Days Notice (upon Oath) to the Juftice or
' Juftices, to the End that the Juftices or the
' Parties concerned may fhew Caufe if they fo
' think

' think fit, againſt the Iſſuing of the *Certiora-ri*.' *Stat.* 13 G. 2. c. 18. ſ. 5.

' No Judgment or Order to be removed by
' *Certiorari* without Sureties found.' *Stat.* 5
G. 2. c. 19. ſ. 2.

Law Caſes.

Adjudged that a *Certiorari* ſhall not be allowed to remove a Preſentment by any Foreſter, for ſelling Wood, before Conviction at the
Swainmote; for if it ſhould, then the Courts
of the Foreſt would be deprived of their Juriſdiction. *The King* againſt *Maxis,* 2 Keb. 81.
Sid. 296.

The Defendant was convicted for ſtealing
Deer, and by Virtue of a Warrant, *&c.* a Diſtreſs was taken for the Forfeiture, and a *Certiorari* was afterwards brought to remove the Conviction into the King's Bench, and after *the Record was removed, the Conſtable ſold the Goods
which he had ſeized, and kept the Money,* and
would not return the Warrant, *&c.* And it
was held, that the Conſtable might proceed in
the Execution of the Warrant after the *Certiorari* was allowed, becauſe it was begun before;
and that the Writ was no more a *Superſedeas,*
than a Writ of Error was to ſtay an Execution
upon a *Fieri Facias already begun*; and that the
Court had no Power over this Warrant, becauſe
it was granted before the *Certiorari* iſſued; therefore they would make no Rule on the Conſtable to return the Warrant, but ſaid the Juſtices
might fine him if he did not return, or pay the
Mone

Money to the Profecutor. *The Queen* againft *Nafh*, 1 *Salk.* 147. See *Law Cafes*, Tit. **Deer.**

If a Motion be made for an Information againft a Juftice of Peace for an illegal Conviction, the Conviction muft be returned by *Certiorari* into the King's Bench. *The King* ver. *Heber*, by whom *A* was convicted *without Summons* for killing the Game.

Chase, (from *Chaffer*, to chafe), is a privileged Place for the Receipt of Deer, and Beafts of the Foreft, and is of a middle Nature betwixt a Foreft and a Park. It is commonly lefs than a Foreft, and not endowed with fo many Liberties, as Officers, Laws, Courts, &c. and yet is of a larger Compafs than a Park, having more Officers, *i. e.* Keepers, Woodwards and Game, than a Park. Every Foreft is a *Chafe*, but every *Chafe* is not a Foreft. It differs from a Park in that it is not inclofed; for if it is inclofed it is a good Caufe of Forfeiture, though it muft have certain Metes and Bounds. But it may be in other Men's Grounds as well as in one's own. It is not lawful to make a *Chafe*, Park or Warren, without Licence under the Broad Seal. *Wood's Inft.* 207. *Manw.* 49.

A *Chafe* is governed by the common Law, and fuch as were never Forefts cannot have any Purlieu. 4 *Inft.* 314, 303.

The Beafts of the *Chafe* are the *Buck*, *Doe*, *Fox*, and formerly the *Martern* and the *Roe*, which are not now in *England*. *Manw.* 50.

The Beafts of the *Chafe* frequent the Fields, Hills and Mountains in the Day-time, and the Vallies,

Vallies, Corn-fields and Meadows in the Night, *Ibid.* 51. and are called *Campestres*, because they frequent the Fields more than the Woods.

If a Man hath a *Chase* adjoining to a Forest, if he deny the Keepers of the Forest to fetch back the hunted Stag, this is fineable; but Red Deer may be in a *Chase* by special Claim. *Ibid.*

A Grant may be made to one to *have a Chase in a Forest*; but yet in such Case the Grantee ought not to hunt or kill any Stag or Red Deer, or other Beast of the Forest, if he doth, 'tis an Offence, and fineable. *W. Jones* 278.

Where a Man hath a Freehold in a free *Chase*, he may cut down Timber without View or Licence of any Person; which he cannot do in a Forest: but if he cut such a Quantity, that there is not enough for *Covert*, and to maintain the Game, he shall be punished at the King's Suit; so if he hath a *Chase* in another Man's Soil, the Owner cannot destroy all the *Covert*, but must leave sufficient for the Deer to browse. 12 *Rep.* 22. *W. Jones* 276. S. P. 2 *Cro.* 155. S. P. 4 *Inst.* 298. S. P.

The Owner of the Soil in a *Chase* may have Common for Sheep, and feeding for his Conies there, either by Grant or Prescription; but he must not surcharge it with more than hath been usual, neither can he make any new Coney-Burrows. 12 *Rep.* 22. 2 *Cro.* 22.

Chief Justice in Eyre, Is an Officer of great Honour and Authority, and is a Peer, and always of the Privy Council. In former Days this great Officer was created by Writ, as other *Justices in Eyre* are, but now by the Stat.

of

of the 27 *H.* 8. *c.* 24. he is made by Letters
Patent under the Great Seal. As his Office is
* Judicial, it was doubted whether he could
lawfully make Deputies ; therefore to avoid
such Ambiguity and Doubt, the Stat. of the
32 *H.* 8. *c.* 35. was made, whereby it is enacted, ' That every Justice of the King's Fo-
' rests, Parks and Chases, may by Writing un-
' der the Hand and Seal of his Office, depute
' as many Deputies as he pleases, which shall
' have the same Power and Authority as if he
' was personally present,'

The *Chief Justice in Eyre* (according to my
Lord *Coke*) is commonly a Man of greater Dignity than Knowlege in the Laws of the Forest,
and therefore where Justice-Seats (the Court
of the *Chief Justice in Eyre*) are to be held,
some other Persons by the King's Appointment
are associated to him, who together are to determine all Pleas of the Forest, and the *Chief
Justice in Eyre*, and those associated, are the
Chief Justices of the Forest, so called in Respect
of the Verderors and others, who, to some Pur-
poses, have judicial Places. 4 *Inst.* 314.

There are two *Chief Justices in* † *Eyre* ; one
for the Forest on this side *Trent*, the other beyond. *Manwood* 57. See **Justice-Seat.**

Chiminage, Is a Toll for Passage thro' a
Forest due by Custom.

---

* By the Common Law a judicial Officer cannot make
a Deputy.
† In *Latin Iter* ; and the *Eyre* of the Forest is the Justice-Seat.

By * *Chart. de Foresta, c.* 14. No *Chiminage* shall be taken in Forests, but by Foresters in Fee, that farm their Bailiwick, and only of such as buy their Bushes, Timber, Bark or Coal, to sell it again, *viz.* 2 *d.* for a Cart, and 1 *d.* for a Horse, to be taken half-yearly; and it shall be only taken where it hath used to be taken, and not elsewhere; neither shall any *Chiminage* be taken of such as carry Burthens of Bushes, Bark or Coal, albeit they sell it, unless they take them out of the King's Demesne Woods.

Claims in Forests. Those who *claim* ought to make it on the first Day of the Justice-Seat, either in Person or by Attorney, otherwise their *Claim* shall not be received without paying a Fine; for if it is once put in, and afterwards it should appear to be faulty, it is not to be amended without a Fine, or if put in and not prosecuted to an Allowance, Judgment shall be entered against them for Default of Prosecution. 4 *Inst.* 297. *Manwood* 80. *W. Jones's Rep.* 297.

If a Man makes his *Claim* by Grant or Prescription, and he and his Counsel mistake his right Title in some material Point, so as the *Claim* is found against him, it is good for him that his true Title be found by the same Verdict specially, for then he may by Petition make a Fine and pray Licence to make a new *Claim*,

---

* This Charter was made at *Westminster* 10 *February* 9 *H.* 3. *Anno Dom.* 1224. (and confirmed 28 *Ed.* 1. *Anno Dom.* 1299.) 208 Years after the Charter of *Canutus* the *Dane.*

and

and thereunto he ought to be admitted.   4. *Inst.* 297.

In Trial of *Claims,* 'tis to be obferved, if a Man claim to be a Forefter in Fee, either by Prefcription, Grant or Tenure, and prayeth, that it may be inquired by Minifters of the Foreft, in this Cafe the Verderors, Regarders and Agiftors fhall try the Title ; but if a Man Claim by Inheritance, or otherwife, any Profits Apprender, as Common of Eftovers or Pafture; in this Cafe the Trial fhall be by the Forefters, Verderors, Regarders, and not by Agiftors. *Munwood* 80.

If a Man makes a *Falfe-claim* by *claiming* more than he ought, he fhall be fined for his *Falfe-claim,* but that which he ought to have fhall not be feized.   4 *Inft.* 297.   See *Appearance.*

Common. By *Chart. de Forefta,* *Art.* 1. ‘ Where the King hath afforefted his own ‘ Woods or Lands, the fame fhall remain a ‘ Foreft, faving Common of Herbage and ‘ other Things within the Foreft, to fuch as ‘ have been accuftomed to enjoy them.’

By *Ord. Forefta,* *Art.* 1.   ‘ Thofe to whom ‘ the King hath granted Purlieus (whereby ‘ their Woods are difafforefted) fhall be quit ‘ of the Charge of the Foreft, but then they ‘ are to have no *Common* within the Foreft. ‘ Howbeit, fuch as are willing to return their ‘ Woods into the Foreft, fhall enjoy *Common* and ‘ other Eafements there, as they did before.’

A Man may claim *Common Appurtenant* in a Foreft by Prefcription for all Manner of Beafts which

which are *commonable* in a Foreſt; ſo likewiſe
he may preſcribe to have *Common by Reaſon of
Vicinage*, or *Common Appendant*; a Man may
alſo have *Common in Groſs*; and he who hath
ſuch a *Common*, may uſe and enjoy it there according to the Purport of his Grant; for this
Sort of *Common* is by Deed only, and not by
Preſcription; but all the other three Sorts of
Commons are by Preſcription only, without
Deed. And no other Title can a Man have to
a *Common* in a Foreſt. *Manwood* 89, 90, 91,
92, 93.

In the Caſe of *Grammer* againſt *Watſon*, a
ſpecial Verdict was found, That *Alamore* Waſte
was in the Foreſt of *Sherwood*; and that the
Meſſuage and 30 Acres of Land, for which
the Defendant preſcribed to have *Common*, was
within the Purlieus of the ſaid Foreſt; and
they found the Defendant had Right of *Common* there, *&c.* but whether ſuch a *Preſcription
to have* Common *in a Foreſt* was good or not,
they left to the Judgment of the Court. In arguing this ſpecial Verdict, the Counſel for the
Plaintiff objected, that the Preſcription alledged
in Bar was ill; it being *to have* Common *in a
Foreſt* abſolutely, without excepting the *Fence-
month*, and alſo for *Sheep* which are not *Commonable* in a Foreſt, becauſe they bite ſo near, that
the Deer may be ſtarved: But theſe Objections
were not allowed, becauſe there are Authorities
in Point, that a Man may *preſcribe for* Common
for Sheep in a Foreſt, *viz.* 2 *Cro.* 155. *W. Jones*
283. and likewiſe without excepting the *Fence-
month*. 3 *Lev.* 98. *Trigg* and *Turner's* Caſe.
And

And the Defendant had Judgment. *Compleat English Copyholder*, Tit. *Alamore*.

All the Inhabitants in *Egham* Foreſt joined to have Claim for all Cattle *commonable*. *Per Cur.* They ought not to have joined in one Claim; it is true, Tenants in Ancient Demeſne may join in a Claim for *Common*, &c. becauſe the King cannot claim for them; but other Men, if Copyholders, they muſt only join who are Tenants to one Lord, and the Lord muſt preſcribe for him and his Tenants. *W. Jones Rep.* 276, 286. See *Staff-herding*.

Preſcription to have *Common* is good, without an Allowance in Eyre, becauſe it is an equitable Preſcriptio, and in Nature of a *Common* Right; for ſince the Deer have fed on my Grounds, it is reaſonable I ſhould have *Common* in the Foreſt.

Note; A Foreſt may be diſafforeſted and laid open, but Right of *Common* ſhall remain. *Poph.* 93.

Coney, Is a Beaſt of Warren, and is called the firſt Year a *Rabbet*, and afterwards an old *Coney*.

By Stat. 3 *J.* 1. *c.* 13. *ſ.* 2. 'If any Perſon ' ſhall in the Night-time enter into any Grounds ' *incloſed*, and uſed for keeping of *Conies*, and ' hunt, drive out, take or kill any *Conies*; ' he ſhall, on Conviction at the Suit of the ' King or the Party, at the Aſſizes or Seſſions, ' on Indictment, Bill, Information, or other- ' wiſe, forfeit 10 *l.* to the Party grieved, or ' treble Damages and Coſts at the Election of ' the Party; and find Sureties for his good ' Abearing

' Abearing for Seven Years, or continue in
' Prifon till he does.
' But this fhall not extend to any Grounds
' to be *inclofed* and ufed for *Conies* after the
' making of this Act, without the King's Li-
' cence.' Same Statute *f.* 7.

By Stat. 22 & 23 *Car.* 2. *c.* 25. *f.* 4 *.
' If any Perfon fhall at any time enter wrong-
' fully into any Warren or Ground kept for
' breeding *Conies*, whether inclofed or not, and
' chafe, take or kill any *Conies* againft the Own-
' er's Will, and fhall be thereof convicted, in
' one Month after the Offence before one
' Juftice, by Confeffion or Oath of one Wit-
' nefs, he fhall render to the Party grieved tre-
' ble Damages and Cofts, and be imprifoned
' three Months, and after till he find Sureties
' for his good Abearing.
' Perfons that kill or take in the Night-time
' *Conies* upon the Borders of Warrens †, or
' on other Grounds lawfully ufed for keeping
' of *Conies*, (except the Owners or Poffeffors
' of the Ground, or Perfons employed by
' them,) fhall on Conviction in one Month
' after the Offence, before one Juftice, by
' Confeffion or Oath of one Witnefs make
' fuch Recompence, to the Party injured, and

---

* *Note*; This Statute extends to all Warrens, whether
inclofed or not. *Hill.* 1 *Geo.* 1. *King* and *Wefton.* And
Note alfo, that a Conviction upon this Statute muft be by
Confeffion, or Oath of one fufficient Witnefs, within a
Month after the Offence, and before one Juftice of the
Divifion.
† See Law Cafes, p.

' withi-

' within such Time, as shall be appointed by
' the Justice, and also pay to the Overseers of
' the Poor of the Parish where the Offence shall
' be committed, such Sum as the said Justice
' shall think fit, not exceeding 10 s. in Default
' whereof they shall be committed to the House
' of Correction, for any time not exceeding a
' Month, and they that use Snares, Hare-pipes,
' and other Engines, shall be liable to the same
' Penalty.' Same Stat. f. 5, 6.

' Persons aggrieved by the Judgment of a
' Justice of Peace, may appeal to the next
' Quarter-Sessions, whose Order shall be final,
' if no Title to any Land or Royalty be therein
' concerned.' Same Stat.

By Stat. 3 Jac. 1. c. 13. f. 5. ' If any Per-
' son not having Lands or Hereditaments of
' 40 l. a Year, or not worth in Goods 200 l.
' shall use any Gun or Bow to kill Conies, or
' shall keep any Ferrets or Coney-Dogs (except
' he have Grounds inclosed for keeping of Co-
' nies, the Increasing of which shall amount to
' 40 s. a Year to be let, and except Warreners
' in their Warrens); in such Cases any Person
' having Lands worth 100 l. a Year may seize
' the same to his own Use.'

A Lease of a Warren of Conies.

THIS Indenture made the 20th Day of
July in the 24th Year of the Reign of our
Sovereign Lord George the Second, by the Grace
of God, of Great Britain, France and Ireland,
King, Defender of the Faith, &c. and in the Year
of

of our Lord 1750. **Between** C. K. *of, &c. of
the one Part, and* W. R. *of, &c. of the other
Part,* **Witnesseth,** *That the said* C. K. *for and
in Consideration of the Yearly Rent and Covenants
herein after mentioned on the Part and Behalf of
the said* W. R. *his Executors, Administrators and
Assigns, to be paid, kept, done and performed,*
Hath *demised, granted and to farm letten, and by
these Presents* **Doth** *demise, grant, and to farm let
unto the said* W. R. **All** *that, &c. and all the*
Conies *in the said Ground being, and to the same
belonging, with the Increase, Gains, Profits and
Advantages from Time to Time arising, coming,
growing and renewing of and from the said* Conies,
*there to hunt, hay, ferret and pitch Nets, or other-
wise to use the same, to and for the most Benefit and
Advantage of the said* W. R. *his Executors, Administrators and Assigns, that he or they can or may
devise, in as large, ample, and beneficial Manner
and Form, as the said* C. K. *or any Person or Persons have heretofore had, held, used, occupied or
enjoyed the same;* **To have and to hold** *all
the said Warren or Piece of Ground, and Game of*
Conies *in the same being or thereunto belonging,
with all the Increase, Gains, Profits and Advantages of the same as aforesaid, unto the said* W.
R. *his Executors, Administrators and Assigns, from
the Feast of* St. Michael *the Archangel next ensuing the Day of the Date of these Presents, for
and during and unto the full End and Term of seven*
Years *from thence next ensuing and fully to be com-
pleated and ended;* **Yielding and Paying**
*therefore Yearly and every Year, during the said
Term of seven Years hereby granted unto the said*

C. K.

C. K. *his Heirs or Assigns, the yearly Rent or
Sum of* 10 l. *of lawful Money of* Great Britain,
*on the four most usual Feasts or Quarter-days for
Payment of Rent in the Year ; that is to say, on
the Feast-day of the Birth of our Lord* Christ, *the
Feast of the Annunciation of the Blessed Virgin* Mary, *the Nativity of* St. John *the* Baptist, *and the
Feast of* St. Michael *the* Archangel, *by even and
equal Portions, and quarterly Payments ; the first
Payment thereof to be made on the Feast-day of the
Birth of our Lord* Christ *next ensuing the Day of
the Date of these Presents.* 𝖆𝖓𝖉 *the said* W. R.
*for himself, his Executors, Administrators and As-
signs, and for every of them, doth covenant, pro-
mise and agree, to and with the said* C. K. *his
Heirs and Assigns, by these Presents, in Manner
and Form following, (that is to say) that he the
said* W. R. *his Executors, Administrators and Assigns, or some or one of them, shall and will well
and truly pay, or cause to be paid, unto the said*
C. K. *his Heirs or Assigns, the said yearly Rent
or Sum of* 10 l. *before hereby reserved, in such
Manner and on the Days and Times herein before
limited and appointed for Payment thereof during
the said Term hereby demised :* [a Covenant to
Repair, and at the End to leave the Berry and
Coney-Clappers sufficiently covered with Thorns,
&c. and leave the same sufficiently stored with
Conies, and a Covenant for quiet Enjoyment.]

Amends pleaded for killing of a *Coney.*

And as to the Taking of the Coney *aforesaid,
that he in going by the publick Highway there
killed*

killed the Coney *aforesaid, leaping before him, for which he often offered to pay the said Plaintiff reasonable Amends (that is to say) ten Pence for that said* Coney, *and is now ready here in Court to satisfy him thereof by the Discretion of the Court,* &c. *and this,* &c.

A Mittimus againſt a Perſon that refuſeth to enter into Recognizance to appear at Seſſions, for offending againſt *Stat.* 22 & 23 *Car.* 2.

To the Keeper, &c.

Middleſex, F*Oraſmuch as* H. H. *of,* &c. *being to wit.* ‾ *this preſent Day brought before me by Warrant, by the Conſtable of,* &c. *and being examined did upon his Examination confeſs, that he had kept and uſed Nets and Ferrets for the taking and killing of* Conies *by the Space of one Year laſt paſt, contrary to the Statutes in that Caſe made and provided; and he the ſaid* H. H. *being required to enter into Recognizance for his Appearance at the next General Quarter-Seſſions of the Peace to be holden for the ſaid County, did refuſe ſo to do; Theſe are therefore in his Majeſty's Name ſtrictly to charge and command you, that you receive into your Cuſtody the Body of the ſaid* H. H. *whom I ſend you by* W. K. *one of the Conſtables of,* &c. *and him ſafely keep until he ſhall enter into ſuch Recogniz..e as aforeſaid, or that he be otherwiſe diſcharged according to Law: And hereof fail not at your Peril.* Given under my Hand and Seal, *&c.*

C

An

An Indictment upon the Stat. of 22 & 23 Car. 2. c. 25.

Middlesex, to wit, THE *Jury for our Sovereign Lord the King upon their Oath say, that* H. O. *of* H. *in the County aforesaid, Yeoman, the* 14th *Day of* August *in the seventh Year of the Reign of our Sovereign Lord* George *the Second, by the Grace of God of* Great Britain, France *and* Ireland *King, Defender of the Faith, and so forth, with Force and Arms, to-wit, with Sticks, Hedging-Bills, Guns, Bows, and other offensive Weapons, the Free-Warren of* R. B. *at* H. *aforesaid in the County aforesaid, about the Hour of Eleven in the Night of the same Day, broke and entered, and in the same Free-Warren, with Greyhounds, Ferrets and Pursenets, without the Licence and against the Will of the aforesaid* R. B. *did come, and fifty Conies of the Value of* 25 s. *of the Goods and Chattels of him the said* R. B. *then and there found took and carried away, to the great Damage of him the said* R. B. *and against the Peace of our now Sovereign Lord the King, his Crown and Dignity, and also against the Form of the Statute in such Case made and provided.* See **Deer.**

Law Cases.

The Statute 22 & 23 *Car.* 2. *c.* 25. *f.* 5. says, *upon the Borders of Warrens;* but if the Conies are out of the Warren, no Person hath any Property in them, and a Man may justify killing them if they eat up his Corn; but no

　　　　　Action

Action lies againſt the Owner of the Warren. *5 Co.* 104.

So a Perſon that hath a Right of Common may kill them, when they are out of the War-ren and deſtroy the Common; but he cannot have an Action on the Caſe againſt the Lord, for that would be to create a Multiplicity of Actions. *Cro. El.* 548. *Cro. Ja.* 195. *Cro. Car.* 388.

If a Man ſhould make *Coney-Burrows* in his own Ground, and put in *Conies*, and they in-creaſe ſo faſt, that they run into his Neigh-bour's Ground and deſtroy his Graſs, it hath been a Queſtion whether he may kill them; and it was adjudged in *Boulſton's* Caſe that he might, and the Reaſon there given is, becauſe they are *feræ Naturæ* [*of wild Nature*]; but a better Reaſon is, becauſe a Man hath a Pro-perty in them *ratione loci* [*by reaſon of the Place*] when they are on his own Land; and therefore he may juſtify the killing *them*. *Boulton's* Caſe, *Rep.* 104.

But 'tis otherwiſe if they are killed by him who hath a *Right of Common* only; as for In-ſtance, In Treſpaſs for digging his Cloſe and killing eighteen *Conies*, the Defendant pleaded Not guilty as to all the Treſpaſs beſides the Killing eighteen *Conies*; and as to them he pleaded, that the Place where, *&c.* was a great Heath in which he had Common of Paſture, and that he found thoſe *Conies* eating the Graſs there, and ſo juſtified the Killing them, *&c.* Adjudged, that though *Conies* are *feræ naturæ*, yet when they are on the Lands of another, he

hath

hath a Property in them by Reafon of the Poffeffion, and therefore an Action lies either for
killing or taking them ; therefore in this Cafe,
the *Conies* being on the Land of the Plaintiff,
who had the Inheritance thereof, and the Defendant having only a Right of Common on
thofe Lands, he might have an Action on the
Cafe, but could not juftify the Killing them.
Coney's Cafe, *Godb.* 122. 4 *Leon.* S. C. By
the Name of *Ould* againft *Lucy,* 2 *Leon.* 201.
S. C.

There is a Cafe in *Cro. Car.* where it was
otherwife refolved, *viz.*

The Plaintiff brought an Action on the Cafe
againft the Defendant, for that he (the Defendant) having a Wood adjoining to a Common
where the Plaintiff and other Copy-holders of
the Manner of *H.* had Right of Common, the
Defendant kept *Conies* in his Wood, which ran
out into the Common, and eat up the Grafs,
&c. Adjudged, that the Action did not lie,
becaufe when the *Conies* were out of the Wood,
the Defendant had no Property in them, and
the Plaintiff could be at no Inconvenience, for
he *might kill them* ; which is very true, if they
had been *on his own Land,* but he had only a
Right of Common there. *Hilfley* againft *Wil-
kinfon, Cro. Car.* 387. *W. Jones* 356. S. C.

And fo are the Authorities both before and
after that Cafe, *(viz.)* In Trefpafs for breaking
and entring his Clofe, and killing his *Conies,*
the Defendant juftified and prefcribed for Common in the Place where the Trefpafs was fuppofed to be done, as appertaining to his Mef-
suage

ſuage in *H.* and becauſe the *Conies* were feeding
on his Common he killed them; and upon a·
Demurrer to this Plea it was inſiſted for the
Defendant, that he might *juſtify the killing Them*,
becauſe he had no other Remedy, as he might
juſtify killing Foxes, or any other Vermin; but
adjudged, that he could not *juſtify the Killing of
Conies,* becauſe the Owner of the Soil where they
are feeding hath a poſſeſſory Property in them
againſt all People when they are there.; and the
Commoner hath no Manner of Right in the
Soil itſelf, for he is only to take his Common,
and may bring an Action againſt him who di-
ſturbs him; beſides, *Conies* are Beaſts of Warren and profitable Beaſts, and therefore are not
to be compared with Vermin, and the keeping
of them is lawful, and the killing of them by
the Commoner unlawful. *Bellow* againſt *Lang-
den, Cro. El.* 876. *Owen* 114. S. C.

So in Treſpaſs for breaking his Cloſe, *necnon
liberam Warreñam intravit,* [*alſo for entering his
free Warren*] and for taking and carrying away
ſo many *Conies*; the Defendant juſtified, for
that he was ſeiſed of a Meſſuage and Lands in,·
&c. and preſcribed to have Common in the
Place where the Treſpaſs was ſuppoſed to be:
done, and that he was there ready to uſe his
Common; and then ſets forth, that many *Conies* were there Damage-feaſant, .thereupon he
entered and chaſed them out; and upon a Demurrer this was adjudged an ill Plea, .becauſe
the Plaintiff being only a *Commoner,* hath no
Intereſt in the Land; he is only to take his
Common, but cannot preſcribe againſt the

Lord,

Lord, for as he may have great Beasts there, so he may have Beasts of Warren, and the Commoner cannot destroy them. *Hoddesden* against *Grissel*, 2 *Cro.* 195. *Palm.* 368. S. C. *Yel.* '44, 143. S. C. 2 *Bulst.* 110. S. C. *Brownl.* 208. S. C. *Winch* 16. S. C. *Bridgm.* 10. S. C. *W. Jones* 12. S. C. by the Name of *Grissel* against *Leigh.* See 1 *Brownl.* 227. *Lawley* against *Park*, S. P.

Upon a Demurrer the Question was, whether a Man who hath Right of Common might destroy the *Conies* feeding on the Land, and fill up the *Coney-Burrows* in the waste Ground; and adjudged that he could not, because he hath no Interest in the Soil, other than to take the Common by feeding his Cattle there; and therefore must not fill up the Burrows, nor destroy the *Conies. Horsey* against *Heyburton*, 2 *Cro.* 229.

In Trespass for hunting Three hundred *Conies*, with a *Continuando* from such a Day to such a Day; the Defendant justified, for that he had Right of Common in the Place where, &c. for 240 Sheep, as to his Messuage in *H.* appertaining, and that he, and all those whose Estate he had therein, &c. have used, when and at such Time as the Common was surcharged with *Conies*, to hunt, kill, and carry them away, *as to his said Messuage belonging,* &c. And upon a Demurrer to this Plea it was adjudged, that the Prescription was void, for as a Man cannot prescribe in the Freehold of another, so he cannot prescribe to hunt and kill *Conies*, *as to his Messuage belonging. Samborn* against *Harrilow. Sandford* against *Howell, Bridgm.* 21. *Godb.* 184.

Case,

Cafe, &c. wherein the Plaintiff made a Title under Coparceners, and prefcribed in them to have a Right of Common in *Hartfhorn*, as appurtenant to his Meffuage there; and that the Defendant had made a Warren in the Common and *Coney-Burrows*, and put in *Conies*, &c. by Reafon whereof he could not enjoy his Common fo beneficially as before; the Defendant prefcribed to have a free Warren within the Manor of *H.* and fo juftified the making *Coney-Burrows*, and putting in *Conies*, &c. and averred, that the Plaintiff had fufficient Common; the Plaintiff replied and maintained his Declaration, and traverfed the Sufficiency of the Common, and the Defendant's Prefcription to a free Warren; and upon a Demurrer to this Replication it was objected againft the Plea, that the Lord of the Soil could not make *Coney-Burrows*, and put in *Conies* there to the Prejudice of the Defendant, who hath Right of Common, fo that he could not enjoy the Benefit thereof; but the Plaintiff had Judgment, by which it appears the Lord might do it; but that if the *Conies* multiply fo faft, that the Plaintiff could not enjoy his Common, he might have an Action on the Cafe againft the Lord. *Haffard* againft *Cantrel*, 1 *Lutw.* 107. *Nelfon*'s *Lutw.* 36.

In Trefpafs for breaking his Clofe and hunting there, and killing *Centum Cuniculos fuos*, &c. upon Not guilty pleaded, the Plaintiff had a Verdict and entire Damages; and it was moved in Arreft of Judgment, that the Declaration was not good, becaufe the Plaintiff could not

have

have any *Property in the Conies,* and therefore could not call them *fuos,* as he did in his Declaration, because they are *feræ naturæ,* and by Consequence *nullius in Bonis;* 'tis true if he had a Warren, then an Action *quare Warrenam fregit & Cuniculos fuos cepit* might be well enough.; but adjudged, that a Warren is only a Franchise to keep the *Conies,* and the Owner of such Warren hath no greater Property in them in the Warren, than any other Man hath; when they are on his Lands; now in the principal Case the *Conies* being on the Plaintiff's Lands, he hath a local Property in them whilst they are there, and no body can justify the Killing them. *Sutton* against *Moody,* 2 *Salk.* 556. *Newton* against *Richards, Gcdb.* 174. S. P. 1 Ld. *Raym.* 251.

In an *Action of Waste* against the Lessee of a Warren, the Waste assigned was, *Stopping Coney-Burrows:* Adjudged, that the *Action* would not lie, because a Man cannot have the *Inheritance of Conies,* nor any Property in them, but only the Possession; 'tis true an *Action* will lie against him who makes Holes in the Land, but not against him who stops them up, because the Land is better by making it plain. *Moyle* against *Moyle, Owen* 66.

One *Yates* was convict of killing Rabbits in a private Warren, by Inquisition taken before a Justice of Peace, and was fined 20 *s.* a Rabbit. Motion to quash the Inquisition, because the Justices of the Peace have no Authority to set a Fine upon a Man for such Offence, for the Stat. 22 *& 23 Car.* 2. *c.* 25. gives treble Costs

and

and Damages, but no Fine; and the Stat. *4 &
5 W. & M. c.* 23. extends only to Game, which
cannot be intended to Rabbits kept in a private Warren * ; and of this Opinion was the
whole Court; and therefore the Inquisition was
quashed. *Rex* v. *Yates*, 1 Ld. *Raym.* 151.

Constable. By *Chart. Foresta*, *c.* 16.
‘ No *Constable*, Castellain or Bailiff, shall hold
‘ Plea of the Forest, neither for green Hue or
‘ Hunting.’

Cottages. The Statute which gives Power
to erect *Cottages* in the Waste for poor People,
doth not extend to Wastes within Forests. 1
Jones Rep. 168, 169.

Coverts, Are those Woods which are
Thickets, and full of Trees touching one another, and signifies a Covering or hiding Place
for the Deer.

Danger, A Duty paid to the Lord for Liberty to Plough and Sow in Mast-time.

Deafforested, Signifies discharged from being a Forest; or Free and Exempt from the
Forest-Laws.

Deawarrened, Is when a Warren is *diswar-
rened*, or broke up and laid in Common.

Deer. By *Chart. Foresta*, *cap.* 10.
‘ None shall lose Life or Member for killing
‘ of *Deer*, but he shall be Fined for it, if he
‘ have any Thing; if not, he shall be Impri-
‘ soned a Year and a Day, and (if he can find
‘ good Sureties) shall then be delivered; but
‘ if not, he shall then abjure the Realm.

* See Ld *Raym.* 151.

By *Stat.* * 3 *Jac.* 1. *c.* 13. ' None fhall
' (without the Owner's Licence) Kill or Chafe
' any *Deer* or *Conies* in any Parks or inclofed
' Grounds, in Pain to fuffer three Months
' Imprifonment, to pay treble Damages to the
' Party grieved, to be affeffed by the Juftices
' before whom he fhall be convicted, after the
' faid three Months expired, and to be bound
' with two good Sureties to his good Beha-
' viour for feven Years, or to remain ftill in
' Prifon till he find fuch Sureties : But the
' Party grieved (being fatisfied) hath Liberty
' to releafe the Behaviour.

' Juftices of *Oyer* and *Terminer*, Affize and
' Peace in Seffions have Power to hear and
' determine thefe Offences ; and Juftices of
' Peace in Seffions (upon Confeffion and Satis-
' faction to the Party grieved) have Power to
' releafe the Behaviour.

' This Act fhall not extend to any Park or
' inclofed Ground hereafter to be made or ufed
' for *Deer* or *Conies*, without the King's Li-
' cence.'

By *Stat.* 7 *Jac.* 1. *c.* 13. ' It fhall be in the
' Election of the Party grieved, whether he will
' take for Satisfaction 10 *l.* in Money, or treble
' Damages, as by the foregoing *Statute.*'

By *Stat.* † 13 *Car.* 2. *c.* 10. ' They that
' courfe, kill, hurt or take away red or fallow

---

* The Statutes before this Time, *viz.* 13 *R.* 2. *c.* 13.
and 5 *Eliz. c.* 21. being found ineffectual to fupprefs Offences of this Nature ; therefore to provide a more cir-
cumfpect Remedy, this Statute was made.

† By this Statute a Reward is given to an Informer,
which was not before.

                                 ' *Deer*

' Deer in any Ground where Deer are kept,
' without the Confent of the Owner, or Per-
' fon chiefly intrufted therewith, or are aiding
' therein, if convicted by Confeffion or Oath
' of one Witnefs before one Juftice of the
' Peace, being profecuted within fix Months
' after the Offence done, fhall forfeit 20 l. to
' be levied by Diftrefs and Sale by Warrant
' under the faid Juftice's Hand ; one Moiety
' thereof to the Informer, the other to the
' Owner of the Deer ; and for want of fuch
' Diftrefs, fhall be committed to the Houfe of
' Correction for fix Months, or the common
' Gaol for a Year, and not to be difcharged
' till Security given for their good Behaviour
' one Year after their Inlargement.

' None punifhed by Virtue of this Act fhall
' incur the Penalty of any other Law for the
' fame Offence.'

By *Stat. 3 & 4. W. & M. c.* 10. f. 2. "If
" any Perfon fhall *unlawfully* * courfe, hunt,
" take in Toils, kill, wound, or take away,
" any red or fallow Deer, *in any Foreft, Chafe,*
" *Purlieu, Paddock, Wood, Park, or other Ground*
" *inclofed, where Deer are, have, or fhall be ufu-*
" *ally kept* †, without the Confent of the Owner
" or Perfon chiefly intrufted with the Cuftody
" thereof ; or fhall be *aiding or affifting* ‡ *theri-*

---

* Where a Man kills Deer in Purfuance of a fuppofed
Right which he has, he is not within the Intent of this, or
any of the other Acts againft Deer ftealing. Ld. *Raym.*
Rep. 584.
† See the Cafe of the *King v. Calcutt* and *Mank,* p.
and p. Ld *Raym.* 791.
‡ See p. Salk. 542, 543.

C 6 " *in*

" in 【】 ; and *shall be convicted thereof, in* 12
" *Months after the Offence* *, by Confession, or
" *Oath of one Witness* †, before one Justice
" where the Offence shall be committed, or the
" Party apprehended, *every such Person so of-*
" *fending* ‡ by unlawful Coursing or hunting on-
" ly, when no Deer is taken wounded or kill-
" ed, shall forfeit for every such Offence 20 *l.*
" And In Case any Deer shall by such Person
" be wounded, taken in Toils, or killed, he
" shall forfeit for every such Deer 30 *l. to be*
" *levied by Distress* ‖ upon the Goods and Chat-
" tels of the Offender *by Warrant of such Ju-*
" *stice* §, *one third to the Informer, one third to*
" *the Poor where the Offence shall be committed,*
" *and one third to the Owner of the Deer* * * : *for*
                 " *Want*

‖ ‖ See the *King* v. *Simpson*, p.   and also p. Note
(a) Tit. Game.
    * By 9 *Geo. 1. c. 22 f. 13.* This Prosecution may be
commenced at any Time within three Years after the Offence.
    † See p.   The *King* v. *Stone* Tit. *Dogs.*
    ‡ Where several Persons are convicted, they forfeit *each*
30 *l.* 1 *Salk.* 182.
    ‖ Tho' Sale of the Goods is not mentioned in the Sta-
tute, yet neverthelefs where the Law gives a Distress for a
publick Benefit, the Officer may sell. 1 *Salk.* 379.
    § Altho' the Constable is not appointed to execute this
Warrant, nor is he so much as named in the Clause ; yet
he is bound to obey the Warrant, and is indictable if he
does not. But he need not return the Warrant itself, for
that is not required, and it may be necessary to keep it for
his own Justification ; but he must either return the Warrant,
or certify what he has done upon it. 1 *Salk.* 381.
    * * The Penalty need not be distributed by the Convicti-
on ; *viz.* 10 *l.* to the Informer, 10 *l.* to the Poor, and 10 *l.*
to the Party grieved ; for the Judgment in such Cases sel-
                      dom

" *Want of sufficient Distress* *; such Person shall
" be imprisoned for a Year, and set in the Pil-
" lory an Hour on some Market-Day in the
" next adjoining Town to the Place where the
" Offence was committed, by the chief Officer of
" such Market Town, or his under Officer."

' Constables, &c. by a Justice's Warrant,
' may enter and search as for Stolen Goods ;
' and if any Venison or Skins of *Deer*, or Toils
' be found, shall carry such Offender before a
' Justice of Peace ; and if he do not give a
' good Account how he came by them, or in
' some convenient Time to be set by the said
' Justice produce the Party of whom he bought
' them, or prove such Sale upon Oath, he shall
' be convicted of such Offence, and be subject
' to the Forfeitures and Penalties hereby inflict-
' ed for killing one *Deer*.' 3 *W. & M. c.* 10, *s.* 3.

And by *Stat.* 9 *G.* 1. *c.* 22. ' Any Justice
' may issue his Warrant for this Purpose, and
' if any Venison or Skin of any Deer shall be
' found in the Custody of any Person, and it
' shall appear that such Person bought such Ve-
' nison or Skin of any one who might be justly
' suspected to have unlawfully come by the
' same, and doth not produce the Party of
' whom he bought it, or prove upon Oath the

---

dom mentions a Distribution; it is enough to say, that he
is convicted, and hath forfeited 30*l.* according to the Statute.   1 *Salk.* 383.

* If the Justice finds there is nothing to distrain, then
he must make a Record thereof, and make an Adjudication
for *Corporal* Punishment; but the Offender is not to pay
Part, and suffer *corporally* for the Residue. Ld. *Raym.*
546, 1195, 6.   See the Case of *Dominus Rex* v. *Whitlock,* p.

' Name

' Name and Place of Abode of fuch Party,
' then the Perfon who bought the fame fhall be
' convicted of fuch Offence by any Juftice of
' the Peace, and fhall be fubject to the Penalty
' above inflicted for killing one Deer.

' After Conviction the Conftable, &c. or
' Perfons profecuting, may detain fuch Offen-
' ders in Cuftody, if they do not prefently pay
' the Monies due on the Conviction, till a Re-
' turn may be made of the Warrant for Diftrefs,
' fuch Detainer not exceeding two Days. *Same*
' *Stat. f.* 4.

' Any Owners of *Deer*, in any inclofed
' Ground, or any acting under them, may re-
' fift fuch Offenders, and be indemnified, as if
' the Fact had been committed in any ancient
' Chafe or Park. *Stat.* 3 *W. & M. c.* 10. *f.* 5.

' No *Certiorari* fhall be allowed, &c. Tit.
Certiorari, p. 65.

' No Offender punifhed by Virtue of this
' Act fhall incur the Penalty of any other Law
' for the fame Offence. *Same Stat.*

' All Perfons profecuted for any Thing done
' in Purfuance of this Act, may plead the ge-
' neral Iffue, and give the fpecial Matter in
' Evidence. *Same Statute.*

' By *Stat.* 5 *Geo.* 1. *c.* 15. ' After Confir-
' mation of any Conviction on the above *Stat.*
' of 3 & 4 *W. & M. c.* 10. by any fuperior
' Court, and delivering the Rule to the Juftice,
' whereby fuch Conviction was confirmed, fuch
' Juftice may proceed as if a *Procedendo* had been
' granted.' See *King* v. *Whitlock,* p.

' In

' In a Profecution on this *Stat.* or the faid
' *Stat. 3 & 4 W. & M. c.* 10. Defendant may
' plead the General Iffue; and if a Verdict paffes
' for the Defendant, or the Plaintiff be non-
' fuited, &c. the Defendant fhall have treble
' Cofts, and a like Remedy for the fame, as
' any Defendant hath in any other Cafe in Law.

' The Perfon convicted upon the *Stat. 3 & 4*
' *W. & M. e.* 10. fhall, before he is difcharged
' out of Cuftody, be bound to the Party grieved
' in 50 *l.* with Condition to be of good Beha-
' viour, and not to offend in the like Manner;
' and if he refufe to give fuch Bond, he fhall
' be committed to Gaol till he doth; and if af-
' ter fuch Bond given he fhall be again con-
' victed for any Matter in the faid Stat. of 3 &
' 4 *W. & M.* the Bond fhall be forfeited, and
' the Penalty with Cofts fhall be recovered in
' any Court at *Weftminfter*, over and above the
' Forfeitures, and diftributed in the fame Man-
' ner as the Forfeitures are by that Statute; and
' the Party convicted fhall be likewife liable to
' the Pains and Forfeitures in the faid Act. And
' the Juftice fhall certify a true Copy of the
' Conviction under his Hand and Seal, to the
' next Quarter-Seffions, there to be kept among
' the Records.'

' If a Keeper, or other Officer of any Foreft,
' Chafe, Purlieu, Paddock, Wood, Park, or
' Place where *Deer* are ufually kept, fhall be
' convicted on the faid Statute of 3 *W. & M.*
' *c.* 10. of killing or taking away any *Deer*, or
' of aiding or affifting therein, without the Con-
' fent of the Owner, or Perfon chiefly intrufted
' with

' with the Cuſtody thereof, ſuch Keeper or
' other Officer ſhall forfeit 50 *l.* for each *Deer*
' ſo killed or taken away, to be levied by Diſ-
' treſs, *&c.* and diſtributed as the Forfeitures in
' the ſaid Act; and for want of Diſtreſs ſhall
' be committed for three Years, and be ſet
' in the Pillory two Hours on ſome Market-
' Day, in the next adjoining Town to the Place
' where the Offence was committed.'

By *Stat.* 5 *Geo.* 1. *c.* 28. *ſect.* 1. ' Entering
' into any Park, Paddock, or other *incloſed*
' Ground where *Deer* are kept, and wilfully
' killing any *Deer* there without Authority, or
' ſhall be aiding or aſſiſting therein, and being
' indicted for the ſame, and convicted before a
' Judge of Aſſize, by Verdict or Confeſſion,
' ſhall be ſent to the Plantations for ſeven
' Years; and the Court may make an Order to
' transfer ſuch Perſon to the Uſe of him who
' ſhall contract for the Performance of ſuch
' Tranſportation.

' *Sect.* 2. Nothing herein ſhall repeal any
' former Law made for the Puniſhment of Deer-
' Stealers; and when any Offender ſhall be pu-
' niſhed by Force of this Act, he ſhall not be
' proſecuted by Force of any other Law.'

In the Reign of King *Geo.* 1. there ſprung
up a Set of deſperate Villains called *Waltham*
Blacks, headed by one whom they ſtiled King
John, who blacking their Faces, and uſing other
Diſguiſes, robbed Foreſts, Parks and Warrens,
deſtroyed Cattle, levied Money on their Neigh-
bours by Threats and Menaces to fire their
Houſes, and committed divers other Violences
and

and Outrages, to the great Terror of the People; therefore by *Stat.* 9 *Geo.* 1. *c.* 22. (made for the preventing such wicked and unlawful Practices), it is enacted, ' that if any Perſon
' or Perſons being armed with Swords, Fire
', Arms, or other offenſive Weapons, and hav-.
' ing his or their Faces blacked, or being
' otherwiſe diſguiſed, ſhall appear in any Foreſt,
' Chaſe, Park, Paddock, or Grounds *incloſed*
' with *any* Wall, Pale or other Fence, wherein
' any *Deer* have been or ſhall be uſually kept,
' or in any Warren or Place where *Hares* or *Co-*
' *nies* have been or ſhall be uſually kept, or
' ſhall unlawfully and wilfully hunt, wound,
' kill, deſtroy, or ſteal any Red or Fallow
' Deer, or unlawfully rob any Warren or Place
' where *Hares* or *Conies* are uſually kept, or
' ſhall unlawfully ſteal or take away *Fiſh* out of
' any River or Pond; or if any Perſon or Per-
' ſons *(whether armed or diſguiſed or not* *) ſhall
' unlawfully and wilfully hunt, wound, kill,
' deſtroy, or ſteal any Red or Fallow Deer, fed
' or kept in any Places in any of his Majeſty's
' Foreſts or Chaſes, which are or ſhall be *in-*
' *cloſed* with Pales, or other Fences, or in any
' Park, Paddock, or Grounds *incloſed*, where
' *Deer* have been or ſhall be uſually kept; or
' ſhall unlawfully and maliciouſly break down
' the Head or Mound of any Fiſh-Pond,
' whereby the Fiſh ſhall be loſt or deſtroyed,
' or ſhall forcibly reſcue any Perſon being law-
' fully in Cuſtody of any Officer or other Per-
' ſon, for any the ſaid Offences; or ſhall by

---

* See *Burn*'s Juſtice, 92. 5th Edit. Fol.

' Gift

' Gift or Promife of Money or other Reward,
', procure any of his Majefty's Subjects to join
' with him or them, in any fuch unlawful Act;
' every Perfon fo offending, being thereof law-
' fully convicted, (*in any County in* England)
' fhall be adjudged guilty of Felony without
' Benefit of Clergy.

' If any Perfon fhall be killed, or wounded
' fo as to lofe an Eye or the Ufe of any Limb,
' in apprehending, or endeavouring to appre-
' hend fuch Offenders, on Proof thereof at the
' General Quarter-Seffions for the County, &c.
' the Juftices fhall give Certificate thereof to
' the Perfon fo wounded, or the Executors, &c.
' of the Party fo killed, which fhall intitle them
' to 50 l. to be paid by the Sheriff in thirty
' Days after Sight of the Certificate, on For-
' feiture of 10 l. for which Sum fuch Perfon
' may bring his Action upon the Cafe againft
' the Sheriff.

' Profecutions on 3 & 4 *W. & M. c.* 10. to
' be commenced in three Years.

' Every Offence againft this Stat. may be
' tried in any County in *England*, as if the Fact
' had been there committed: But no Attainder
' for any of the Offences in this Act fhall make
' any Corruption of Blood, Lofs of Dower, or
' Forfeiture of Lands, Tenements, Goods or
' Chattels.

' By *Stat.* 10 *Geo.* 2. *c.* 32. ' Perfons a fe-
' cond Time convicted, by Indictment or In-
' formation, of Hunting, taking in Toils, Kill-
' ing, Wounding or taking away any Red or
' Fallow *Deer* out of open or *uninclofed* Forefts

or

' or Chafes, during the Continuance of the Act
' of the 9 *Geo.* 1. to be tranfported for feven
' Years, and to return, *&c.* is Felony without
' Benefit of Clergy.'

Note; The Stat. 9 *Geo.* 1. *c.* 22. extends only
to Forefts, Chafes, Parks, Paddocks, or
Grounds *inclofed* for *Deer*, (except the Offender
be withal armed or difguifed) and therefore the
firft Offences in *uninclofed* Places are punifhable
by 3 & 4 *W. & M.* which inflicts only a pecuniary Penalty ; and fecond Offences by the
Claufe in Stat. 10 *Geo.* 2. *c.* 32. above ; and Offenders are by this Stat. ' ordered to be tried
' for fuch fecond Offence before the Juftices of
' Affife, *&c.* for that Place where the fecond
' Offence was committed, and the Juftice of
' the Peace before whom fuch Offender was
' convicted of fuch firft Offence, to certify a
' true Copy of fuch Conviction, under Hand
' and Seal, to the next Quarter-Seffions ; and
' the Clerk of the Peace (on Application) to
' certify a Tranfcript of fuch Conviction, and
' the fame to be a fufficient Proof of fuch Of-
' fender's firft Offence.'

And by another Claufe in the faid Act of 10
Geo. 2. *c.* 32. ' Perfons coming armed, (during
' the Continuance of faid Act 9 *Geo.* 1. *c.* 22.)
' into a Foreft, Chafe, or Park, wherein *Deer*
' are ufually kept *(whether inclofed or not)* with
' an Intent to courfe, hunt, take in Toils,
' kill, wound, or take away any Red or Fal-
' low *Deer*, and fhall there unlawfully beat or
' wound any Keeper or Page of any fuch Fo-
' reft, Chafe, or Park, their Servants or Affift-
' ants

'ants in the Execution of their Office, and be
' thereof lawfully convicted, he fhall be tranf-
' ported for feven Years.'

By *Stat.* 31 *Geo.* 2 p. 1039. the Claufes in
Stat. 10 *Geo.* 2. *c.* 32. relating to the unlawful
hunting or taking of any Red or Fallow *Deer*
in Forefts or Chafes, or beating and wounding
the Keepers or other Officers in Forefts, Chafes,
or Parks, and which were to continue in Force
during the Continuance of Stat. 9 *Geo.* 1. *c.* 22.
and which by feveral fubfequent Acts were to
be continued until 1 *September* 1757 and from
thence *&c.* are made perpetual.

By *Stat.* 28 *Geo.* 2. *c.* 19. *f.* 3. ' If any Per-
' fon, not having a legal Licence, fhall fet fire
' to, burn or deftroy (or be aiding therein) any
' Gofs, Furze, or Fern, in any Foreft or
' Chafe, without Confent of the Owner or Per-
' fon chiefly intrufted with the Cuftody of fuch
' Foreft or Chafe, or of fome Part thereof, and
' being brought before a Juftice fhall be thereof
' convicted of deftroying Covert for *Deer* and
' Game, by Confeffion or Oath of one Witnefs,
' or on View of the Juftice, he fhall forfeit not
' exceeding 5 *l.* nor lefs than 40 *s.* half to the
' Informer, half to the Poor; if not forth-
' with paid, to be levied by Diftrefs; and if
' no fufficient Diftrefs can be found, the Juftice
' fhall commit him to the common Gaol, for
' any Time not exceeding three Months, nor
' lefs than one Month.'

An

An Information againſt *Deer-Stealers.*

The Information of *F. F.* of, *&c.* taken by *W. H.* Eſq; one of his Majeſty's Juſtices of the Peace for the County of, *&c.* the 27th Day of, *&c.*

THIS Informant *upon his Oath ſaith,* **That** *on,* &c. *laſt paſt in the Night-time,* W. P. *of,* &c. *and* A. T. *of,* &c. *did enter into the Park of* T. D. *Eſq; ſituate,* &c. *And then and there, with Harneſs made for that Purpoſe, did take and kill one fallow* Deer *of the ſaid* T. D.'s, *and when they had ſo killed the ſaid* Deer, *they laid the ſame upon a* Horſe, *and carried away the ſame to,* &c.

F. F.

A Warrant Dormant for *Deer.*

KNOW *all Men by theſe Preſents,* **That** *I* P. M. *have given and granted,* **And by theſe Preſents** *do give and grant unto my well-beloved Friend* R. P. *one Stag, and two Bucks in Summer, and one Hind and two Does in Winter, yearly, to be taken in my two Parks called* H. *and* W. *of my Gift yearly, during his Life.* **And** *I licenſe, give Authority and Power to the ſaid* R. P. *and his ſufficient Deputy, yearly, in the Seaſon, to go into my ſaid Parks, calling the Keeper or Keepers thereof with him, there to hunt and kill the ſame* Deer, *and them to bear and carry away at his Liberty and Pleaſure, with ſuch convenient Number of Perſons as he ſhall like, for and about*

doing

doing the fame. **And** *my further Will is, that i,
the faid* R. P. *yearly fometimes will not, come him
felf for the fame, then I will that my Keeper or
Keepers of my faid two Parks for the Time being.
upon Sight of a Bill figned with the Hand of the
faid* R. P. *concerning the fame, fhall kill and deliver from Year to Year the faid, Summer and Winter* Deer, *without any Reftraint or Gainfaying by
them or any of them, in any wife to be made or
done.* **In Witnefs** *whereof,* &c.

A Warrant for Courfing *Deer* in a Park.
(Stat. 3 & 4 *W. & M. c.* 10.) The like
Warrant, &c. *mutatis mutandis*, to levy
30 *l.* for taking in Toils, &c. aiding and
affifting.

To the Conftable of, &c.

Somerfet, **W**Hereas *it hath been duly proved be-
to wit.* fore me, *That* G. P. *of* B. *in the
County aforefaid, did on the 5th Day of* September *laft unlawfully Courfe* (or as the Fact is) *one
fallow* Deer *in the Park of* J. S. *of* T. *without his
Confent, or Perfon intrufted with the Keeping thereof : Thefe are therefore in his Majefty's Name to
require you to levy by Diftrefs and Sale of the Goods
of the faid* G. P. *the Sum of* 20 *l.* * *which was
adjudged to be forfeited by him on his Conviction before me for the faid Offence, and that you pay one
third Part to* A. B. *the Informer, another third
Part to the Churchwardens or Overfeers of the Poor*

* For every Deer wounded, 30 *l.* by the fame Statute.

of the Parish of L. *where the said Offence was committed, for the Use of the Poor of the said Parish, and the other third Part to* J. S. *Owner of the said* Deer, *according to the Act of Parliament in that Case made : And if no Distress can be found, that then you certify the same to me.*

The Form for the Commitment, Tit. 𝕻𝖆𝖗𝖐, p.   will serve in this Case, *mutatis mutandis.*

No Precedent for killing *Deer, &c.* because it is Felony, by Stat. 5 *Geo.* 1. *c.* 28. 9 *Geo.* 1. *c.* 22. 10 *Geo.* 2. *c.* 32.

A Warrant to search after Venison and *Deer-*Skins. (*Vide Shaw's Justice,* Vol. 1. *p.* 297. for a Precedent of this Kind.)

To the Constable of, *&c.*

Essex, ⎱ *B*Y *Virtue of an Act of Parliament*
to wit. ⎰ *made in the third and fourth of*
King *William and* Queen *Mary, These are to authorise and require you, on Sight hereof, to enter into and search the Houses, Outhouses, (as for stolen Goods) and all other Places belonging to such Person or Persons, within your Precincts, as you shall justly suspect or be informed to have in their Custody any Venison or Skins of* Deer; *not being lawfully qualified ; and if on your Search, you shall find Venison or Skins of* Deer, *then you are presently to bring such Person, or Persons, in whose Custody the same shall be found, before me or some other of his Majesty's Justices of*
the

the Peace for this County, to be proceeded against for such Offence, according to Law. Given, &c.

A Warrant to levy the Penalty. *(Vide Shaw's Justice, Vol. 1. p. 297.)*

To the Constable of, &c.

Essex, } W*Hereas* A. B. *of your Parish is*
to wit. } W *brought before me (being one of his Majesty's Justices of the Peace for this County) for having Venison or Skins of Deer in his Possession, and upon his Examination before me he cannot give a good Account how he came by the same, nor produce a credible Witness to prove on Oath the Sale thereof; whereby he hath forfeited the Sum of* 30 l. *of lawful Money; one third Part to the Informer, another third Part to the Poor of the Parish where the Offence was committed, and the other Part to the Owner of the* Deer, *according to the Act of Parliament in that Case made: These are therefore to authorize and require you, on Sight hereof, to levy the said Sum of* 30 l. *by Distress and Sale of the Goods of the said* A. B. *for the Uses aforesaid, rendering to him the Overplus; but for want of sufficient Distress whereon to levy the same, you are forthwith to convey the said* A. B. *to the Gaol at* ——— *for the said County, to be by the Keeper thereof safely kept for twelve Months, and then to be set on the Pillory for one Hour, in the next Market Town.* Given, &c.

An Indictment for hunting and taking *Deer* in the Park of *E. T.* Efq;

Effex, to wit. } **T**HE *Jury,* &c. *That* O. D. *of* E. *in the County aforefaid, Yeoman, the third Day of* July *in the feventh Year of the Reign,* &c. *about the Hour of Twelve in the Night of the fame Day, gathered to himfelf divers other evil difpofed Perfons unknown, and the Peace of our Sovereign Lord the King that now is broke, with Force and Arms,* to wit, *with Sticks, Swords, Daggers, Knives, and other Weapons, the Clofe and Park of* E. T. *Efq; at* A. *in the County aforefaid, unlawfully broke and entered, and the* Deer *of him the faid* E. T. *then and there feeding and lying in the Park aforefaid, with two Greyhounds did hunt, and with a Buckftall which the aforefaid* O. D. *in the Park aforefaid then had, and the Dogs aforefaid then and there two Does took, killed, and carried away, againft the Peace,* &c. *to the great Damage of him the faid* E. T. *and againft the Form of the Statute,* &c.

Law Cafes.

Deer in a Park fhall go to the Heir, and not the Executor. 1 *Inft.* 8.

He that hath Land adjoining to a Chafe, may hunt *Deer* out of his Ground with a little Dog, but not with Beagles; and by fome, if the Dog follow them into the Chafe, and the Owner beat them back, yet if they kill the *Beaft,* Trefpafs doth not lie. See 18 *H.* 6. *fo.*

21. Held, that if a Man go in the way adjoining to a Park, and his Dogs break his Leaſh and kill a *Deer* in the Park againſt his Will, and he call them back, he ſhall not be puniſhed; but it ſeems that if he do not what he can to hinder them, it ſhall be a Treſpaſs. 48 *Ed. 3. fol.* 8. *Kitchin* 119, 120.

If a Perſon kill another by ſhooting *Deer,* &c. in a third Perſon's Park, he is guilty of Manſlaughter. *Hawkins's Pleas of the Crown,* 1 *B.* 74.

The Defendant was convicted upon the Statute 13 *Car.* 2. and immediately brought a Writ of Error, and moved to be bailed till the Error was determined; but it was denied, becauſe he was in Execution for a Fine; and thereupon he was committed to the *Marſhalſea*; and there being another Indictment againſt him at the Seſſions for *Deer-ſtealing,* to which he pleaded Not guilty, it was ruled upon a Motion, that it ſhould be removed and tried in the Court of King's Bench. One *Stirt* was convicted upon the ſaid Statute, and a Warrant being made to levy the Penalty of 20 *l.* by Diſtreſs and Sale of his Goods, the Defendant, to whom the ſaid Warrant was directed, refuſed to execute it; whereupon he was indicted, which being removed by *Certiorari,* it was objected, that it did not appear *where the Warrant was made, or that it was made by the ſame Juſtice before whom the Party was convicted* (which is expreſly required by the Statute); beſides the Indictment was inſufficient, it being *pro injuſtâ Venatione,* &c. which is not good upon this Statute with-

out

out *killing the Deer*: The Indictment was quashed. *The King* againſt *Whitmore,* Sid. 286. *The King* againſt *Marſhall,* Sid. 320. S. P.

A Conviction upon this Statute was removed by *Certiorari* into *B. R.* but it was moved, that it might not be filed, becauſe if the Court ſhould be poſſeſſed of the Cauſe, they cannot puniſh the Offender; for the Statute appoints the Execution to be by Diſtreſs and Sale, by Virtue of a Warrant made *by the Juſtice before whom the Party was convicted*; and becauſe a Writ of Error doth not lie upon ſuch a Conviction, therefore a *Procedendo* was granted. *Gawdy* againſt *Felton,* 1 *Keb.* 813.

The Defendant was indicted on the 3 & 4 *W. & M.* for *Deer-ſtealing,* and the Exception to it was, that it did not appear *in what Year, or on what Day,* the *Deer* was killed; then as to the Form of the Indictment, it was objected that it did not appear how or in what Manner he was convicted, either by *Confeſſion* or by *Witneſs,* as the *Statute* requires: but it was adjudged, that if the *Deer* was killed within a Year before the Indictment, it was ſufficient, and that the Indictment was good, though it did not appear in what Manner the Defendant was convicted. 1 *Salk.* 381.

A Perſon was convicted upon the *Statute* of *Deer-ſtealing,* and it appeared by the Conviction, that the *Deer* were not in a Park *incloſed, &c.* upon Motion in the *King's Bench* the Conviction was *quaſhed.* *Mich.* 9 *W.* 3. *B. R.* *The King* againſt *Pennoyer.*

       A Con-

A Conviction for killing *Deer* was quashed, becaufe it faid only that he killed *Deer in a certain Place where Deer had been ufually kept*, and did not fay *inclofed* *. Ld. *Raym.* 791.

A Conviction againft the Defendant for killing *Deer* was removed into *B. R.* by *Certiorari*, and was quafhed, becaufe it faid only, that he killed *Deer in quodam loco*, where they had been ufually kept, and did not fay *inclofed*. *Trin.* 1 *Ann. Regina* v. *Moore,* 2 Ld. *Raym. Rep.* 791.

At every Juftice-Seat, the Number of *Deer* muft be prefented which have been given away by Warrant, and fuch as have died, or have been otherwife killed fince the laft Court. *Manwood* 104.

Convictions (two or more) of *Deer-ftealing*, before Juftices of the Peace upon Stat. 3 *&* 4 *W. & M. c.* 10. were removed by *Certiorari* into *B. R.* and Exceptions being taken, the Queftion was, whether upon the faid Statute Juftices of the Peace might convict the Offender in his Abfence, upon his Default to appear, being duly fummoned. The whole Court (upon great Confideration) were of Opinion, that the Convictions were good Convictions, though taken in the Abfence of the Party. The *Queen* and *Simpfon*, *B. R. Lucas Rep.* 378.

A *Deer-ftealer* may be convicted upon the Statute 3 *&* 4 *W. & M. before Appearance, if duly fummoned,* but an Attorney in thefe Cafes may be made to defend, for the Offender may intruft his Defence with another, and the Juftices cannot enforce him to appear in Perfon. *Hil.* 3

* See *Stat.* 3 *W. & M. c.* 10.

Geo.

Geo. 1. *Dominus Rex* v. *Simpſon,* in *B. R.* 1
Str. 44.

Certiorari to remove a Conviction for *Deer-
ſtealing*; it was objected, that the *Conviction* appeared to be a Year after the Day when the Information was exhibited; but adjudged, that if
the Information is proſecuted within a Year after the Fact, 'tis well enough, becauſe it is
a good Commencement of the Suit, and 'tis
from the Conviction that the Time in ſuch Caſes
is to be computed.

Then it was objected, that the Diſtribution
of the Forfeiture ought to have been made by
the Judgment, *(viz.)* ten Pounds to the Informer, ten Pounds to the Party grieved, and
ten Pounds to the Poor, *&c.* but here it was,
that the Defendant *convictus eſt & forisfaciat ſum-
mam* 30 l. *juxta formam ſtatuti* [*is convicted and
hath forfeited the Sum of* 30 l. *according to the
Form of the Statute*;] but adjudged, that the
Judgment in ſuch Caſes ſeldom or never makes
any Diſtribution, becauſe it is only conditional;
for if the Offender hath not Goods to be diſtrained, he cannot forfeit, but muſt be puniſhed in another Manner. *The Queen* againſt *Bar-
ret,* 1 *Salk.* 383.

The Defendant was convicted upon the *Statute* 3 *&* 4 *W.* by a Juſtice, who entered into a
Glover's Houſe, and finding a *Deer-Skin* there
aſked him how he came by it, who anſwered,
that he bought it of *T. S.* who not giving a
good Account of himſelf, he the ſaid *T. S.* was
convicted; and adjudged, that the Juſtice might
enter

enter and convict the said *T. S.* who sold it, *The Queen* against *Jennings*, 1 *Salk.* 383.

Two Persons were convicted upon the said Statute for *Deer-stealing*, and Judgment was given, that each of them should forfeit 30 *l.* and this being removed into *B. R.* it was insisted, that this being but one Offence, there ought to be but one Forfeiture, *viz.* 30 *l.* and no more ; but adjudged, that the Forfeiture is not in Nature of Satisfaction to the Party grieved, but a Punishment of the Offender, and Crimes are several, though Debts are joint. *Partridge* against *Nailour, Cro. Eliz.* 480. *The Queen* against *King, Noy* 60. S. C. *Moor* 453. S. C.

The Question was, whether he, who *lent Dogs* to another to course *Deer*, was *aiding and assisting in the Hunting* ; and by the Opinion of the three Judges he was ; but *Holt* Chief Justice was of a contrary Opinion ; for this being a Question upon a penal Law, which ought to be construed strictly, then he who *lent the Dogs* could not be *assisting in the Act of Hunting*, and so not within the Words of the Statute, which are *aiding and assisting* therein ; now he was not assisting *therein* though by lending his Dogs he, might be assisting *thereunto*. See p. 57.

A. lends his Dogs to kill *Deer* in a Park, and Horses to hunt and carry it away ; *A.* is aiding and assisting therein within the Stat. of 3 & 4 *W.* & *M. c.* 10. tho' he be not actually present. *Hil.* 1 *Anna.*

A Conviction for *Deer-stealing* was removed into *B. R.* and there it was confirmed ; and
upon

upon a *Levari facias* directed to the Sheriff, he
levied the 30 *l.* Forfeiture by Sale of the Goods;
and adjudged, that the Sale was good, becaufe
the Court being poffeffed of the Caufe, the Record could not be fent back again to the Juftices; and as they have Power to confirm the
Conviction, by Confequence they have Power
to award Execution, which muft be by the
Sheriff, who is the Officer of the Court, and
not by the Conftable; and it muft be by *Levari
facias*, becaufe the Words of the Statute are,
that the Offender fhall forfeit,. *&c.* to be levied
by Diftrefs and Sale, *&c.* and where the Law
gives a Diftrefs for a publick Benefit, the Officer may fell. *The King* againft *Speed*, 1 *Salk.*
379. See *Certiorari.*

He who fteals tame *Deer*, knowing them to
be tame, is guilty of Felony. 2 *Inft.* 201.

At a Juftice-Seat for the Foreft of *Windfor*
one *Newfham* was convicted, and fined 5 *l.* for
concealing the killing a Stag by another Perfon. *W. Jones*, 275.

The Defendant was a Juftice of Peace for
the County of *Bucks*, and the Court having
granted an Information againft him for har-
bouring of *Deer-ftealers*, Mr. Attorney General
moved, that it might be tried at the Bar of this
Court; and faid, that it had been done before
in Cafes of this Kind, and produced an Affidavit of the Defendant's having an Eftate of 700 *l.*
per Ann.

The Defendant's Counfel oppofed the Motion, upon Affidavits that he had a large Fami-
ly, and was not able to be at the Expence of

trying

trying it in this Manner, and that several of his Witnesses were old and infirm, and not able to travel: But by the whole Court a Trial at Bar was ordered, for they held that this was so very great an Offence that it required the most pub-lick Examination. *Mich.* 12 *Geo.* 1. *Rex* v. *Johnson, M. S. Rep.*

If an Offender for Deer-stealing be but once convicted, and hath Goods only sufficient to sa-tisfy Part of the Sum forfeited, his Goods in such Case cannot be taken, but he must be im-prisoned for a Year and set in the Pillory: But in case he is twice convicted, and has Goods sufficient to satisfy one Conviction but not both, he shall pay one, and suffer corporal Punish-ment for the other. 2 Ld. *Raym.* 1195.

The Description of a Place *where Deer have been usually kept* in 3 *W. & M. c.* 10. does not refer to the Words Forest, Chase, &c. The The Case was this: There were five several Con-victions for *Deer-stealing* returned, four of which being either for killing, or aiding in killing *Deer,* in *Waltham* Forest, had no material Ob-jections made to them; but as to the fifth, which was for *Deer-stealing* in a *Purlieu* of the Forest, objected, that it was not averred, that *Deer* were usually kept in the *Purlieu,* but only that they were usually kept in the Forest; where-as by 3 *W. & M. c.* 10. that seems to be re-quired. The Clause is, ' If any Person shall ' unlawfully course, &c. any Red or Fallow ' *Deer* in any Forest, Chase, *Purlieu,* Paddock, ' Wood, Park, *or other Ground inclosed, where* ' Deer *have or shall be usually kept,* without the
' Consent

'Confent of the Owner or Perfon chiefly in-
'trufted with the Cuftody thereof, he fhall for-
'feit, &c.' Anfwered that fuch Averment
could not extend to a *Purlieu*; for 4 *Inft.* 303.
defcribes it as a Place where by Law *Deer* cannot be kept, it being difafforefted as well with·
regard to all others as the Owner, and the Oath
of the Ranger is to drive Deer out of the *Purlieu* into the Foreft, *Manwood* 292. Secondly,
The Averment as to Forefts, Chafes, and *Purlieus*, is not made neceffary by the Act; for the
Words, *where* Deer *are ufually kept,* extend only
to Grounds inclofed; elfe the Words *other
Ground* will make it neceffary to aver that the
Foreft, &c. was inclofed, which is not the Cafe
in any Part of *England.* And *per Curiam,* the
Anfwer is right in both Refpects. Another
Objection was, that it did not appear, but that
the Defendant was Owner of the *Purlieu*; in
which Cafe he had a Right to chafe the *Deer*
off his Ground. *Sed per Curiam,* That would
be Matter of Defence, and fhould be fhewn on
his Part, according to the Refolution in the
Cafe of the King v. *Bryan**. So the Conviction
was confirmed. *M.* 13 *Geo.* 2. *Dominus Rex*
v. *Calcutt & Monk,* 2 *Str.* 1119.

On a Conviction the Queftion was, whether
he who lent Dogs to another to hunt, was aiding and affifting therein; to wit, in the hunting: And by the Opinion of three Judges he
was; but *Holt Ch. J.* was of a contrary Opi·
nion, for this being a penal Law, fhall be conftrued ftrictly; and if fo, then he who lent the

---

* 2 *Str.* 1101.

Dog

Dogs could not be affifting in the Act of hunting, and fo not within the Words of the Statute, *aiding or affifting therein* *, tho' he might be *affifting thereunto*, 2 *Salk.* 542, 543.

Defendant being brought up from *Newgate* by *Habeas Corpus*, it appeared upon the Return, that he was committed for *Deer-ftealing*, as the Statute 3 & 4 *W. & M. c.* 10. directs, not having fufficient Diftrefs, and that this was done by one Juftice under *Stat.* 5. *Geo.* 1. †—Two Exceptions were taken to the Warrant. 1. Becaufe it does not appear that the Conviction was ever confirmed in this Court, or that the Rule for Confirmation was delivered to the Juftice; and the Words of the Statute are, ' That *after* the ' Confirmation of any Conviction, and *deliver-* ' *ing the Rule* to the Juftice, it fhall and may be ' lawful, &c.' Now this Statute gives the Juftice a Jurifdiction after Confirmation which he had not before, and therefore he ought to fhew every thing requifite to found his Jurifdiction. The Word *after* makes what comes under it to be in the Nature of a Condition precedent, and imports fomething previous to found the Jurifdiction. 2. The Juftice only fays, that it has been certified to him by the Conftable, that there was *no fufficient Diftrefs*, whereas there ought to have been a Warrant to levy, and a Return to that, that there was no Diftrefs : It may be the Conftable only told him fo. But *per Cur.* the Warrant is well enough; for the Word *certified* imports it to be in a legal Manner. And

* See *Stat.* 3 *W. & M. c.* 10.
† *C.* 15. *S.* 2.

as to the other Objection we take Notice of our own Records, and by them it appears that the Conviction is confirmed: And the Statute does not give the Juſtice a new Juriſdiction, but only revives his old one, which was ſuſpended by the *Certiorari.* And the Defendant was remanded. *Hil.* 6 *Geo.* 1. *Dominus Rex* v. *Whitlock, Str.* 263.

𝕯𝖊𝖊𝖗-𝖋𝖊𝖑𝖉, A Park or *Deer-fold.* Stabulum.

𝕯𝖊𝖊𝖗-𝖍𝖆𝖞𝖘, Are great Nets made of Cords to catch *Deer.*

By *Stat.* 19 *H.* 7. *c.* 11. ' None ſhall keep ' any *Deer-hays* or Buckſtalls, ſave in his own ' Foreſt or Park, in Pain to forfeit for every ' Month 40 *s.* Any two Juſtices of Peace in ' Seſſions may examine the Offenders, and ' commit them to Priſon till they have ſatis- ' fied the Forfeiture, whereof the ſaid Juſtices ' are to have the tenth Part.'

𝕯𝖊𝖗. The Names of Places beginning with this Word, ſignify, that formerly wild Beaſts herded there; it comes from the Sax. *Deor, Fera.*

𝕯𝖊𝖘𝖈𝖗𝖎𝖕𝖙𝖎𝖔𝖓. Exception was taken to an Indictment of Treſpaſs for entring into his Cloſe, called *South-Kelſey* Warren, and killing two Conies, Price 10*d.* againſt the Form of the Statute; and it was quaſhed, becauſe this is but a *Deſcription* of the Place, and no poſitive Affirmation that it is a Warren. 2 *Keb.* 389. *The King* againſt *Smith.*

𝕯𝖎𝖘𝖋𝖔𝖗𝖊𝖘𝖙, Is to diſplant or cut down the Trees of a Foreſt.

𝕯𝖎𝖘𝖕𝖆𝖗𝖐.

Difpark. A *modus decimandi* for a Park ; Prefcription for two a Year, and a Shoulder of every third Deer killed in the Park, in Confideration of all Tithes in the faid Park. The Defendant denied the Prefcription, and pleaded, That the Park is *Difparked*, and turned into arable Land. *By the Court*, It yet remains a Park *in Form*, and the *Difparking* the Park of the Deer was not any *Difparking* of the Park; fo as to take away the Prefcription ; but if a Man doth pull down his Park-Pales, the fame is a *Difparking* without any Seizure of the Liberty into the King's Hands, by a *Quo Warranto. Hob.* 39. *Godb.* 237.

If a Man grants the Cuftody of his Park, he may neverthelefs *Difpark* it ; but if he leafe his Park he may not *Difpark* it. *Dyer* 17.

The King may *difpark* his Park, and by his *Difparking* the Office of Keeper is gone ; but if there be an annual Fee, that remains, be he difcharged, or the Park *difparked. Hutton* 87. *Sir Charles Howard's* Cafe, 1 *Cro.* 59.

Diftrefs. If any of the Officers of the Foreft, or others, who ought to appear at the Court of *Swainmote*, make Default, the fame fhall be inrolled in the Rolls of the Court, and the Defaulters fhall be amerced, for which Amerciament the chief Warden of the Foreft, his Lieutenant, or the Beadle, may *diftrain* on any Lands within the Foreft. *Manwood* 99, 100.

If no *Diftrefs* can be found in the Foreft, it ought to be certified by the proper Officer to the chief Juftice in Eyre, and upon a *Teftatum* there, that

that such a Person, who ought to appear, did make Default, and was amerced for the same, and that he had not any Goods or Lands in the Forest that he might be distrained, but that he hath Lands out of the Forest, and in such County ; then the Justices of the Forest may cause a Precept to be directed to the Sheriff of the County out of the Forest, to levy the Amerciament. *Manwood* 101. *Hesket* 37.

If the Officer coming to *Distrain*, is prevented by the Owner of the Cattle, by conveying them out of the Forest, or otherwise ; in such Case, though the Officer freshly pursue them, yet he cannot lawfully take them, being out of the Bounds of the Forest ; but if such Cattle had once been *distrained* for the Amerciament, and then the Owner had by Force taken them away, and driven them out of the Forest, in such Case he may *retake* them in any Place out of the Forest. *Manwood* 101.

Doe, Is the second Beast of the Chase, and is called the first Year a *Fawn*, 2d a *Pricket's-Sister*, 3d a *Doe*. The Season begins on *Holy-Rood-Day*, and lasteth till *Candlemas*.

Dogs. The Laws of the Forest do so much regard the necessary Use of *Dogs*, for the Safety of Mens Goods and Houses who live within the Boundaries, that certain *Dogs* are suffered to be kept therein by any Person whatsoever: But some Sorts are not suffered to be kept there, but only by particular Men. *Manwood* 107.

Mastiffs expeditated, and *little Dogs*, may be kept in a Forest ; but no other *Dogs* without a
good

good Claim ; as for *Greyhounds*, it was unlawful to keep them from the very Beginning of
the Foreſt-Laws, they being prohibited by the
31ſt of the Laws of *Canutus*. *Manwood* 110,
111, 401.

By the *Aſſizes and Cuſtoms of the Foreſt*, *Artic*.
17. ' Of theſe which claim to have Privileges,
' as *Dogs* unlawed, and *Greyhounds*, within the
' Bounds of the *Foreſt*, there ſhall be nothing
' done to them without our Lord the King's
' Warrant, or his Juſtices.' By which it appeareth, That he who hath a lawful Claim, by
good Title, may keep *Maſtiffs*, in a Foreſt,
unexpeditated, and *Greyhounds* alſo ; but ſuch a
Claim muſt be by Virtue of a Grant from the
King, rather than by Preſcription : But *Quare*.
Manwood 110, 411.

By **Stat.** 23 *Eliz*. *c*. 10. ' If any manner
' of Perſon ſhall hawk or hunt with *Spaniels* in
' any Ground where Corn or other Grain ſhall
' then grow, (except in his own Grounds) at
' ſuch Time as any eared Corn or Grain ſhall
' be growing thereon, and before it be ſhocked
' or cocked, and be thereof convicted at the
' Aſſizes, Seſſions or Leet ; he ſhall forfeit
' 40 *s*. to the Owner of the Corn ; and if not
' paid in ten days, he ſhall be impriſoned for
' one Month. And any Juſtice may examine
' the Offender, and bind him over to appear
' at the next Seſſions to anſwer the Offence,
' and to pay the Penalty, or receive the Pu-
' niſhment.'

By

By **Stat.** 5 *Ann.* *Sect.* 2. *c.* 14. * ' If any
' Perſon not *qualified* ſhall *keep or uſe* any *Grey-*
' *hound, Lurcher, Setting-Dog, Hays, Tunnels,* or
' any Engine to kill and deſtroy Game, and
' ſhall be thereof convicted, on the Oath of
' one *credible Witneſs,* † before one Juſtice of
' Peace where the Offence is committed, he
' ſhall forfeit 5*l.* one Half to the Informer,
' the other to the Poor of the Pariſh; to be
' levied by Diſtreſs and Sale of Goods by the
' Warrant of the Juſtice before whom convict-
' ed; and *for want of ſuch Diſtreſs, to be ſent*
' *to the Houſe of Correction* ‡ for three Months
' for the firſt Offence, and every other Offence
' four Months.'

Queen and *Green,* *Eaſter* 13 *Ann.* The Defendant was convicted by two Juſtices *(one ſuffi-*
cient) on this Stat. and committed for want of
Diſtreſs, till delivered by due Courſe of Law; this
makes the Commitment *void;* for the Time of
Impriſonment is directed by the Act, and it
ought to have been for that Space of Time, and
not a General Concluſion, therefore quaſhed.

---

* By Stat. 9 *Ann.* *c.* 25. this Act is made perpetual.
See Tit. **Guns,** p. for a Caſe on this Act.

† A Conviction was quaſhed, becauſe the Informer was
the Witneſs; diverſe Convictions having been quaſhed for
the ſame Reaſon before. *M.* 2 *Geo.* 2. *King* and *Stone,*
Ld. *Raym.* 1545. The ſame adjudged in the Caſe of *K.*
and *Blaney, T.* 11 *Geo.* 2. *Andr.* 240. A Conviction for
Deer-ſtealing quaſhed, becauſe the ſame Perſon is both
Informer and Witneſs, and is intitled to a Part of the Penalty. *T.* 6 *Geo.* 1. *Dominus Rex* v. *Tilly,* 1 *Str.* 316.

‡ See *Hill* and *Batcman.*

By

By **Stat.** *5 Geo.* 1. *c.* 11. ' If any Perſon,
' not qualified by Law, or not truly and pro-
' perly a Servant of the Lord or Lady of a
' Manor, or not immediately appointed to kill
' the Game for their ſole Uſe, under Colour of
' any Deputation from any Lord or Lady, ſhall
' keep or uſe any *Greyhounds, Setting-Dogs,* or
' *Lurchers,* to kill and deſtroy the Game, he
' ſhall incur ſuch Pains and Forfeitures, as by
' the Statute *5 Annæ* laſt mentioned.'

N. B. *There are ſeveral other* Statutes *relating
to* Dogs; *but they not properly coming under this
Head, I therefore refer the Reader to the Table.*

A Declaration for keeping and uſing *Grey-hounds,* not being qualified.

Somerſet, **W**Illiam Brooks, *Eſq; who as well
to wit.* for *himſelf, as the Poor of the
Pariſh of* T. *in the ſaid County, in this Behalf
proſecutes, complains of* Johnſon Trevor *in the
Cuſtody of the Marſhal of the* Marſhalſea *of the
Lord the King, before the King himſelf, of a Plea,
that he render to him and to the ſaid Poor of the
ſaid Pariſh of* T. *five Pounds, which to the ſaid*
William *and to Poor of the ſaid Pariſh he owes,
and unjuſtly detains; for that, to wit, that whereas the ſaid* Johnſon 21ſt *Day of* September *in the
ſixth Year of the Reign of the ſaid Lord* George
the Second, now King of Great Britain, *and ſo
forth, at the ſaid Pariſh of* T. *in the County
aforeſaid, uſed two* Greyhounds *to kill and deſtroy*
Game, *againſt the Statute in that Caſe lately made*
and

and provided ; *be the said* Johnson, *by Force of
the Laws of this Realm, not being qualified so to
do* ; *by which, and by Force of the Statute in that
Case lately made and provided, the said* Johnson
*forfeited the said Sum of five Pounds, and by Force
of the Statute in that Case lately made and provided, the Action accrued to the said* William, *as
well for himself, as for the said Poor of the said
Parish of* T. *in the County aforesaid, to have and
receive from the said* Johnson *the aforesaid five
Pounds* : *Yet the said* Johnson, *although often
requested, the said five Pounds to the said* William, *who as well, and so forth, hath not ren-
dred, but the same to the said* William, *who as
well, and so forth, to render hath hitherto altogether refused, and still doth refuse* ; *wherefore
the said* William, *who as well, and so forth,
said he is prejudiced, and hath Damage to the Value of ten Pounds* ; *And for that, as well for himself, as for the said Poor of the Parish of* T. *he
brings his Suit.*

A Licence to hunt, *&c.* and to seize Dogs, *&c.*

T𝔒 **all** *Christian People to whom this present
Writing shall come, I* H. H. *of, &c. Lord
of the Manor of* H. *send Greeting* : 𝕶𝖓𝖔𝖜 𝖞𝖊,
That I the said H. H. *have given and granted,*
𝖆𝖓𝖉 *do hereby give and grant, unto* W. P. *of,
&c. full Liberty and Authority to hunt at all sea-
sonable Times hereafter, for the Space of five Years
next ensuing, within the said Manor of* H. *in the
County aforesaid, and upon the Lands and within*
the

the Limits thereof, in the same Manner as I my-self might or could do, without any Let, Denial or Disturbance whatsoever : **Giving likewise** *hereby full Power and Authority to the said* W. P. *and his Assigns, from Time to Time during the said Term, to seize all* Spaniels *and* Dogs *whatsoever, of any Person or Persons who are prohibited by the Laws or Statutes of this Realm to keep the same, and who shall, during the Term abovementioned, hunt within the said Manor without his Consent, and the said* Dogs *to keep and detain to and for my Use.* Given *under my Hand and Seal,* &c.

A Warrant to a Game-keeper, or any other Person, to search for *Dogs*.

On 22 & 23 *Car.* 2. *c.* 25.

To the Constable of, &c. and to *W. P.* of, &c. in the County, &c. Yeoman.

Somerset, ⎱ **These are** *to require you, or either*
to wit, ⎰ *of you, to search in the Day-time the Houses, Outhouses or Places of any Person or Persons within,* &c. *whom you shall have just Occasion to suspect, or be informed to keep Set-ting-Dogs, Greyhounds, Lurchers, Tumblers, or other* Dogs, *to destroy Partridges, Hares or Co-nies, not being qualified by Law to keep the same ; and the* Dogs, *which you shall find in the Posses-sion of such Person or Persons, to seize and keep to and for the Use of the Lord of the Manor where they shall be taken :* **But** *you are not to*
search

fearch the Houfe of any Perfon who hath an Eftate of 100 l. a Year, a Leafe for any long Term of Years of the clear yearly Value of 150 l. or of him who is Son and Heir apparent of an Efquire, or any Perfon of higher Degree, or of thofe who are Keepers or Owners of Forefts, Chafes, Parks or Warrens; And you are to certify me with all convenient Speed what you do in the Premiffes. Given, &c.

Law Cafe.

In Trefpafs the Plaintiff declared, that he was poffeffed of a *Greyhound ut de bonis fuis propriis* [as of his own proper Goods]; and that on fuch a Day he loft it, and that afterwards, in Confideration thereof, the Defendant promifed to deliver the faid *Greyhound* to the Plaintiff; and upon a Demurrer to this Declaration, it was objected that this Action would not lie, for the *Dog* being out of the Poffeffion of the Plaintiff, he had no Property in him, becaufe he was *feræ naturæ* [of a wild Nature] and that by a Grant of *omnia bona & catalla* [of all Goods and Chattels] a Dog will not pafs. *Incledon* againft *Higgins*, 3 *Leon.* 219. *Cro. El.* 125. S. C. *Owen* 93. *Hetly* 80.

But *Quære*, for 'tis every Day's Experience, that he is *domitæ naturæ*; a Beaft brought up and tamed by the Induftry of Man, which is fo univerfally known, that the Plaintiff need not aver in his Declaration that the *Dog* was tame, becaufe it fhall be fo intended, and it being a Beaft of Ufe to catch the Game, for
those

those who are qualified to keep them; and therefore the Law regards it, as it doth many other *Dogs*, of which there are four Sorts, (*viz.*) a *Mastiff*, a *Hound*, which comprehends a *Greyhound*, a *Spaniel* and a *Tumbler*; and *Tanfield* (who was afterwards Chief Baron) in arguing this Case tells us, that he had seen a Precedent *Anno* 13 *H.* 7. *Rot.* 35. where in an Action of Assault and Battery, the Defendant justified that *T. S.* was possessed of a *Dog ut de bonis suis propriis*, and delivered it him to keep, and that the Plaintiff would have taken it from him (the Defendant); and thereupon he resisted him (the Plaintiff) and beat him in Defence of the *Dog*, &c. and that that Hurt was of his own Wrong; and that upon a Demurrer to this Plea the Defendant had Judgment; which shews, that a Man may have a Property in a *Dog*, when 'tis lawful for him to justify the Beating another Man in Defence of it. *Dyer* 306.

In Trespass the Plaintiff declared, that *T. S. Vi & Armis*, at such a Place and in such a Year, took and led away *an Hound*; and upon a Demurrer to the Declaration, it was adjudged that the Action did lie. *Edwards* against *Ingleton, Hob.* 283.

Trespass was brought for taking away a *Blood-hound*; upon Not guilty pleaded, the Plaintiff had a Verdict, and 10 *l.* Damages. *Cro. Eliz.* 125, 126.

Trover was brought for a *Spaniel Dog*; and upon a Demurrer to the Declaration it was held,

held, that the Action was well brought. *Pells* against *Lemon*, Hob. 363.

Trespass for taking away a *Greyhound*; the Defendant pleaded, that the *Dog* was coursing a Hare on his (the Defendant's) Lands, and thereupon he took and led him away; and upon a Demurrer to this Plea it was held frivolous; which shews that Trespass will lie for taking a *Greyhound*; and in this Case it was the Opinion of the Court, that an Action of Trespass will lie for killing a *Mastiff*. *Athill* against *Corbett*, 2 *Cro*. 463.

Trespass was brought against the Defendant for killing *two Greyhounds*; who justified, for that the *Greyhounds* did chase a *Deer* in his (the Defendant's) Park, whereupon to prevent further Mischief he killed them; the Plaintiff replied, that the *Deer* was out of the Defendant's Park, and upon his (the Plaintiff's) Lands, and that he let loose the *Greyhounds* at the *Deer* to chase him off his Lands, and that the *Greyhounds* pursued the *Deer* into the Park, and there killed him; and upon a Demurrer to this Replication, it was held ill; because the Plaintiff did not set forth, that he endeavoured to stop the *Dogs* before they came into the Park; but then it was insisted that the Plea was naught, because though it was unlawful to chase a *Deer* in the Defendant's Park, yet he could not justify the Killing the *Dog*; but adjudged that he might. *Barrington* against *Turner*, 3 *Lev.* 28.

In *Trespass* the Plaintiff declared, that the Defendant beat and killed his (the Plaintiff's) *Mast.*[*]

Maſtiff, *&c.* the Defendant pleaded in Bar, that the Plaintiff ſuffered his *Maſtiff* to go in the Street without a *Muzzle*; and thereupon he ran upon another *Dog* of one *Ellen Bagſhaw*, which he did bite, (which *Dog* was kept by the ſaid *Ellen* for the better Security of her Houſe), and that the Defendant as her Servant *killed the Maſtiff* left he ſhould do any further Damage; and upon a Demurrer to this Plea it was adjudged ill, becauſe a *Maſtiff* is a valuable *Dog*, and therefore the Defendant could not juſtify killing it without a reaſonable Cauſe; 'tis true he might juſtify the Beating it to prevent farther Miſchief, but not to *kill it*, unleſs it could not be otherwiſe prevented; but by this Plea it doth not appear but that the Defendant might have ſaved his Miſtreſs's *Dog* without killing the *Maſtiff*; and that was the Caſe of *Wadhurſt Damm*, where the Defendant juſtified the Killing a *Maſtiff*, becauſe he could not be otherwiſe prevented from doing Damage in the Warren. *Wright* againſt *Ramſcot*, 1 *Saund.* 84. *Sid.* 336. S. C. *Lev.* 216. S. C. 3 *Salk.* 139.

Trover, *&c.* and amongſt other Things *de ſex Catulis*; after a Verdict for the Plaintiff, upon Not guilty pleaded, it was moved in Arreſt of Judgment, that *Catulus* ſignified *Whelps* of any *Species*, as of *Foxes*, *Bears*, *&c.* but adjudged, that it ſhall be intended *Dog-Whelps*; and that a Man may have a Property in a *Dog.* 3 *Lev.* 326. *Chambers* againſt *Warkhouſe.*

The Defendant ſold a *Lurcher* to the Plaintiff, who promiſed to redeliver him to the Plaintiff, as often as he ſhould return to the Defendant,

dant, which he had not done ; and it was held that the Action was well brought. *Elliot* againſt *Richardſon,* 1 *Keb.* 608.

In an Action on the Caſe the Plaintiff declared, that the Defendant in ſuch a Pariſh *knowingly did keep a Dog,* which uſually did bite Men ; upon Not guilty pleaded the Plaintiff had a Verdict, and 100 *l.* Damages; and it was moved in Arreſt of Judgment, that the Declaration was ill, becauſe the Plaintiff did not ſet forth, that the Defendant did know the *Dog* was accuſtomed to worry Men ; for the Word *Knowingly* in this Declaration muſt relate to the Keeping the *Dog* ; and ſo is the Caſe of *Kinion* and *Davis, Cro. Car.* 350, 487. in Point, which is very true; but the Rule in that Caſe was made without any Debate of the Point ; and it was, that the Defendant ſhould have Judgment, unleſs Cauſe, *&c.* ſo that it might be the Negligence of the Plaintiff in that Caſe that the Rule did ſtand ; therefore in the principal Caſe there was a contrary Judgment, and that it would be impertinent, that the Word *Knowingly* ſhould only relate *to the Keeping the Dog,* becauſe he who keeps a *Dog* muſt know that he keeps it : The Judgment was affirmed. *Cropper* againſt *Matthews, Sid.* 127.

Caſe, *&c.* againſt the Defendant for keeping a Maſtiff, *knowing the Dog* was accuſtomed to *bite Hogs* ; upon a Demurrer to the Declaration it was adjudged, that this Action would not lie, becauſe 'tis not only common, but in many Caſes neceſſary, for *Dogs* to *bite Hogs* ;

and

and therefore not like the Cafe where an Action is brought for keeping a *Dog*, which ufually did bite Sheep. *Dyer* 25.

The Defendant was convicted upon **Stat.** 5 *Ann. c.* 14. for keeping a *Greyhound*, and *killing four Hares*, not being qualified, *which Conviction was upon his own Confeffion*; now by the faid Statute the Forfeiture of 5 *l.* relates to the Conviction, fo that if 'tis not made according to the Statute, nothing js forfeited ; now it was infifted that the Conviction in this Cafe was not according to the Statute, becaufe that directs it fhould be *by the Oath of one credible Witnefs before one Juftice*, but here it was *by his own Confeffion*; befides the Juftice, before whom the Party was convicted, having no Power but what he derives from the Statute, for that Reafon it ought to be purfued ; but adjudged, that the *Confeffion of the Offender* is the ftrongeft Evidence againft himfelf ; and though 'tis not within the Letter, yet 'tis within the Reafon and Meaning of the Statute ; therefore where the Conviction is upon a ftronger Evidence than required by the Statute, it muft be good. *The King* againft *Gage*, 9 *G. B R. M. S. Rep.* — *Str.* 546. S. C. ftates it thus. The Defendant was convicted on 5 *Ann. c.* 14. for ufing a *Greyhound* in killing four Hares, *per quod* he forfeited 20 *l. Reeve* excepted to the Conviction, that the Act not only gives the Juftices Jurifdiction to convict upon the Oath of one or more credible Witneffes, whereas this was upon his own Confeffion, which he infifted the Juftice had no Power to take ; and it follows in the Act, that

the

the Perfon *fo* convicted fhall forfeit, which Word *fo* is relative to the former Method, by Oath of one or more credible Witneffes : And he put the common Cafe upon the Removal of a poor Perfon, which muft be upon the Com--plaint of the Churchwardens or Overfeers, the Juftices having Jurifdiction in that Manner. *Sed per Curiam, (præter Eyre* J.) The Conviction muft be confirmed. The Intent of mentioning the Oath of one Witnefs was only to direct the Juftices, that they fhould not convict on lefs Evidence : Suppofe the Confeffion had not been before the Juftices, but before two Witneffes who had fworn it, that would be convicting him on the Oaths of Witneffes, and yet the Evidence would not be fo ftrong as this. By the Civil Law Confeffion is efteemed the higheft Evidence, and in fome Cafes, though there are one hundred Witneffes, the Party is tortured to confefs. Here the Juftices had a better Evidence than the Oath of any fingle Witnefs; and it is a monftrous thing to fay, that a better Sort of Evidence fhall not do. *Eyre* J. *contra,* there was no Occafion to carry this Act fo far, the 22 *&* 23 *Car.* 2. *c.* 26. giving Power to convict for this Offence upon *Confeffion,* with a different Penalty, and he faid that it ought to have been a Conviction upon that Statute. The Conviction was confirmed.

Queen and *Cobbold, Mich.* 12 *Ann.* Defendant was convicted upon 5 *Ann. c.* 14. for keeping a *Greyhound,* not being qualified. Objection, that the Conviction was upon the fingle Teftimony of the Informer ; *Per Cur.* 'Tis a

E   fatal

fatal Objection; for should the Informer be allowed to be a sufficient Evidence, it would induce profligate Persons to commit Perjury for the sake of the Reward, more especially since they cannot be convicted of it; when the Statute says a credible Witness, 'tis such a one as is allowed *per Legem.*

In *Trespass* the Defendant pleaded, that the Plaintiff's Sheep were in his (the Defendant's) Ground, and that he chased them from thence with his *Dog*, which pursued them into the Plaintiff's Ground adjoining, and that he immediately chid his *Dog*, *quæ est eadem transgressio, &c.* [*which is the same Trespass*]; and upon a Demurrer to this Plea, it was objected, that though 'tis lawful to chase Cattle out of his Ground with a *Dog*, yet he ought not to exceed that Authority which he hath by Law, *(viz.)* (to pursue them into another Man's Ground), for if he doth, 'tis void in all; but adjudged, that the Plea was good, for 'tis the Nature of a *Dog* not to be ruled on a sudden; therefore the Defendant had not abused that Authority, which he lawfully had. *Miller* against *Cowdry*, *Poph.* 161.

In an Action of Debt, upon the Statute 5 *Ann.* for keeping and using a *Dog* to kill the Game, it is necessary to shew what sort of *Dog* it was; for a *Mastiff-Dog* or a *Lap-Dog* may chance to kill Game, and the Statute mentions only *Greyhounds, Setting-Dogs* and *Lurchers.* See the *Table.*

Conviction before one Justice for keeping a *Greyhound*; reciting that one *William Tonne* came

and

and informed, that the Defendant, being a Person *not qualified* to keep a *Greyhound*, did nevertheless keep one at *A.* and another at *B.* and with them killed one Hare at *A.* and two at *B.* and that he being summoned did appear; and being asked what he had to say, offered nothing in excuse, and *ideo* the Justice convicted him. The Conviction was quashed, because the Witness swore *generally* that the Defendant was not qualified, and had taken upon himself to judge of the Qualifications. *M.* 4 *Geo.* 1. *Dominus Rex* v. *Marriott.* 1 *Str.* 66. See 10 *Mod.* 26.

Conviction on *Stat.* 5 *Ann. c.* 14. for *keeping a Lurcher* to destroy Game, not being qualified, good, without shewing Defendant made *use of the Dog to destroy Game.* For *per Cur'* the Statute is in the Disjunctive, *keep or use*, so that the bare keeping a *Lurcher* is an Offence, and so it was determined in the Case of the *King* v. *King,* * *E.* 3 *Geo.* 1. *B. R.* which was a Conviction for *keeping a Gun*, and it was not doubted by the Court, whether the *Keeping* was not enough to be shewn; but the only Question they made was, whether a *Gun* was such an Engine as is within that Statute; and in that Case a Difference was taken as to *keeping a Dog*, which could only be to destroy the Game, and the *keeping a Gun,* which a Man might do for the Defence of his House. *Hil.* 8 *Geo.* 1. *Dominus Rex* v. *Tiler.* 1 *Str.* 496.

* In this Case *Parker,* Ch. J. said, that walking about with Intent to kill Game, is Evidence of *using* the Instrument for that Purpose. *Seff. C.* V. 1. 88.

Debt

Debt on 8 *Geo.* 1. *c.* 13. for the Penalty of 30*l.* for ufing a *Hound* to deftroy Game. After a Verdict for the Plaintiff Judgment was arrefted, for 5 *Ann. c.* 14. has not the Word *Hound,* and the Words *other Engines* come after *Nets, &c.* and are applicable only to inanimate Things; and this being a penal Law, cannot be extended. The *Stat.* 22 & 23 *Car.* 2. *c.* 25. has indeed general Words, *or any other Dogs to deftroy Game,* but this is not a Conviction on that Statute. *H.* 13 *Geo.* 2. *Hooker* v. *Wilks,* 2 *Str.* 1126.

Dove and **Dove-cote.** There are feveral *Statutes* made for the Prefervation of *Doves;* and which are inferted under other Heads, for which fee the *Table.*

A Declaration for taking *Doves.*

Huntingdon,
to wit. } T M. *Complains of* E. F. *in the Cuftody of the Marfhal and fo forth, for that he the faid* E. *with Force and Arms, the third Day of* September, *in the feventh Year of the Reign of our Sovereign Lord* George *the Second, now King of* Great Britain, *the Clofe and Houfe of him the faid* T. *at* G. *in the faid County, did break, and then and there* 144 *Doves of the Dove-cote of him the faid* T. *with Nets and other Engines did take, to the Value of* 50 l. *by which Taking he the faid* T. *his Flight of his Doves aforefaid wholly loft, and other Enormities to him did, againft the Peace of the faid Lord*
the

the now King, and to the Damage of the faid T. ten Pounds ; and therefore he brings his Suit.

An Indictment for erecting a *Dove-cote.*

Huntingdon, ⎰ 𝕿 Ⓗ Ⓔ 𝕵𝖚𝖗𝖞, &c. *That* A. B.
 to wit. ⎱ *of* G. *in the faid County of*
H. *Yeoman, not being Lord of the Manor of* G.
aforefaid, nor Rector of the Parifh Church of G.
*aforefaid (*fuch *a Day and Year,* &c.*) at* G.
aforefaid in the County aforefaid, a Dove-cote *did
erect or caufe to be erected, to the common Nufance of the Subjects of our faid Lord the King,
and alfo againft the Peace of our faid Lord the
King, his Crown and Dignity.*

Law Cafes.

Doves in a *Dove-houfe, young* and *old,* fhall
go to the *Heir,* and not the *Executcr.* 1 *Inft.* 8.

A Freeholder erected a *Dove-cote* on his Freehold Land, where there was none before, and
ftored it with *Pigeons* ; this was *prefented at the
Leet for a Nufance,* and the Defendant was ordered to remove it by fuch a Day ; which not
being done, he was amerced to 20 *s.* and the
Lord of the Leet diftrained for the fame.

And firft, The Court doubted whether this
could be prefented as a *Nufance* ; and my Lord
Coke, who was now Chief Juftice, faid, that
there was no Reafon why a Lord of a Manor
fhould have a *Dove-cote* more than another Freeholder ; and it being infifted, that this is an Offence *punifhable in the Leet,* becaufe by 𝕾𝖙𝖆𝖙.

E 3   18 *Ed.*

18 *Ed.* 2. reciting the Articles of the Charge at a Leet, it appears, that one of thofe Articles is to make Inquiry of *Dove-cotes* erected without Licence; my Lord *Coke* thereupon afked a very material Queftion, *(viz.) Who fhall give fuch Licence?* The Lord of the Manor cannot; for if 'tis a *Nufance*, he himfelf cannot erect a *Dove-cote*; and the King cannot, becaufe 'tis a *Nufance*; but in the principal Cafe, the Prefentment was quafhed, becaufe it did not fet forth, that the Building the *Dove-cote* was *ad commune nocumentum Ligeorum Domini Regis,* [*to the common Nufance of his Majefty's Liege Subjects*]. *Pratt* againft *Sterne*, 2 *Cro.* 382. *Godb.* 259. S. C.

In *Trefpafs* upon a Demurrer the Cafe was, The Plaintiff being a Freeholder within the Manor of *Ifleworth* in *Middlefex*, erected a *Dove-cote* on his own Lands, and ftored it with *Pigeons*, and fuffered them to fly out, which was prefented at the Leet as a common Nufance, and a Pain of 10 *l.* was impofed on him, if he did not remove it before fuch a Day; which not being done, it was prefented at the next Court, and the Pain thus impofed was affeered to 8 *l.* and for Non-payment thereof a Diftrefs was made on his Goods and Chattels; whereupon he gave Bond for the Payment of the Money, and afterwards brought an Action of Trefpafs for taking and detaining his Cattle, till he entered into the faid Bond: The Defendant pleaded fpecially, and fet forth all the Matter before mentioned; to which Plea the Plaintiff demurred; and it was adjudged by the whole

Court,

Court, that the Erecting a *Dove-house* by a Freeholder on his own Land, and storing it with *Pigeons*, is *not a Nusance inquirable in a Leet*, because 'tis not a common Nusance to all People; for if 'tis any Nusance, 'tis only so to those whose Corn they eat; besides a Man hath *jus proprietatis & privilegii* in *Pigeons*, and both in respect to the Place where they are, *(viz.)* in his *Dove-cote.* *Dewell* against *Sanders*, 2 *Cro.* 490. *Poph.* 141. S. C.

To steal *Wild-Pigeons* in a *Dove-house* shut up, or Hares or Deer in a House, or even in a Park inclosed in such a Manner, that the Owner may take them whensoever he pleases, without the least Danger of their escaping, in which Case they are as much in his Power as Fish in a Pond, or young *Pigeons*, or Hawks in a Nest, *&c.* in taking of which, for the like Reason, it seems to be agreed, that Felony may be committed. *Hawk. P. C.* 1. *B.* 94.

If *Pigeons* come upon my Land, and I kill them, the Owner hath no Remedy against me; though I may be liable to the Statutes which make it penal to destroy them. *Cro. Jac.* 492.

Drifts of the Forests. The *Drifts of the Forests* are said to be when all the Cattle, as well of Commoners as of Strangers, are driven by the Officers of the Forest to some certain Pound or Place inclosed, and the End thereof is three-fold, *viz.* 1*st*, to see whether those that ought to Common do Common with such Kind of Cattle as by Prescription or Grant they ought. 2*dly*, If they Common with such Cattle as they ought, whether they do surcharge or no. 3*dly*,

E 4 If

If the Cattle of any Stranger be there which ought not to Common at all.

By **Stat.** 32 *H.* 8. *c.* 13. ' Forests, Chafes,
' and Common Ground fhall yearly be driven,
' either at *Michaelmas,* or within fifteen Days
' after, by the Keepers and Officers of the Fo-
' refts and Common Grounds, on Pain of 40*s.*
' who have alfo Power by the Statute to drive
' them at any other Time in the Year, as they
' fhall think fit; and the Owners of thofe
' Grounds have the like Power.'

Lord *Coke* makes the following Obfervations on this Act: That if the Foreft is in the King's Hands, the *Drift* muft be made by all the King's Officers of Attendance in the Foreft, and by four Men and the Reeve of every Town within the Foreft. If in a Subject's Hand, then by the Owner or Poffeffors, or by the Conftable, *&c.*. And likewife in this Statute the Purlieus are included. 4 *Inft.* 309.

Duck. See **Pheafant, Wild-Duck.**

Eggs. By **Stat.** 11 *Hen.* 7. *c.* 17. ' None
' fhall take out of the Neft any *Eggs* of Falcon,
' Gofhawk, Laner, or Swan, on Pain (being
' convicted thereof before the Juftices of the
' Peace) of a Year and a Day's Imprifonment,
' and to incur a Fine at the King's Pleafure,
' to be divided between the King and the
' Owner of the Ground, where the *Eggs* fhall
' be fo taken.'

By **Stat.** 25 *Hen.* 8. *c.* 11. ' None, from
' *March* 31 to *June* 30, fhall deftroy or take
' away the *Eggs* of any Wild-Fowl, upon Pain
' of

' of Imprifonment for a Year, and to forfeit
' for every *Egg* of a Crane or Buftard fo taken
' or deftroyed, 20 *d.* of a Bittern, Heron or Sho-
' velard, 8 *d.* and of a Mallard, Teal, and other
' Wild-Fowl (except Crows, Ravens, Bof-
' cards, and other Fowl not ufed to be eaten)'
' 1 *d.* Half to the King and Half to him that
' will fue by Action of Debt; alfo Juftices of
' the Peace may determine the fame, as in Cafes
' of Trefpaffes.'

By **Stat.** 5 *Eliz. c.* 21. ' None fhall take
' any Hawk's *Eggs,* on Pain to fuffer three
' Months Imprifonment, and to be bound with
' good Sureties to his good Behaviour for fe-
' ven Years after, or remain in Prifon till he
' doth.'

By **Stat.** 1 *Jac.* 1. *c.* 27. ' Every Perfon
' convicted by his own Confeffion, or by two
' Witneffes upon Oath before two or more Juf-
' tices of Peace, to have taken or deftroyed the
' *Eggs* of Pheafants, Partridges or Swans, fhall
' be committed to Prifon without Bail for three
' Months, unlefs he immediately pay to the
' Ufe of the Poor where the Offence is com-
' mitted, or he apprehended, 20 *s.* for every
' *Egg* ; and after one Month's Commitment,
' fhall before two or more Juftices of Peace be
' bound with two fufficient Sureties in 20 *l.*
' apiece, with Condition never to offend in the
' like again.'

A War-

A Warrant againſt a Perſon for Deſtroying
of Pheaſants *Eggs.*

(On 1 *Jac.* 1. *cap.* 27.)

To *A. B.* the Conſtable of, *&c.*

WHereas *it hath been this Day duly proved
before us* W. T. *and* J. F. *Eſquires, two
of his Majeſty's Juſtices of the Peace for the County
of* H. *That* A. J. *of* D. *in,* &c. *on or about,* &c.
*laſt paſt, did take away from and deſtroy three Phea-
ſants* Eggs *in a Neſt at* H. *contrary to an Act
of Parliament in that Caſe made and provided:*
Theſe *are therefore in his Majeſty's Name to command you to apprehend the ſaid* A. J. *and to convey
him to the common Gaol of,* &c. *there to be kept
ſafely by the Keeper of the ſame, for the Space of
three Months; except he forthwith pay to the
Churchwardens of the Pariſh of* D. *for the Uſe of
the Poor there, the Sum of* 60s. *according to the
Direction of the Statute in that Behalf made and
provided.* **Given** *under,* &c. *See* Table.

Ejectment. See *Table.*

Esbrancatura, Cutting of Branches or
Boughs in a Foreſt.

Estovers, Signifies to ſupply with Neceſſa-
ries; every Man may take *Eſtovers* in his own
Woods by the View of the Foreſters, and not
otherwiſe; and the Foreſters muſt not take any
Thing for their View; if they do, 'tis Extortion. *W. Jones's Rep.* 277.

IF

If a Man hath *Eſtovers* allowed for making a Hedge, which Hedge would have laſted two Years, but is burned the firſt Year; in this Caſe, he ſhall not be allowed new *Eſtovers*; and if he take more *Eſtovers* than he ought at one Time, they ſhall be ſeized, and the Party fined. *Itin. Pick. fol.* 3. *Manwood* 388.

If he who hath *Eſtovers* in a Foreſt, make Hurdles of them, and ſell thoſe Hurdles, he is puniſhable. *Manwood* 388.

𝕰𝖝𝖕𝖊𝖉𝖎𝖙𝖆𝖙𝖎𝖓𝖌 𝖔𝖋 𝕯𝖔𝖌𝖘. The Dogs which are allowed to be kept in the Foreſt, muſt be ſuch which are not able of themſelves to hurt the Deer; or ſuch which are diſabled, by the Laws of the Foreſt, to hurt them; which *Diſabling* or *Lawing* of Dogs, was called *Hambling* by the ancient Foreſters, but now *Expeditating*; and it was inſtituted for the Quiet and Safety of the Wild-Beaſts, and relates to every Man's Dog who lives near the Foreſt.

By **𝕮𝖍𝖆𝖗𝖙. 𝕱𝖔𝖗𝖊𝖘𝖙𝖆𝖊,** *c.* 6. '*Lawing* of Dogs ' ſhall be made in Foreſts from three Years to ' three Years by the View and Teſtimony of ' lawful Men, and not otherwiſe; and he that ' hath not his Dog *lawed* ſhall be amerced 3 *s.* ' alſo no Ox ſhall be taken, for *Lawing* of ' Dogs: And it ſhall be done by the uſual Aſ- ' ſize, *viz.* That three Claws of the Forefoot be ' cut off by the Skin. Howbeit, ſuch *Lawing* ' ſhall not be but where it hath been uſed from ' the Coronation of *H.* 2.'

The Regarders of the Foreſt ſhall view all the Maſtiffs in the Foreſt whether they are *Expeditated*, and at the next Swainmote after they have

E 6   made

made their Regard, prefent what Maftiffs are not *Expeditated*, and who are the Owners; then the Court of Swainmote or Attachments may caufe all thofe Maftiffs to be brought before them, and appoint a Perfon, with Inftruments convenient for the Purpofe, to *Expeditate* them according to Law; and then upon fuch Matter of Record, the Court may award Procefs to levy the 3*s*. and not before. *Manwood* 114, 119.

Though the Forfeiture for keeping a Maftiff not *Expeditated*, is no more than 3*s*. yet if the Dog doth hurt or kill a wild Beaft of the Foreft, then the Owner is to be punifhed according to the Quality of that Offence, and above the faid Forfeiture. *Ibid.* 119.

By *The Affize and Cuftoms of the Foreft*, If a Maftiff be found upon any Deer, and fhall be *Expeditated*, he whofe Maftiff he is, fhall be quit of the Deed: but if it be not *Expeditated*, the Owner of the Maftiff fhall be guilty, as if he had given it with his own Hands; and he fhall be put by fix Pledges, whofe Names fhall be written, and alfo what Kind of Dog it was.

If the Regarders find and prefent fuch a Dog kept at or in the Houfe of *D. A.* in the Foreft, he fhall not be amerced upon this Prefentment; but if they prefent, that *D. A.* kept the Dog, this is good, and he fhall be fined the 3*s*. *Manwood* 121.

If a Peer of the Realm, or a Bifhop, is prefented for keeping fuch a Dog, he fhall pay only 3*s*. and not according to his Quality; but if a Peer is prefented and indicted before the Juftices

of

of the Foreſt for keeping a Greyhound, and hunting with him there, in ſuch Caſe he may be amerced by the ſaid Juſtices, according to his Dignity and Eſtate. *Ibid.* 122.

In Purlieus or Places deafforeſted, a Man may keep a Maſtiff without being *Expeditated.* 4 *Inſt.* 300.

Felony. In ſome Caſes Offenders in Foreſts may be guilty of *Felony*; as if a Foreſter hath killed a Deer, and leaves it in the Foreſt whilſt he goes to the Lodge for a Horſe, and in the mean Time another Perſon carries it away, this is *Felony*, and the Offender is to ſuffer as in other Caſes of *Felony*. *Manwood* 215.

A Foreſter was indicted for *Feloniouſly* cutting down and carrying away ſeveral Trees; but the Judges would not ſuffer him to be arraigned for *Felony* upon that Indictment, becauſe the Trees which are growing are annexed to the Freehold, of which a Man cannot commit *Felony*; but if they had been cut down by the Owner, and then the Foreſter had carried them away, this had been *Felony*. 12 *Aſſi. Placito* 32. *Manwood* 215.

Where *Felony* is committed in a Foreſt, Hue and Cry may purſue the *Felon* whereſoever he goes, as after a *Felon* at Common Law, till he is apprehended. *Manwood* 216. See the *Table.*

Fence-month. The *Fence-month*, by the ancient Foreſters was called the *Defence-Month*, and is the Fawning Time; during which, Watch and Ward is kept, (ſince the Time of *Canutus*) to defend the wild Beaſts and their young ones from Danger; and every Man is
forbidden

forbidden to wander up and down in the Foreft, or otherwife to difquiet the Deer, and the Forefters, Verderors, Regarders, Agiftors and Woodwards, are all to be affifting each other in fuch Watch and Ward, and the Verderors give a Charge, which fee in *Manwood* 137. It begins fifteen Days before *Midfummer*, and ends fifteen Days after. 4 *Inft.* 313. *Manwood* 135, 136.

If any Swine, Goats or Sheep are found in the Foreft in *this Month*, they are forfeited to the King. *Itin. Lancaftr. fol.* 7. *Manwood* 136, 139. See the *Table*.

Ferret, Is a little Creature like a Weafel, ufed in catching Rabbits, for which a Replevin lies. *Cro. Jac.* 463.

Ferry. One *Blagrave* having erected a *Ferry* where there was none before, was fined 5 *l.* becaufe the Deer by this Means may be ftolen, and carried over the Water, fo as no Blood-hound can follow. *W. Jones's Rep.* 273.

Fish. By *Weftm.* 2. *c.* 47. ' None fhall ' take *Salmon* * betwixt the eighth of *September* ' and the eleventh of *November*, nor young *Salmon* with Nets or Engines, at Mill-pools, be- ' twixt the Midft of *April* and twentieth of ' *June*, on Pain of having their Nets and Engines burnt for the firft Offence ; for the fecond a Quarter of a Year's Imprifonment ; ' for the third a Year's, and after to have their

---

* The Salmon every Year afcend from the Sea up a River, fome 4 or 500 Miles perhaps, to caft their Spawn, and fecure it in Banks of Sand, until the Young is hatched, or excluded, and then return to the Sea again.

' Punifh-

' Puniſhment increaſed according to the Treſ-
' paſs. And in Places where freſh Waters be,
' Overſeers of this *Stat.* ſhall be aſſigned and
' ſworn to inquire of the Offenders.'

By **Stat.** 13 *Ric.* 2. *c.* 19. ' No *Fiſher* ſhall
' uſe any Engine by which the Fry of *Fiſh* may
' be deſtroyed, on the Pains mentioned in Sta-
' tute *Weſtm.* 2. *c.* 47.

' *Salmon* in *Lancaſhire* ſhall not be taken be-
' twixt *Michaelmas* and *Candlemas.*'

' Conſervators ſhall be ſworn to ſee this Sta-
' tute obſerved, and the Offender puniſhed.'

By **Stat.** 17 *Ric.* 2. *c.* 19. ' Juſtices of
' Peace ſhall be Conſervators of the Statutes of
' *Weſtm.* 2. *c.* 47. and 13 *Ric.* 2. *c.* 19. and
' ſhall have Power to ſearch all Wears, left by
' their Straitneſs the Fry of *Fiſh* may be de-
' ſtroyed.'

' Juſtices of Peace ſhall have Power to ap-
' point and ſwear Under-Conſervators; the ſame
' Juſtices ſhall hear and determine in Seſſions
' Offences of this Kind, and puniſh the Offen-
' ders by Fine and Impriſonment; and half the
' Fine is to go to the Under-Conſervator who
' informs.'

' The Mayor of *London* hath like Power in
' the *Thames* from *Staines* to *London*, and in
' *Medway* as far as the Citizens Grant ex-
' tends.'

By **Stat.** 2 *Hen.* 6. *c.* 15. ' None ſhall faſ-
' ten Trunks or other Nets over Rivers to the
' Deſtruction of the Fry of *Fiſh*, and Diſturb-
' ance of the common Paſſage of Veſſels, on
' Pain to forfeit 5*l.* to the King: Howbeit
' they

' they may uſe them at ſeaſonable Times, ſo
' they draw them as other *Fiſhers* do in their
' Nets, without faſtening them. And every
' Man's Right of *Fiſhing* is ſaved.'

By **Stat.** 1 *Eliz. c.* 17. ' None ſhall uſe
' any Net or Engine to deſtroy the Spawn or
' Fry of *Fiſh*, or take *Salmons* or *Trouts* out of
' Seaſon, or *Pike* ſhorter than ten Inches, *Sal-*
' *mon* than ſixteen, *Trouts* than eight, and *Bar-*
' *bels* than twelve; or ſhall uſe any Engine to
' take *Fiſh*, other than *Angle* or Net, or a Tra-
' mel of two Inches and an half Meſh, on
' Pain to forfeit 20*s.* the *Fiſh* ſo wrongfully
' taken, and the Net or Engine ſo wrongfully
' uſed.'

' All Perſons having Juriſdiction of Confer-
' vancy upon Streams of Waters, and Lords of
' Leets, have Power, upon the Oaths of 12
' Men, to hear and determine theſe Offences,
' and ſhall have all the Forfeitures which ac-
' crue thereupon.'

' The Steward of a Leet ſhall give this Sta-
' tute in Charge to the Jury, on Pain of 40*s.*
' to be divided betwixt the Queen and the In-
' former.

' If the Jury wilfully forbear to preſent Of-
' fences of this Kind, the Steward or Bailiff
' ſhall impanel another Jury to inquire of their
' Default, which being found, the firſt Jury
' ſhall forfeit 20*s.* apiece.

' Upon Default of Preſentment in Leets
' within one Year, Juſtices of Peace in Seſ-
' ſions, Juſtices of *Oyer* and *Terminer*, and Ju-
' ſtices

' ſtices of Aſſize in Circuits, have Power to
' hear and determine the ſaid Offences.'

' This Act ſhall not reſtrain the Taking of
' *Smelts, Loches, Minews, Bullheads, Gudgeons* or
' *Eels,* with Nets or Engines formerly uſed,
' ſo that no other *Fiſh* be taken therewith ; nor
' ſhall extend to abridge any former Privilege
' of Conſervancy lawfully enjoyed, or *Fiſhing*
' in *Tweed, Uſſſe, Wye,* or in Waters let to
' Farm by the Queen, ſo that the Spawn or
' Fry of *Fiſh* be wilfully deſtroyed.'

By **Stat.** 5 *Eliz. c.* 21. ' None ſhall unlaw-
' fully break down *Fiſh-Pond* Heads, or *fiſh*
' there, without Licence of the Owners, &c.
' on Pain to ſuffer three Months Impriſonment,
' and to be bound with good Sureties to the
' good Behaviour for ſeven Years.'

' The Party grieved ſhall in Seſſions or elſe-
' where recover treble Damages againſt the De-
' linquent, and on Satisfaction ſhall have Li-
' berty to procure his Releaſe of Behaviour.'

' Juſtices of *Oyer* and *Terminer,* Aſſize, Peace
' and Gaol-delivery in Seſſions, have Power to
' hear and determine theſe Offences.'

' Juſtices of Peace upon the Offenders Ac-
' knowledgment in Seſſions, and Satisfaction
' to the Party grieved, ſhall have Power to re-
' leaſe the Behaviour.'

By **Stat.** 3 *Jac.* 1. *c.* 12. ' None ſhall erect
' any Wear along the Shore, or in any Haven
' or Creek, or within five Miles of the Mouth
' of any Haven or Creek, or ſhall willingly
' deſtroy the Spawn or Fry of *Fiſh,* on Pain of
' 10*l.* to be divided between the King and the
' Proſecu-

' Proſecutor; nor ſhall any Perſon *Fiſh* in any
' of the ſaid Places, with any Net of a leſs
' Meſh than three Inches and an half from
' Knot to Knot (except for the taking Smoulds
' in *Norfolk* only) or with a Canvas Net or
' other Engine, whereby the Spawn or Fry of
' *Fiſh* may be deſtroyed, on Forfeiture of the
' ſaid Net or Engine, and 10*s*. in Money, to
' be divided betwixt the Poor of the Pariſh
' and the Proſecutor, and to be levied in Cor-
' porations by the Head-Officers, and in other
' Places by Diſtreſs and Sale of Goods, upon
' a Warrant of a Juſtice of Peace, directed unto
' the Conſtable and Churchwardens of the ſame
' Pariſh for that Purpoſe.'

' By **Stat.** 22 & 23 *Car.* 2. ' A Perſon
' convicted by Confeſſion or Oath of one Wit-
' neſs, within one Month after the Offence com-
' mitted, before a Juſtice of the Peace, of ta-
' king *Fiſh* by any Device whatſoever, in any
' Water or River, or aiding therein, ſhall make
' ſuch Recompence, and within ſuch Time, as
' the Juſtice ſhall appoint, not exceeding treble
' Damages, and pay down to the Overſeers of
' the Poor ſuch Sum as the Juſtice ſhall think
' meet, not exceeding 10*s*. in Default to be le-
' vied by Diſtreſs; and for Want thereof the
' Offender to be committed, not exceeding one
' Month, unleſs he enters into Bond with Sure-
' ties to the Party injured, not exceeding 10*l*.
' never to offend in like Manner; the Juſtice
' before whom convicted may deſtroy the En-
' gines; and Perſons aggrieved may appeal to
' the

' the Quarter-Seffions, whofe Order fhall be
' final, if no Title to any Land, Royalty or
' Fifhery be therein concerned.' *

By **Stat.** 30 *Car.* 2. *c.* 9. ' None fhall in
' the River *Severn fifh* with or ufe any Net,
' Engine or Device, whereby any *Salmon, Sal-*
' *mon-mart, Salmon-peal, Pike, Carp, Trout, Bar-*
' *bel, Chub* or *Grayling*, the Mefh whereof fhall
' be under two Inches and an Half Square from
' Knot to Knot, or above twenty Yards in
' Length, and fix in Breadth, or above fifty
' in Length, and fix in Breadth, in the Wing
' of the Net, in the faid River from *Ripley*
' *Lockftake* to *Gloucefter*-Bridge, or above fixty
' in Length below *Gloucefter*-Bridge, and fix in
' Breadth in the Wing of the Net; or fhall
' *fifh* with more than one of thofe Nets at once,
' nor fhall ufe any Device for taking the Fry of
' *Eels,* on Forfeiture of 5*l.* for every Offence,
' with the *Fifh* fo taken, and the Inftruments
' with which, *&c.*

' None between the firft of *March* and laft
' of *May* fhall do any Act whereby the *Spawn*
' of *Fifh* fhall be deftroyed, on Forfeiture of
' 40*s.* for every Offence, and the Inftruments.'

' The Juftices of Peace in the Counties of
' *Worcefter, Salop* and *Gloucefter*, fhall be Con-
' fervators of the Rivers in their refpective
' Counties, and make one or more Conferva-
' tors in their Limits; to whom or to any
' Conftable, *&c.* upon their Knowledge or In-

---

* See the Form of a Warrant to levy the Forfeiture incurred by this Stat. on a Perfon fifhing in a River or Pond,
p. See alfo *Stat.* 9 *Geo.* 1. *p.* 92.

' formation

' formation of any ſuch Offence, any two of
' them ſhall iſſue Warrants to ſearch ſuſpected
' Houſes, &c. for unlawful Inſtruments, to
' ſeize and bring them to the Quarter-Seſſions
' to be deſtroyed.'

' None ſhall be puniſhed for the ſaid Offences
' but by Information or Indictment before the
' Juſtices of *Aſſize* and *Niſi Prius*, *Oyer* and *Ter-*
' *miner*, and Gaol-delivery, or in the General
' Seſſions of Peace ; one Moiety of the Forfei-
' ture ſhall be to the Poor of the Pariſh where
' the Offence ſhall be committed, the other to
' the Proſecutor, to be levied by *Fieri Facias* or
' *Capias ad Satisfaciendum.*'

' The Juriſdiction of the Lords of Leets or
' Franchiſes ſaved, and all Rights, &c. of the
' King and others in the ſaid River.'

By **Stat.** 4 & 5 *Ann. c.* 21. 'The Acts 4 &
' 5 *W.* & *M.* & *Weſtm.* 2. to be duly put in
' Execution, and to extend to all Rivers,
' Creeks, &c. in the County of *Southampton*
' and Southern Parts of *Wiltſhire*, &c. in like
' Manner and under the ſame Penalties, as are
' contained in the above-mentioned Act, which
' ſee under **Nets.**'

' Juſtices reſiding near the Rivers ſhall aſſign
' Overſeers of this Act, who ſhall inquire after
' Offenders againſt this Statute, and apprehend
' them and deſtroy their Nets, &c. every Of-
' fender to be brought before a Juſtice of Peace,
' and being convicted by the Oath of one or
' more Witneſſes, or by his own Confeſſion,
' ſhall forfeit for the firſt Offence a Sum to be
' aſcertained by the Juſtice, not under 20 *s.* nor
' above

' above 5 *l.* and for the second, not under 40*s.*
' nor more than 10*l.* and as the Offence shall
' increase, the Justice shall double the Penalty;
' one Half thereof to the Informer, the other
' to the Poor of the Parish where the Offence
' is committed; and if the Offender do not on
' Demand pay the Penalty, or be not able, the
' Justice shall send him to the House of Correc-
' tion for three Months.'

' No Person (not duly qualified) shall here-
' after kill *Salmon,* or any other *Fish*; and no
' Person whatsoever shall take, kill, &c. any
' *Salmon, Salmon-Peal,* or *Salmon-Kind,* by
' Hawks, Racks, Gins, &c. at any Time after
' *June* the thirtieth till *November* the eleventh,
' under the Penalties afore mentioned.'

' Owners of Meadow-Grounds, &c. to let
' *Salmon* pass out of Dikes, &c. into the Ri-
' vers and not destroy them, under the like
' Penalty.'

' Owners of Mills, &c. to keep open one
' Scuttle of a Foot Square in the Waste-hatch,
' for *Salmon* to pass up and down, from the
' eleventh of *November* to the thirty-first of
' *May* every Year, and not to use any Nets,
' &c. in the said Scuttle during the said Term,
' on like Penalty; and not to lay any Pots or
' Nets to catch *Eels* after the first of *January* to
' the tenth of *March,* unless Racks be set be-
' fore them, &c.'

' No *Bouges* or *Sea-Trouts* shall be taken, or
' *Salmon* sold, after the thirtieth of *June* till the
' eleventh of *November* every Year, under like
' Penalties.'

4   ' The

' The Forfeitures to be levied by Diſtreſs
' and Sale, of the Offender's Goods, by War-
' rant of the Juſtice before whom convicted ;
' and for want of Diſtreſs, to be ſent to the
' Houſe of Correction: But this Act ſhall not
' extend to any Country or Place in this King-
' dom, ſave only to the County of *Southampton*
' and Southern Parts of *Wiltſhire.*'

By **Stat.** 1 *Geo.* 1. *c.* 18. ' The Clauſe in
' the Act of 4 & 5 *Ann. c.* 21. relating to the
' catching of *Salmon,* &*c.* from the thirtieth of
' *June* till the eleventh of *November,* ſo far as
' relates to the Owners of *Fiſheries* in the Rivers
' mentioned in the ſaid Act, is repealed : And
' ſuch Owners may take *Salmon,* &*c.* from the
' eleventh of *November* to the firſt of *Auguſt* ;
' but no ſuch Owner ſhall between the firſt of
' *Auguſt* and the eleventh of *November* follow-
' ing take any *Salmon,* or offer the ſame to Sale,
' under the Penalties in the ſaid Act of 4 & 5
' *Ann. c.* 21.'

' Perſons deſtroying the Fry of *Salmon* in the
' Rivers *Severn, Dee, Wye, Teame, Ware, Tees,*
' *Ribble, Merſey, Dun, Air, Ouze, Swaile, Cal-*
' *der, Wharf, Eure, Darwent* and *Trent,* with
' Nets, Engines, &*c.* whereby the Spawn of
' *Salmon,* or any *Kepper* or *Shedder-Salmon,* or
' any not being eighteen Inches in Length from
' the Eye to the Extent of the Middle of the
' Tail; or who ſhall erect any Bank, Dam,
' Hedge, or Nets, croſs any of the ſaid Rivers,
' whereby the *Salmon* may be hindered from
' paſſing up the ſaid Rivers to ſpawn ; or ſhall
' take any *Salmon* in the ſaid Rivers between
' the

' the laſt Day of *July* and the twelfth of *No-*
' *vember*, or who ſhall after the twelfth of *No-*
' *vember* *fiſh* there for *Salmon* with other Nets,
' *&c.* than are allowed by 1 *Eliz. c.* 17. and 30.
' *Car.* 2. *c.* 9. being convicted thereof before
' one Juſtice of the Peace of the County where
' the Offence ſhall be committed, either upon
' View of ſuch Juſtice, by Confeſſion, or by
' one Witneſs upon Oath, ſhall forfeit 5*l.* for
' every Offence, beſides the *Fiſh* * ſo taken,
' and the Nets, *&c.* one Half to the Informer,
' the other to the Poor of the Pariſh where the
' Offence ſhall be committed, to be levied by
' Diſtreſs and Sale of Goods, rendering the
' Overplus, above the Charges of the Diſtreſs;
' and for want of ſuch Diſtreſs, the Offender to
' be committed to the Houſe of Correction,
' or other County Gaol, for any Time not ex-
' ceeding three Months, or leſs than one, there
' to be kept to hard Labour, and ſuffer ſuch
' other corporal Puniſhment as the Juſtices
' ſhall think fit; the Nets, *&c.* to be forfeited,
' and the Banks, *&c.* to be removed at the
' Charge of the Offender, which if not paid on
' Conviction, to be levied as the ſaid 5*l.*

' Perſons convicted of ſending to *London*
' from any of the ſaid Rivers, to Fiſhmongers
' or their Agents, or buying or ſelling any ſuch
' *Salmon*, weighing leſs than ſix Pounds each,
' ſhall forfeit 5*l.* and the *Fiſh*; one Half of
' the ſaid Sum and *Fiſh* to the Informer, the

---

* *Note*, It is not ſaid who ſhall have the Fiſh, ſo that
it ſeemeth that they are forfeited to the King. *Burn's*
Juſtice, p. 326. 5th Edit. in fol.

                  ' other

' other to the Poor where the Offence ſhall be
' committed, to be levied by Diſtreſs, if the
' Sum be not paid on Conviction; .and for
' want of ſuch Diſtreſs the Offender ſhall be
' committed to the Houſe of Correction or
' County Gaol, there to be kept to hard La-
' bour for three Months, unleſs the Forfeiture
' be paid in the mean Time.'

' Offenders in the ſaid Rivers puniſhed by
' this Act, ſhall not be proſecuted on any other
' for the ſame Offence.'

' Perſons aggrieved by any Judgment of Ju-
' ſtices, in the Caſes aforeſaid, may appeal to
' the Quarter-Seſſions of the County, &c. who
' are hereby impowered to hear and finally de-
' termine the ſame.'

' This Act ſhall not extend to any ancient
' Wears or Locks on any Rivers; but the Pro-
' prietors thereof may repair, rebuild, remove
' or take down any of them, as they might
' have done if this Act had not been made.'

By Stat. 9 *Geo.* 1. *c.* 22. Stealing *Fiſh* out of
any River or Pond, or breaking down the
Head or Mound of any *Fiſh* Pond, whereby
the *Fiſh* ſhall be loſt or deſtroyed, made Felony
without Benefit of Clergy. Continued by 2
Geo. 2. *c.* 57. to *Sept.* 1, 1757, and from thence,
&c. See *antea*, p.

A Wa

A Warrant againſt a *Fiſher* for taking *Sal-mon* under Size, in order to convict him. (*1 Geo. 1. cap.* 18.)

To the Conſtable of, *&c.*

W𝔥𝔢𝔯𝔢𝔞𝔰 *Complaint hath been made unto me by* H. W. *of,* &c. *That* C. C. *of your Pariſh hath lately killed and deſtroyed ſeveral* Salmons, *not being of the Size the Law requires,* to wit, *not eighteen Inches in Length from the Eye to the Extent of the Tail;* 𝔗𝔥𝔢𝔰𝔢 *are therefore to command you to apprehend the ſaid* C. C. *and to bring him before me or ſome other of his Majeſty's Juſtices of the Peace for this County, to anſwer the Premiſſes, and be dealt with according to Law.* 𝔊𝔦𝔳𝔢𝔫, &c.

A Warrant to levy the Forfeiture on a *Miller* for deſtroying *Salmon.* (4 *& 5 Ann. cap.* 21.)

W𝔥𝔢𝔯𝔢𝔞𝔰 *it hath been duly proved before me* J. A. *Eſq; one of his Majeſty's Juſtices of the Peace for the County of* Southampton, *reſiding near the River of,* &c. *in the ſaid County, which runs into the Sea there, That* D. J. *of,* &c. Miller, *living in the Mill called,* &c. *on the River aforeſaid, hath not kept open a Hatch for the* Salmon *to paſs and repaſs from the eleventh Day of* November *to the thirty-firſt of* May *laſt, as the Statute in that Behalf directs and requires,*

F

but

but *bath lately taken and deſtroyed ſeveral* Salmons
*in Pots, and by other Means in the ſaid River out
of Seaſon, contrary to Law :* **Theſe** *are therefore
to command you to demand of the ſaid* D. J. *the
Sum of* 20 s. *which be bath forfeited by the Offence
aforeſaid ; and if the ſaid* D. J. *refuſes to pay the
ſame, that you do levy it by Diſtreſs and Sale of the
Goods of the ſaid* D. J. *and if no ſuch Diſtreſs
can be found, that you convey him to the Houſe of
Correction, there to remain for the Space of three
Months, according to the Direction of the ſaid
Statute in that Caſe made and provided.* **Given,** &c.

A Warrant for taking Nets and *Fiſh*, (4 &
5 *W.* & *M. cap.* 23.) *Vide Shaw's Juſtice,*
Vol. 1. *p.* 400. for a Precedent on this
Act.

         To the Conſtable of, &c.

——— } *to wit.* **B**Y *Virtue of an Act of Parliament
in that Caſe made ; Theſe are to
require you, on Sight hereof, (in the Day-time) to
make ſtrict Search in Houſes and Outhouſes of all
Perſons in your Pariſh not qualified to take* Fiſh *in
Rivers or* Fiſheries, *except navigable Rivers, and
Makers and Sellers of ſuch Nets, or Owners of*
Fiſheries ; *and if on your Search, or you ſhall be
informed of ſuch Nets laid in any River or* Fiſhery,
*then you are to ſeize them and bring them to the
Lord of the Manor, to be kept for his Uſe, or deſtroyed, as he ſhall think fit.* Given, &c.

         A Decla-

A Declaration in Trespass for breaking the Plaintiff's Clóse, and *Fishing* in his *Fishery.*

Southampton, } **T** P. *complains of* J. K. L.
to wit.   }   . W. *and* E. J. *being in the.
Cuſtody of the Marſhal of the* Marſhalſea *of our
Sovereign Lord the King, before the King himſelf,
for that on the nineteenth Day of* May *in the ſe-
venth Year of the Reign of our preſent Sovereign
Lord* George *the Second, and ſo forth, they the
ſaid* J. K. L. W. *and* E. J. *with Force and
Arms broke and entered into the Clóse of the ſaid*
T. P. *called,* &c. *at,* &c. *in the ſaid County of*
Southampton; *and in walking in the ſaid Clóse,
trod down and deſtroyed the Graſs of the ſaid* T.
P. *then and there growing, to the Value of* 40 s.
*And alſo for that afterwards, that is to ſay, the
ſame Day and Year, at,* &c. *aforeſaid, in the ſaid
County of* Southampton, *with Force and Arms
they the ſaid* J. K. L. W. *and* E. J. *Fiſhed in
the ſeparate* Fiſhery *of the ſaid* T. P. *in the River of,* &c. *in the,* &c. *aforeſaid, and then took
and carried away* Fiſhes *from his the ſaid* T. P.'s
ſaid ſeparate Fiſhery *there found, that is to ſay,*
1000 *Dacos, and* 1000 *Gudgeons, to the Value of*
50 l. *And then and there committed other Injuries
againſt the ſaid* T. P. *againſt the Peace of our ſaid
Sovereign Lord the King, and to the Damage of the
ſaid* T. P. 200 l. *and therefore he brings his Suit,*
&c.

An Indictment (at Common Law) for *Fiſh-ing* without the Conſent of the Owner.

Middleſex, } **T**HE Jurors &c. That D. P.
to wit. } of, &c. *in the County afore-ſaid, Yeoman, the third Day of* June *in the ſeventh Year,* &c. *with Force and Arms, the Cloſe of* M. A. *at* A *in the County aforeſaid broke, and in the ſeveral* Fiſhery *of the ſaid* D. P. *un-lawfully did* fiſh, *and* Fiſh *there,* to wit, *two* Salmons *and ten* Trouts, &c. *to the Value of,* &c. *then and there took and carried away, and his Graſs to the Value of,* &c. *there lately growing did tread down and deſtroy, and other Enormities to him did, againſt the Peace,* &c.

An Indictment for *Fiſhing* in a Pond.

Middleſex, } **T**HE Jurors, &c. That C. D.
to wit. } of B. *in the ſaid County, Yeo-man, on the* —— *Day of* —— *in the* —— *Year of the Reign,* &c. *and on divers Days and Times, as well before as after the ſaid* —— *Day of* —— *at* B. *aforeſaid in the ſaid County, with Force and Arms, did unlawfully* fiſh *with Nets and other Engines in a certain Pond there, being the Freehold of* E. F. *Eſq; and did then and there take and carry away divers* Fiſh, *that is to ſay, fifty Trouts, fifty Carps,* &c. *againſt the Peace,* &c.

Taking

Taking *Fish* out of a Net, Trunk or Pond is Felony, becaufe they have not their natural Li﹣ berty as in Rivers. 1 *Vent.* 122.

Law Cafes.

Any Man may erect a *Fish* Pond without Li﹣ cence ; becaufe it is a Matter of Profit, and for the Increafe of Victuals. 2 *Inft.* 199.

In Trefpafs for breaking and entring his Clofe, and *fifhing* in *feparali pifcaria fua,* [*in his feparate Fifhery*] and for taking *his Fifh* there, *(viz)* one hundred *Eels*; upon Not guilty pleaded, the Plaintiff had a Verdict, and intire Damages; but it was moved in Arreft of Judgment, that the Declaration was ill, becaufe it was for ta﹣ king *his Fifh*; whereas he cannot have a Pro﹣ perty in them, fo as to call them *his Fifh,* till they are taken, and in his Poffeffion ; but ad﹣ judged, that he having fet forth, that they were taken in his *feparate Fifhery,* he hath a Property in them; for no other Perfon can enter and take them there; if it had been *extra liberam pifca-riam fuam* [*out of his Free Fifhery*] the Action would not lie. *Child* againft *Greenbill,* Cro. Car. 390, 399, 553. *March* 48. S. C.

The Queftion at a Trial at Bar concerning the *River of Wallfleet* was, whether *T. S.* had a Right of *Fifhing* there, exclufive of all other Perfons; and the Lord Chief *Juftice Hale* thus diftinguifhed;

ff. That a Lord of a Manor having the Soil of a private River, 'tis good Evidence to prove that he hath the Right of *Fifhing,* exclufive of all others, and that he who will claim *free Fish-ing* in such a River, must prove his Right; but that where a River *ebbs* and *flows*, and is an Arm of the Sea, in such Case the *Fishing* there is common to all People; and if an Action of Trespass is brought against any Man for *fishing* there, 'tis a good Justification for the Defendant to plead, that the Place where the Trespass is supposed to be done, is an *Arm of the Sea,* in which every Subject of the King hath and ought to have *free Fishing*; that in the River *Severn* there are several Restraints as *Gurgites*; but that on each Side of the said River, the Soil doth belong to the respective Lords on those Sides, and they have a peculiar Sort of *Fishery*; but that the common *Fishery* belongs to all People; that the Soil of the River *Thames* is in the King, and that the Lord Mayor of *London* for the Time being is Conservator of that River, and that it is common to all Fishermen. 1 *Mod.* 105.

Trespass, &c. for breaking his Close, &c. the Defendant justified, for that the Place where the Trespass was supposed to be done is in *B.* in which Place he had a Right of *Fishing* by Prescription; and upon a Demurrer to this Plea, it was adjudged not good; because there are several Sorts of Fisheries, (viz.) *free Fishing, several Fishing,* and *common Fishing*; and he (the Defendant) did not set forth to what Kind of *Fishing* he had a Right, nor whether it was a Right as appertaining to any Manor or Messuage, but made it a mere Personal Thing by this Plea; 'tis true an *Easement* (as a Way) may be claimed without setting forth to what it appertains, and so may

a

a *Liberty*, but an *Intereſt* cannot; as for Inſtance, a *Common* cannot, becauſe 'tis an *Intereſt*, and ſo is a *Right of Fiſhing*. *Hardres* 407.

The Defendant was indicted for taking out of the Pond of *T. S.* at *H. &c.* certain *Fiſh*, called *Carp Fiſh*, *de bonis & catallis ipſius* T. S. *propriis* [*the proper Goods and Chattels of him the ſaid* T. S.] An Exception was taken to this Indictment, becauſe it did not ſet forth how many *Fiſh* the Defendant did take; and for this Purpoſe, 5 *Rep.* 34. *Playter's* Caſe was cited, which was an Action of Treſpaſs *Quare clauſum fregit, & piſces ſuos cepit* [*wherefore he broke his Cloſe, and took his Fiſh*]; the Plaintiff had a Verdict and intire Damages, but the Judgment was ſtayed for the *Incertainty of the Number and Nature of the Fiſhes taken*; but the principal Caſe being upon an Indictment, Damages are not to be recovered, but the Offender is to be fined at the Diſcretion of the Court, according to the Circumſtances of the Fact, and not according to the Number of the *Fiſh* he took; 'tis true, in Actions of Treſpaſs the Modern Reſolutions have been according to *Playter's* Caſe; as for Inſtance, in Treſpaſs, *&c.* for taking his *Fiſh*, not ſetting forth *what Number, or of what Kind*; the Plaintiff had a Verdict, but could never get Judgment; for the Chief Juſtice *Hale* was of Opinion, that both the *Kind* and *Number* ought to be ſet forth; and that where the Plaintiff declares for *Fiſhing* in his *ſeveral Fiſhery*, and taking *Eels* there, 'tis uſually ſaid what Numbers. *The King* againſt *Wetwany,* 1 *Lev.* 203. 1 *Keb.* 178. S. C. 3 *Keb.* 107. *Burrage's* Caſe.

F 4   The

The Defendants were indicted, for that they *Vi & Armis*, and without Licence and unlawfully did fish *in quadam piscinâ* of *T. S.* and took and carried away several *Fish* in the Night with Nets, against the Form of the Statute 5 *Eliz. c.* 21. It was held, that if this had been an Indictment at Common Law, it had been ill; because the Words *riotofe affemblaverunt* were left out, but that it was well enough upon the Statute; however this Indictment was quashed, because of that infenfible Word *Piscina*, whereas *Piscaria* is the proper Word to exprefs a *Fishery*. *The King* against *Marshal and others*, 2 *Keb.* 594.

Trefpafs, &c. for that the Defendant *with Force and Arms* on fuch a Day, &c. and in fuch a Place, did fish in his (the Plaintiff's) *free Fishery*, and did take *Fish* there, &c. upon Not guilty pleaded the Plaintiff had a Verdict; and it was moved in Arreft of Judgment, that he who had a *free Fishery* could not maintain this Action, because it was only a Freedom of *Fishing* with others, and the fame as *Communis piscaria*, and that fuch a Grantee had only a Liberty to take *Fish*, and no Property in them till they are taken; that *libera piscaria* was not like *libera warrena*; for a Grantee of the laft might maintain Trefpafs against any one but the Owner of the Soil, for hunting in his *free Warren*, becaufe that is a Liberty to hunt in his own or another's Ground exclufive of others; and this Grant the King may make, who is Mafter of all the Game; but a *free Fishery* is only a Freedom of *fishing* with others. But *Holt* Chief Juftice held there were three Sorts of *Fisheries*, (viz.) a *feveral Fishery*,

Fishery, and he who has such a *Fishery*, is the
Owner of the Soil where the Water doth run;
and therefore if *T. S.* should bring an Action,
&c. for *fishing* therein, the Defendant may plead
that 'tis *liberum tenementum* of another; the next
is *libera piscaria, free Fishery*, which is where
the Right of *fishing* is granted to *T. S.* in such
Case he hath the Property of the *Fish*, and may
bring a possessory Action for them without making any Title; the last is *communis piscaria*, and
this is like the Case of other Commons. See
Regist. 95. in Point. *Smith* against *Kemp*, 2
Salk. 637. 4 *Mod.* 355. S. C. 1 *Inst.* 122.
was denied to be Law.

Trespass, &c. in which the Plaintiff declared
quare pisces suos eepit in separali piscaria; upon
Not guilty pleaded the Plaintiff had a Verdict;
and now it was moved in Arrest of Judgment,
that the Declaration was ill, because the Plaintiff could not declare for taking *Pisces suos*, unless they had been in a Stew or Trunk; but it
was adjudged, that after a Verdict any Thing
shall be intended to make the Declaration good.

Foot-geld, In *Saxon* For-ʒelban, is an
Amerciament for not expeditating Dogs in the
Forest.

A Man claimed to be quit of *Foot-Geld* * and
produced a Grant for the same, which was allowed: But a Man cannot prescribe for the same,
because such Prescription cannot have any reasonable Commencement. *Assizes of Pickering,
Anno* 10 *Ed.* 3. *Manwood* 109.

* *i. e.* To keep Dogs in the Forest without being expeditated.

Forest,

Forest, Is a certain Territory of Woody Grounds, and fruitful Pastures, privileged for Wild Beasts and Fowls of *Forest*, Chase, and Warren, to rest and abide there in the safe Protection of the King, for his Delight and Pleasure; and is in its Nature the highest Franchise of Princely Pleasure, comprehending a Chase, a Park, and a Warren; which Territory of Ground so privileged is meered and bounded with unremoveable Marks, Meers and Boundaries, either known by Record or Prescription; and also replenished with Wild-Beasts of Venary or Chase, * and with great Coverts of *Vert*, for the Succour of the Beasts there to abide: For the Preservation and Continuance of which Place, together with the Vert and Venison, there are particular Officers, Laws, and Privileges belonging to the same, requisite for that Purpose, and proper only to a *Forest*, and to no other Place. *Manw.* 146. *All which will be inserted under their Heads.*

The Beasts of the *Forest* frequent the Coverts in the Day-time, and feed on the Lawns, Meadows and Pasture Grounds in the Night, and they are properly the *Hart*, the *Hind*, the *Buck*, the *Hare*, the *Boar*, and the *Wolf*; but legally all Wild Beasts of Venary. 1 *Inst.* 233.

* A Forest must be replenished with wild Beasts of Venary or Chase, † otherwise 'tis no Forest. *Manwood* 145, 163. And this Privilege distinguishes a Forest from other Places, having Woods, Coverts and Fruitful Pastures.

† *Vert* comprehends every Thing which bears green Leaves in a Forest. *Manw.* 146.

'Ti

'Tis a general Opinion amongſt the Learned in the Law, That the King only by the Law of Nations, or Common Law, may make a Foreſt. *Braċt. Lib.* 2. *c.* 24. *Heſket, fol.* 8. *Man-wood* 153.

The King being ſeiſed of a *Foreſt*, did grant the Foreſt to another in Fee, the Grantee ſhall have no *Foreſt*, becauſe he hath no Power to make Juſtices and Officers of the *Foreſt* to hold Courts, *&c.* but yet though it cannot take Effect by Force of the Grant as a *Foreſt*, yet the ſame ſhall paſs as a Free-Chaſe. But if the King grants a *Foreſt* to a Subjeċt, and granteth further, that upon Requeſt made in Chancery, he and his Heirs ſhall have the Juſtice of the *Foreſt*, then the *Subjeċt* hath a *Foreſt* in Law. 4 *Inſt.* 314.

The Oath of the Inhabitants of the *Foreſt*, being of the Age of twelve Years, was antiently uſed in theſe Old Rhymes.

You ſhall true Liege-Man be,
Unto the King's Majeſty :
Unto the Beaſts of the Foreſt *you ſhall no Hurt do;*
Nor to any Thing that doth belong thereunto :
The Offences of others you ſhall not conceal,
But to the utmoſt of your Power, you ſhall them reveal
Unto the Officers of the Foreſt,
Or to them who may ſee them redreſs :
All theſe Things you ſhall ſee done,
So help you GOD at his Holy Doom.

By 𝔖tat. 17 *Car.* 1. *c.* 16. ' 'Tis enaċted, ' that the Metes, Limits, and Bounds of every
F 6 ' Foreſt,

' *Forest*, fhall be adjudged to extend no farther
' than they were commonly known or reputed
' to extend in the 20th Year of the Reign of
' King *James*; and no Place in *England* or *Wales*
' fhall be adjuged a *Forest*, or within the Bounds
' of a *Forest*, where no *Justice-Seat*, *Swainmote*,
' or *Court of Attachments* have been held ; or
' where no *Verderors* have been chosen, or *Re-*
' *gard* made within *sixty Years* before the first
' Year of the Reign of King *Car.* 1. but the
' fame Place fhall be disafforested, and exempt-
' ed from the Laws of the *Forest*.

' Provided, That for the better ascertaining
' the *Metes and Bounds of the Forests*, the *Lord*
' *Chancellor*, or *Keeper of the Great Seal* for the
' Time being, fhall upon Request of any of
' the Peers, or Knights of Shires, or Burgesses
' of Parliament, grant Commissions under the
' Great Seal to Commissioners, to be nominated
' by them respectively, or by any of them, to
' make Inquisition, by the Oaths of Witnesses,
' concerning the *Metes and Bounds* of any *Forests*,
' which were commonly known to be such in the
' 20th Year of King *James*, and to return into
' Chancery the Inquest so taken ; and the She-
' riffs, &c. of every County where such Inqui-
' sition fhall be taken, and the *Verderors*, *Fo-*
' *resters*, *Rangers*, and other Officers of the *Forest*
' respectively, fhall be assisting to the Execu-
' tion of such Commissions ; or where there are
' no such Officers, or where there are any and
' they fhall neglect to attend, the Commissioners
' may proceed without them.'

' And

' And the *Metes and Bounds* of the *Foreſt* ſo
' returned, ſhall not be adjudged to extend far-
' ther; and all Places, which ſhall be without
' ſuch Metes and Bounds ſo returned ſhall be
' free, as if they had never been Part of the
' *Foreſt*, or ſo reputed.'

' Provided, That all Grounds diſafforeſted
' by Letters Patent, or otherwiſe, ſince the 20th
' Year of the Reign of King *James*, ſhall be
' excluded and left out of the Metes and Bounds
' of *Foreſts*, to be inquired into by the ſaid Com-
' miſſioners, and are hereby declared to be diſ-
' afforeſted ; and the Owners, of Grounds diſ-
' afforeſted ſhall enjoy Common in the *Foreſt*
' as heretofore.'

Law Caſes.

Hen. 8. granted a Leaſe to *T. S.* of the *Foreſt*
of Wayland and *Sapley* ; in which the Leſſee
covenanted to keep 100 Deer there, during the
Term demiſed, and at the End thereof to leave
the like Number there ; and afterwards the
King granted the Reverſion thereof to the Lord
North : Adjudged, that by the Grant of this
Leaſe of theſe *Foreſts*, the Deer paſſed to
Leſſee, and that the Grantee of the Reverſion
could not kill them, becauſe that would be to
diſable the Leſſee to perform his Covenant.
Dyer 149.

Where the King granted the Herbage of his
Foreſt, and a Stranger puts in his Cattle ; adjudged, that the Grantee might either diſtrain
them damage-feaſant, or he might have an
Action

Action of Trefpafs *quare clauſum fregit*; but he cannot take the Fruit of the Trees, or cut them down. *Dyer* 287.

A Man ſhall not enter the *Foreſt* in the Night-time; therefore if his Horſe is paſtured there, and he enter in the Night, and take out his Horſe, he ſhall be impriſoned, or ranſomed and bound to the Good Behaviour of the *Foreſt*. *Manwood* 214. See *Table*.

Foꝛeſter, Is an Officer made by Letters Patent under the Great Seal, and is ſworn to preferve *Vert* and *Veniſon* in the Foreſt; and to attend upon the Wild-Beaſts within his Bailiwick; to attach Offenders there, either in *Vert* or *Veniſon*, and to preſent the ſame at the Courts of the Foreſt, that they may be puniſhed according to the Quantity and Quality of their Offences and Treſpaſſes: Some *Foreſters* have their Office in Fee, paying to the King a Fee-Farm Rent: And a Man may be a *Foreſter* in Fee in Right of his Wife. Some have their Office for Life, and others only during Pleaſure. And *Foreſters* muſt not walk or make any Attachments in the Foreſt before they are ſworn, *Manwood* 162, 163,

The Oath of a *Foreſter*.

YOU *ſhall truly execute the Office of a* Foreſter, *or Keeper of the King's Wild-Beaſts, in the Walk called* P. *within the Foreſt of* W. *you ſhall be of good Behaviour yourſelf towards his Majeſty's Wild-Beaſts, and the Vert and Veniſon of the ſame; you ſhall not conceal the Offence of any*
other

*other Person, either in Vert or Venison, that shall
be done within your Charge, but as well the same
Offence, as also all Attachments, you shall present
at the next Court of Attachment, or Swainmote,
which shall happen to be holden for the same Forest;
And you shall to the uttermost of your Power maintain and keep the Assize of the Forest; and in all
Things the King's Right defend concerning the same
so long as you shall be Keeper there.*

So help you God.

Every *Forester* is bound to appear at the
Justice-Seat, and when he is first called, he
ought to deliver his Horn upon his Knees to the
Chief Justice in Eyre, which is then delivered
to the Marshal, and he pays a Fine of 6s. 8d.
before it is redelivered. *Manwood* 173.

A *Forester* cannot hunt or kill any Deer in
the Forest without a lawful Warrant; for if he
doth, he forfeits his Office: And so it is if he
is negligent in apprehending Offenders, or willingly suffers them to kill or destroy the Game.
Manwood 164, 165. 5 *Ed.* 4. *fol.* 26. *Trin.* 5
Ed. 4. *fol.* 5. *Placito* 64.

By **Stat.** 21 *Ed.* 1. ' A *Forester*, Parker,
' or Warrener shall not be questioned for kil-
' ling a Trespasser, who (after the Peace cried
' unto him) will not yield himself, so it be not
' done out of some other Malice.'

By **Stat.** 25 *Ed.* 3. *Stat.* 5. *c.* 7. ' No *Fo-
' rester*, or other Minister of the Forest, shall
' gather any Victuals, or other Thing, by Co-
' lour of his Office, but, what is due of old
' Right.' See *Table.*

Forest-Law,

Forest-Law, Is a private Law, and muſt be
pleaded. 2 *Leon.* 209, 210. See *Laws of the
Foreſt.*

Forest-Service. *Stanhope,* together with
Walſingham and *Aukland,* in the Biſhoprick of
Durham, were held of the Biſhop by *Foreſt-
Service,* beſides Demeſnes and other Tenures.
Particularly upon his great Huntings, the Tenants in thoſe Parts were bound to ſet up for him
a *Field-houſe* or *Tabernacle,* with a Chapel, and
all Manner of Rooms and Offices ; as alſo to
furniſh him with Dogs and Horſes, and to carry
his Proviſion, and to attend him during his Stay,
for the Supply of all Conveniencies. *Compleat
Engliſh Copy-holder* 511. ſub Tit. *Stanhope.*

Fowl. See **Wild-Duck.**

Fox. The *Fox* is the third Beaſt of Chaſe,
and is called the 1ſt Year a *Cub,* and the 2d a
Fox, * and ſo afterwards ; his Seaſon of Hunting begins at *Chriſtmas,* and laſteth till *Lady-
Day.*

Though the Common Law warrants the
Hunting of Beaſts of Prey in other Men's
Grounds, as the Fox and the Badger; yet 'tis
not lawful to dig the Ground to unearth them,
as appears by the following Caſe :

In Treſpaſs for entering on and digging his
Lands, the Defendant pleaded in Bar, that the
common Voice was, that *quædam melis* a noiſome
Vermin called a Badger, was on the ſaid Land,

---

* *Canutus* did not account a *Fox* a Beaſt of Chaſe, yet
he was privileged in a Foreſt, and was not to be hurt
there.

and had done much Harm there, and therefore
he (the Defendant) came thither with his Dogs
and hunted him ; and in Pursuit of the said
Badger he followed his Dogs to kill it, and
found him in the Plaintiff's Ground, which he
digged, and killed him there, and filled up the
Trench with Earth again *quæ est eadem trans-*
gressio & soditio (which is the same Trespass and
Digging) ; and upon a Demurrer, this was adjudged an ill Plea ; for there is a Difference
where a Man enters on the Land of another
without his Leave to find such Vermin, and
where he enters in Pursuit of them when found ;
for in the first Case 'tis unlawful, but in the other
Case 'tis justifiable ; besides this Plea is ill, for,
the Defendant cannot justify the Digging ; he
might have found other Means to kill the Badger.
Gedge or *Guest* against *Mimms*, 2 *Cro.* 321. 2
Bulst. 60. S. C.

In Trespass for hunting and breaking his
Hedges, the Case was, 'A man unkennelled a
Fox on his own Lands, and his Hounds pursued
the same *Fox* into the Grounds of the Plaintiff ;
and if his Hedges were broke, it was done in-
voluntarily, in Pursuit of the *Fox* ; this was adjudged a good Plea, and that he might lawfully
pursue the *Fox*, because 'tis a noisome Creature
to the Publick. *Popb.* 163. in *Miller* and *Cowdry's*
Case.

Justification

Juftification in Trefpafs, where the Defendant was fued, and juftified for hunting and killing *Foxes* and Badgers.

A N D the aforefaid T. S. as to the whole Trefpafs aforefaid, in the aforefaid Place called B. with the Appurtenances, fuppofed to be, except the Breaking of the Clofe aforefaid and digging of the Soil aforefaid, faith, that he is not thereof guilty; and of this he puts himfelf upon the Country, &c. And as to the Breaking of the Clofe aforefaid and the Soil in the aforefaid Clofe called B. above fuppofed to be done, faith, that the aforefaid (Plaintiff) his Action aforefaid, against the faid (Defendant) ought not to have, becaufe he faith, That within the Clofe aforefaid, called B. before the Time aforefaid, in which the Trefpafs aforefaid is above fuppofed to be done, there were certain Earths and Kennels, wherein Badgers and Foxes, being hurtful living Creatures, and which were wont to kill Lambs, and other living Creatures, profitable and neceffary for the Food and Suftenance of Men, did Earth and Kennel themfelves: And the fame T. further faith, that he the faid T. (on fuch a Day and Year) in a certain Clofe of Land called W. did find the Footing of two Badgers, being hurtful Creatures, and which were ufually accuftomed to kill Lambs, and other fuch like living Creatures as aforefaid; and the fame Footing of the faid Badgers fo found, from the aforefaid Clofe called W. into the aforefaid Clofe B. called at the aforefaid Time, &c. did follow and hunt, into which faid Clofe the aforefaid two Badgers, the aforefaid Time in
which

*which, &c. in the said Earths had Earthed them-
selves there, by which the same T. S. the aforesaid
Time in which, &c. to kill and destroy them so under
the Earth, (as aforesaid) Earthing in the Soil
aforesaid, in the said Close called B. then and there
did dig, and them then and there did kill and destroy,
as it was lawful for him; which said Following
and Hunting of the Badgers aforesaid into the aforesaid Close called B. are the same Breaking of the
Close aforesaid, and Digging of the Soil aforesaid,
whereof the aforesaid (Plaintiff) above against him
complaineth; and this he is ready to verify, &c.*

The Laws for paying Rewards for *Foxes,
Crows,* and other ravenous Creatures are expired. See the *Table.*

𝔉𝔯𝔞𝔫𝔨-𝔠𝔥𝔞𝔰𝔢, Is a Liberty of *Free-Chase*;
by which all Persons, that have Lands within
the Compass thereof, are prohibited to cut down
any Wood, &c. without the View of the Forester,
though it be in his own Demesnes. *Cromp, Jur.*
187.

𝔉𝔯𝔢𝔰𝔥-𝔖𝔲𝔦𝔱 *within the View,* impowers the
Officers that pursue Trespassers in the Forest to
seize them, even without the Bounds of it.

𝔊𝔞𝔪𝔢. By 𝔖𝔱𝔞𝔱. 4 & 5 *W. & M. c.*
23. ' All the Laws now in Force, for the better
' Preservation of the *Games* of this Kingdom,
' shall be duly put in Execution.'

By 𝔖𝔱𝔞𝔱. 3 *Geo.* 1. *c.* 11. ' The Stat. 5 &
' 9 , *Ann.* * and all others now in Force, for
' the better Preservation of the *Game,* and all

* See Tit 𝔇𝔬𝔤𝔰,

' Things

' Things therein contained, not hereby altered,
' ſhall remain in full Force.'

- By **Stat.** 8 *Geo.* 1. *c.* 19. for the better
Recovery of the Penalties inflicted upon Perſons
who deſtroy the *Game*, it is enacted, ' That
' wherever any Perſon ſhall, for any Offence
' hereafter to be committed againſt any Law
' now in Being, for the better Preſervation of
' the *Game*, be liable to pay any pecuniary Pe-
' nalty, upon Conviction before any Juſtice or
' Juſtices of the Peace, it ſhall be lawful for any
' other Perſon whatever either to proceed to re-
' cover the ſaid Penalty by Information and
' Conviction before a Juſtice, or to ſue for the
' ſame by Action of Debt, *&c.* in any Court of
' Record, wherein no Eſſoin, *&c.* ſhall be allowed
' or more than one Imparlánce; and the Plain-
' tiff, if he recover, ſhall have double Coſts.'

- ' Provided, That all Suits and Actions to
' be brought by Force of this Act, ſhall be
' brought before the End of the next † Term
' after the Offence committed; and that no
' Offender againſt any of the Laws now in being
' for the better Preſervation of the *Game*, ſhall
' be proſecuted for the ſame Offence, both by the
' Ways preſcribed by this Law and by the Way
' preſcribed by any of the former Laws; and that
' in Caſe of a ſecond Proſecution, the Perſon ſo
' doubly proſecuted may plead in his Defence
' the former Proſecution pending, or the Con-
' viction or Judgment thereupon had, '

† By Stat. 26 *Geo.* 2. c. 2. before the End of the 2d
Term after the Offence committed.

The

The Form of an Information exhibited
against one for killing and deſtroying the
Game.

—————}**B**ⱦ **it remembereɒ,** *That on the*
to wit. *Day of*   *in*
the   *Year of the Reign of our Sovereign*
Lord   *by the Grace of God, of* Great
Britain, France *and* Ireland *King, Defender of the*
Faith, and ſo forth, at the Pariſh of   *in the*
County of   *who proſecuteth as well for the*
Poor of the Pariſh of   *as for himſelf in this*
Behalf, cometh before   *of the Juſtices*
of our ſaid Lord the King, aſſigned to keep the
Peace of our ſaid Lord the King in the ſaid County,
and alſo to hear and determine divers Felonies, Treſ-
paſſes, and other Miſdemeanors in the ſame County
perpetrated ; and giveth   *the ſaid Juſtice to be*
informed, that   *not having on the*   *Day*
of   *in his own proper Right, or in the*
Right of his Wife, Lands, Tenements, or any
other Eſtate of Inheritance of the clear yearly
Value of 100 l. *or for Term of Life, nor then hav-*
ing any Leaſe or Leaſes, or Eſtate, of or for
ninety-nine Years, or for a longer Term, of the
clear yearly value of 150 l. *nor then being the Son*
and Heir apparent of an Eſquire, or other Perſon
of higher Degree ; nor being then the Lord of any
Manor, nor the Owner or Keeper of any Foreſt,
Park, Chaſe or Warren, being ſtocked with Deer
or Conies for his neceſſary Uſe, nor being a Game-
keeper of any Lord or Lady of a Lordſhip or Manor,
nor being truly and properly a Servant of any Lord
                             or

or Lady of a Manor, nor immediately employed and appointed to take and kill the Game *for the sole Use or immediate Benefit of any such Lord or Lady, nor then having any lawful Right, Title, Appointment or Authority to have keep, or use, nor then being lawfully qualified to have, keep or use a Gun, Greyhound, Lurcher, setting Dog,* or *other Engine to kill and destroy the* Game, *did nevertheless, and contrary to the Statutes and Laws of this Realm, on the said* Day of *in the said Parish of* to kill and destroy the Game, *whereby he hath forfeited the Sum of* 5 l. *one Half to* the said the Informer, *and the other Half to the Poor of the said Parish of* where the Offence was committed. And the said prayeth the Judgment of the said Justice in the Premisses, and that the said may be summoned to answer the same.*

The Form of the Summons *.

To of in the County of

——— ⎱ Y OU *are hereby to take Notice,*
to wit. ⎰ that *this Day cometh*
before *of his Majesty's Justices of the Peace in and for the said County, and exhibiteth to* an Information and Complaint against you, *for having, contrary to the Statutes and Laws of this Realm, on the* Day of at *to kill and destroy the*

---

* A Defence cures all Defects in Summons's. 1 Str. 261. See Salk. 181, 383.

Game,

Game, *you not having then any legal Right, Title, Power, Appointment or Authority so to do, nor being thereunto qualified, according to the said Laws or Statutes; whereby you have forfeited, as he alledgeth, the Sum of 5 l. And the said prayeth of   to summon you to answer the Matters contained in the said Information : These are therefore to require and summon you the said to be and appear before   at on the   Day of by   of the Clock in the Forenoon of the same Day, then and there to answer to the said Information, and the Matters therein contained, and to make your Defence thereto. And take Notice, that if you neglect so to do,   shall then and there proceed to examine into the Cause of the said Information, and into the Matters contained and alledged therein, and proceed to give such Judgment thereupon, as shall appear to   to be just and agreeable to Law. And do appoint and require   to serve this Summons, and to attend at the Time and Place above mentioned, then and there to make a Return to   of the Execution hereof.   Given at   on the Day of   under   Hand and Seal*

Note ; A Copy of the above Summons muſt be ſerved on the Offender.

The

The Return.

BY *Virtue of the* *written Precept, I*
have fummoned *the* *named*
to be and appear as I am
authorized and required to do.

To　　　　　Conftable of the Parfh of
　　in the County of　　　and to all other the
　　Conftables and Peace Officers of his Majefty
　　in the faid County of

───── ⎰ **F**Orafmuch as　　　　　　of
to wit. ⎱ upon the Information of
who profecuteth as well for the Poor of the Parifh
of -　　　　in the faid County of
as for himfelf in this Behalf, is, by and upon the
Oath of　　　　　credible Witnefs, made this
*　　　　- Day of　　　　before -　　　　of*
his Majefty's Juftices of the Peace of and for
the faid County, convicted before　　　　of
and for　　　in the faid Parifh, on the
Day of　　　　to kill and deftroy the Game,
contrary to the Statutes and Laws of this Realm ;
be the faid　　　　not having then any lawful
Right, Title, Appointment, Power or Authority
to keep or ufe, nor being lawfully qualified to keep
or ufe, a　　　　or any other Engine, to kill and
deftroy the Game : By Reafon whereof the faid
*　　　　hath forfeited the Sum of 5 l. one Half*
to be paid to the faid ·　　　the Informer, and
the other Half to the Poor of the faid Parifh of
*　　　　where the Offence was committed : Thefe*
*　　　　　　　　　　　　　　　　are*

are therefore in his Majesty's Name to command
you to levy by Diſtreſs and Sale of the Goods of the
ſaid   the ſaid Sum of 5 l. and to pay one
Half of the ſame to the ſaid   the Informer,
and the other Half to the Poor of the ſaid Pariſh
of   And what you ſhall do in the Execution
of this Precept you are to certify to   as (men-
tioning the Place) on the   Day of
Given under   Hand and Seal at
this   Day of

Note ; The *Time* and *Place* muſt be mentioned in the Warrant : For muſt the Conſtable
ſeek the Juſtice all over the County ? Surely
it is but reaſonable for the Juſtices of Peace,
where they have but a ſpecial Authority, (as in
ſuch Caſes they only have) to inſert a Time and
Place of Return in their Warrants.

The Conſtable not obliged to return the Warrant itſelf to the Juſtice, but may keep it for
his own Juſtification in Caſe he ſhall be que-
ſtioned for what he has done ; but he muſt
give the Juſtice an Account of what he has done
upon it.

The Form of a Declaration in Debt, upon
  the Statute of the 8 *Geo.* 1. *cap.* 19.

Wilts,   } T S. *Gent. who as well for the*
to wit.   } **T.** *Poor of the Pariſh of* Biddiſon
in the County aforeſaid, as for himſelf in this Behalf
proſecutes, complains of L. R. *in the Cuſtody of*
the Marſhal of the Marſhalſea, &c. *of a Plea,*
that be render to the ſaid Poor, and to the ſaid T.

G

S. 20 *s.* of *lawful Money of* Great Britain, *which
to the* said *Poor and the* said T. S. *who as well,
and so forth, he owes, and unjustly detains* ; *for
that, to wit, Whereas by a certain* Act *of Parliament of our late Sovereign Lord* George *the First,
of* Great Britain, France *and* Ireland *late King,
Defender of the Faith, and so forth, held at* Weſt-
minſter *in the eighth Year of his Reign, it was
amongſt other Things enacted, by the King's moſt
Excellent Majeſty, by and with the Advice and
Conſent of the Lords Spiritual and Temporal and
Commons in the same Parliament aſſembled, and by
the Authority of the same, That whereſoever any
Perſon ſhall, for any Offence to be hereafter committed againſt any Law now in Being for the better
Preſervation of the* Game, *be liable or ſubject to
pay any pecuniary Penalty or Sum of Money, upon
Conviction before any Juſtice or Juſtices of the
Peace, it ſhall and may be lawful for any other
Perſon whatſoever, either to proceed to recover the
said Penalty, by Information and Conviction before
a Juſtice or Juſtices of the Peace, in ſuch Manner
as is in ſuch Law contained, or to ſue for the same
by Action of Debt, in any of his Majeſty's Courts
of Record, wherein no Eſſoin, Protection, Wager
of Law, or more than one Imparlance ſhall be
allowed* ; *and wherein the Plaintiff, if he recovers,
ſhall likewise have his double Coſts* ; *as in and by
the said* Act *more fully it doth and may appear.
And the said* T. S. *who as well, and so forth, further saith, That by another* Act *in Parliament of
our late Sovereign Lord and Lady* William *and*
Mary, *of* England, Scotland, France *and* Ireland *late King and Queen, Defenders of the Faith,
and*

and so forth, held at Westminster *in the fourth
and fifth Years of their Reign, it was amongst
other Things enacted by the King's and Queen's most
excellent Majesties, by and with the Advice and
Consent of the Lords Spiritual and Temporal and
Commons in the same Parliament assembled, and
by the Authority of the same, That if any Tradesmen,
Apprentices, and other dissolute Persons, neglecting
their Trades and Imployments, shall presume
to hunt, hawk, fish or fowl, (unless in Company
with the Master of such Apprentice, duly qualified
by Law) such Person or Persons, upon Conviction
before some Justice of Peace of the same County,
shall forfeit the Sum of* 20 s. *one Moiety to be paid
to the Informer, and the other Moiety to the Poor
of the Parish where the Offence is committed, as in
and by the said last recited Act it doth more fully and
at large appear: And the aforesaid* T. S. *saith,
That after the making of the Statute aforesaid, to
wit, the 28th Day of* September *in the seventh
Year of the Reign of our Sovereign Lord* George the
Second, *by the Grace of God now of* Great Britain,
France *and* Ireland, *King, Defender of the Faith,
and so forth, the aforesaid* L. *being a dissolute
Person neglecting his Trade and Imployment, at* H.
*in the Parish aforesaid, the Day and Year last mentioned,
unlawfully did hunt and follow Greyhounds,
and Hounds, in and upon the Lands of the said* T. S.
*who as well, and so forth, in the Parish aforesaid;
which Hunting is an Offence committed since the
making the Statute aforesaid, and against the Law
then and now still in Being for the better Preservation
of the Game; by Virtue whereof the aforesaid*
L. *is subject and liable to pay a pecuniary Penalty*

upon

upon Conviction before a Justice or Justices of the Peace ; from whence this Action accrued, for the said Poor of the said Parish of Biddison, *where the Offence aforesaid was committed, and also to the said* T. S. *who as well, and so forth, to receive and have of the aforesaid* L. 20 s. *of lawful Money, by the aforesaid* L. *by Virtue of the Statute aforesaid forfeited : Yet the said* L. *although often requested, the said* 20 s. *to the Poor aforesaid and the said* T. S. *who as well, and so forth, hath not rendered, but the same to the said Poor and to the said* T. S. *who as well, and so forth, to render hath hitherto altogether refused, and still doth refuse ; wherefore the said* T. S. *who as well, and so forth, saith he is prejudiced, and hath Damage to the Value of* 5 l. *and therefore, as well for the Poor of the said Parish of* Biddison, *as for himself, he brings this Suit.*

By 4 & 5 W. & M. c. 23. f. 11. For the better preserving the Red and Black *Game* of Grouse, commonly called Heath-Cocks and Heath-Polts, ' No Person shall on any Moun-
' tains, Hills, Heaths, Moors, Forests, Chases,
' or other Wastes, between the 2d of *February*
' and the 24th of *June,* burn any Grigg, Ling,
' Heath, Furz, Gors, or Fern, on Pain of
' being committed to the House of Correction
' for any Time not exceeding a Month, nor
' under ten Days, there to be whipt and kept
' to hard Labour.'

As here is no Method of Conviction directed for this Offence, the Justices of Peace seem to have no Cognizance thereof ; but the Trial and Conviction must be at the Assizes, or in the
Courts

Courts at *Weftminfter.* *Burn's* Juftice, p. 324. Edit. 5. in Fo.

By Stat. 5 *Ann. c.* 14. for the better Prefer-vation of the (Breed of) *Game,* ' None fhall cut ' or burn into Afhes on the Ground in the Foreft ' of *Sherwood,* or any Wafte or Land in the ' County of *Nottingham,* without. Licence. from ' the Owner of the Soil, any Ling, Heath or ' Brakes, *i. e.* Fern, on Forfeiture of 10*s.* and ' of the Afhes fo burnt, to the faid Owner ; ' and Perfons buying fuch Fern-Afhes fhall ' forfeit 10*s. per* Peck ; one Moiety to the ' Poor, *&c.* the other to the Informer ; the ' Officers of the Foreft and the Owners of the ' Land may take away the Inftruments ufed for ' the faid Purpofes, and keep them to their own ' Ufe. A Juftice of the Peace may, on Com-' plaint, iffue his Warrant to apprehend an ' Offender, and if the Party be convicted by the ' Oath of one or more Witnefles, and do not ' immediately pay the Forfeitures, he fhall be ' committed to the Houfe of Correction, and ' kept to hard Labour for a Month, unlefs the ' Penalties be fooner paid.' (See **Hare**).

Search for *Game,* fee *poftea,* p. and for a Warrant to fearch for *Game, vid.* p.

Law Cafes.

The Defendant *B.* being a Juftice of Peace had convicted the Plaintiff for deftroying *Game,* and though, as it was proved, the Plaintiff had Effects of his own which might have been di-ftrained, which were fufficient to anfwer the

Penalty

Penalty he had incurred, yet *B.* sent him immediately to *Bridewell*, without endeavouring to
levy the Penalty upon his Goods ; and an
Action of Trespass and false Imprisonment being
brought against *B.* for this Commitment, *Ray-
mond* Chief Justice was of Opinion that the
Action well lay. The other Defendant was the
Constable who had executed this Warrant ; and
as to him it was agreed, That the Warrant was
a sufficient Justification, it being *in a Matter
within the Jurisdiction of the Justice of Peace.*
Trin. 12 Geo. 1. *in* B. R. Hill *and* Bateman
& al' M. S. Rep. — Str. 710. S. C.

Note *it was agreed, That where Actions of this
kind are brought against Justices of the Peace, they
are obliged to shew the Regularity of their Convictions; and the Informations, &c. laid before them,
upon which their Convictions are grounded, must
be produced and proved in Court.* Str. 711. in S. C.

Game-Keeper, Is one who has the Care of
Keeping and Preserving of the *Game,* being
appointed thereto by Lords of Manors, *&c.*
he has a limited Authority, and if he transgresses
his Bounds, the Law no longer looks on him
as qualified.

By **Stat.** 22 *&* 23 *Car.* 2. *c.* 25. *sect.* 2.
' Lords of Manors or other Royalties, not
' under the Degree of an Esquire, may by
' Writing under their Hands and Seals autho-
' rize one or more * *Game-Keeper* or *Game-
' Keepers,* within their respective Manors or Roy-
' alties, and may impower them upon their own

* See 9 *Annæ,* c. 25. p. 127. by which only one *Game-
keeper* is to be appointed.

                                   ' Manors

' Manors to kill Hare, Pheasant, Partridge, or
' any other *Game*, and such *Game-Keepers* may
' seize all Guns, Bows, Greyhounds, setting
' Dogs, Lurchers, or other Dogs to kill Hares,
' or Conies ; Ferrits, Tramels, Lowbells, Hays
' or other Nets, Hare-pipes, Snares or other
' Engines for taking Conies, Hares, Pheasants,
' Patridges or other *Game*, used within such
' Manors by Persons prohibited by this Act
' to use the same : [See **Qualification**] Such
' *Game-Keepers* and others, by Warrant from
' a Justice of Peace, may search the Houses
' of such Persons so prohibited, as shall be
' suspected to keep such Guns, &c. and seize
' them for the Use of the Lord of the Manor, or
' otherwise destroy them.' *Vide* Tit. **Gun.**

By **Stat.** 5 *Ann.* Seff. 2. c. 14. ' Any
' Lord of a Manor may, by Writing under
' his Hand and Seal, impower his *Game-Keeper*
' to kill any *Game* whatsoever; but if such
' *Game-Keeper*, under Colour of such Power to
' kill or take for the Use of such Lord, sell or
' dispose thereof without the Consent or Know-
' ledge of such Lord, and shall be convicted
' upon Complaint of such Lord, by the Oath
' of one or more Witnesses, before a Justice
' of Peace, such *Game-Keeper* shall be commit-
' ted to the House of Correction for three
' Months, and be kept to hard Labour.'

By **Stat.** 9 *Ann.* c. 25. the *Stat.* 5 *Ann.*
c. 14. is made perpetual ; ' And no Lord of
' a Manor shall appoint more than one *Game-*
' *Keeper* in one Manor with Power to kill and
' destroy the *Game*, and his Name shall be en-

' tered

' tered with the Clerk of the Peace without
' Fee, who shall give him a Certificate thereof,
' paying one Shilling; and if any *Game-Keeper*
' whose Name shall not be so entered, or who
' shall not be otherwise qualified by the Laws
' of this Kingdom to kill *Game*, shall kill, sell,
' or expose to Sale, any Hare, Pheasant, Par-
' tridge, Moor, Heath *Game*, or Grouse, he
' shall, on Conviction before One Justice, on
' Oath of One Witness, forfeit for every Of-
' fence, 5 *l.* Half to the Informer, and Half
' to the Poor, by Distress: For Want of Dis-
' tress, to be sent to the House of Correction for
' three Months for the first Offence, and for
' every other Offence, four Months.'

Who shall not be otherwise qualified]. From
these Words it seemeth clear, that a *Game-
Keeper*, who is qualified in his own Right to
kill *Game*, need not be entered with the Clerk
of the Peace. *Burn*'s Justice, 304. Fo. Edit.

' And if any Person not being qualified so to
' do, or not being truly and properly a Servant
' of any Lord, *&c.* of a Manor, or not im-
' mediately employed and appointed to take
' and kill the *Game*, for the Use or immediate
' Benefit of the said Lord, *&c.* shall under
' Colour or Pretence of any Power or Authority,
' Deputation, or Qualification, to him granted
' by any Lord, *&c.* of a Manor, take or
' kill any Hare, Pheasant, Partridge, or other
' *Game* whatsoever, or shall keep or use any
' Greyhounds, Setting Dogs, Hays, Lurchers,
' Guns, Tunnels, or any other Engine, to kill
                 ' and

' and deſtroy the *Game*; he ſhall forfeit 5 *l.* in
' like Manner as mentioned, *Ann. c.* 25.'

By **Stat.** 3 *Geo.* 1. *c.* 11. ' No Lord or
' Lady of a Manor ſhall appoint any Perſon
' to be a *Game-Keeper*, with Power to kill or
' take *Game*, unleſs ſuch Perſon be qualified
' ſo to do by the Laws of this Realm, or be
' truly and properly a Servant to the ſaid Lord
' or Lady, or be immediately employed and ap-
' pointed to take and kill the *Game*, for the
' ſole Uſe of the Lord or Lady, and not
' otherwiſe.

A Commiſſion for a *Game-Keeper.*

GEORGE the Second, *by the Grace of God,
of* Great Britain, France *and* Ireland, *King,
Defender of the Faith,* &c. **To** *all to whom theſe
Preſents ſhall come, Greeting:* **Know ye,** *That
we of our ſpecial Grace, and by the Advice and
Conſent of the Chancellor and Council of our Duchy
of Lancaſter, have appointed, authorized, and impowered; and by theſe Preſents do for us, our
Heir and Succeſſors, appoint, authorize, and impower our truſty and well beloved* H. M. *of our
County of* S. *Gent. to be* Game-Keeper *of and
within our Manors of* H. *and* P. *with their and
every of their Royalties, Members and Appurtenances
in our ſaid County, during our Pleaſure; And we
do hereby give and grant unto him the ſaid* H. M.
*during our Pleaſure, full Power and Authority to
ſeize and take all and all Manner of Guns, Bows,
Greyhounds, Setting Dogs, Lurchers, and other
Dogs, Trammels, Lowbels, Hays or other Nets, Hare-*

G 5 ' *pipes,*

pipes, Snares *or other Engines for taking Conies,* Hares, Pheafants, Partridges *or other* Game ; *and alfo all and all Manner of fifhing Nets,* Angles, Leaps, Pipes *and other Inftruments, or Engines for taking of Fifh, ufed and imployed within the faid* Manors *or either of them, or the Royalties, Members and Precincts thereof, by any Perfon or Perfons whatfoever, prohibited by the Laws of this Realm in any wife to ufe, imploy and keep the fame, as any other* Game-keeper *may lawfully do.* **And** *further we do hereby for us, our Heirs and Succeffors, give and grant unto the faid* H. M. *during our Pleafure, full Power and Authority to do all and every Act or Acts, Thing or Things, which and as by the Law of this Realm are requifite and neceffary for the Prefervation of our* Game *within our faid Manors and Precincts, and for the Difcovery of Offenders therein againft the Laws and Statutes in that Cafe made and provided.* **And** *laftly, we do hereby command all* Mayors, Bailiffs, Juftices, Conftables *and all other Perfons whatfoever, whom it may concern, that they be diligently aiding and affifting unto him the faid* H. M. *in the due Execution of this Commiffion.* **Given** *at our Palace,* &c.

A Deputation for a *Game-Keeper.*

Vide Stat. 22 & 23 Car. 2. c. 25. f. 2. — 5 Ann. c. 14. f. 4. — 3 Geo. 1. c. 11. f. 1.

To all *People whom thefe Prefents may concern:* **Know** ye, *That I* R. P. *of,* &c. *Efq ; Lord of the Manor of* G. *in the County of* H. *do hereby make, nominate, authorize, and appoint*

appoint W. W. *of,* &c. *who is truly and properly
my Servant,* [*or,* a Perſon immediately appointed
and imployed to take and kill *Game,* for my
ſole Uſe and Benefit ; *or,* being qualified by the
Laws of this Realm to take and kill the *Game,*
as the Caſe is] *to be my* Game-keeper *within my
ſaid Manor, according to an Act of Parliament in
that Caſe made in the third Year of the Reign
of King* George *the Firſt, during my Will and
Pleaſure ;* 𝖆𝖓𝖉 *I do alſo hereby authorize the
ſaid* W. W. *by Virtue of another Act of Parliament in that Caſe made, to take away any
Hare, Pheaſant, Partridge or any other Game,
which he ſhall find in the Cuſtody of any Perſon
or Perſons within my ſaid Manor, not being duly
qualified to kill the* Game ; 𝖆𝖓𝖉 *alſo to ſeize and
take away, for my Uſe, all Greyhounds, Setting
Dogs, Lurchers or other Inſtruments for the Deſtruction of the* Game, *from any Perſon or Perſons
within my ſaid Manor, not being duly qualified to
uſe the ſame:* 𝖆𝖓𝖉 *further to act and do all and
every Thing and Things which belong to the Office of
a* Game-Keeper, *purſuant to the ſeveral Acts of
Parliament made for the Preſervation of the* Game.
𝕲𝖎𝖛𝖊𝖓, &c.

The Entry of it with the Clerk of the
Peace.

June 6, 1735.

Huntingdon, ⎱ **B** E it remembered, *That the*
to wit. ⎰ *Day and Year above-writ-
ten, the within Deputation from* R. P. *Eſq ; to*

his Game-Keeper W. W. *was entered by me*
W. C. *Clerk of the Peace for the said County,
on Behalf of the said* R. P. *according to the Direction of the Statute.*

         W. C. Clerk of the Peace.

The Clerk of the Peace's Certificate.

June 6, 1735.

Hunt'don, ⎱ **T**HESE *are to certify, That*
to wit. ⎰ *the Day and Year above-written, the Deputation from* R. P. *Esq; to his*
Game-Keeper W. W. *was duly entered by me*
W. C. *Clerk of the Peace for the said County,
according to the Direction of the Statute in that
Case made.*

         W. C. Clerk of the Peace.

His Fee by Statute 9 *Ann.* is one Shilling.

A Mittimus *of a* Game-Keeper *to the House
of Correction, for disposing of the Game,
on* 5 Ann. *c.* 14.

         To the Constable of *&c.* and to
         D. E. Keeper of the House of
         Correction.

Huntingdon, ⎱ **W**Hereas W. W. *of,* &c.
to wit. ⎰ *being impowered under*
the Hand and Seal of R. P. *Esq; Lord of the*
                           Manor

Manor of G. *in the said County, to kill Game.
in his said Manor, and did on the next Day sell,
the same to* A. S. *of,* &c. *without the Consent or
Knowledge of the said* R. P. *And whereas the
said* W. W. *hath on the Day of the Date hereof,
and upon the Complaint of the said* R. P. *been
duly convicted before me of the said Offence, by the
Oath of* G. A. *of,* &c. *These are therefore to
require you to convey the said* W. W. *to the House
of Correction, at,* &c. *and to deliver him to the
Keeper thereof, who is hereby required to receive him
into his Custody, and safely to keep him in the House
of Correction, for the Space of three Months next
ensuing, there to be kept to hard Labour.* Given,
under my Hand and Seal, &c.

A Warrant to levy 5 *l.* upon one (not qualified) for killing a Hare, under Pretence
of being a *Game-Keeper.* (3 *Geo.* 1. *c.* 11.
5 *Ann. c.* 14. *sect.* 2. 9 *Ann. c.* 23.)

To the Constable of, &c.

Middlesex, **W**HEREAS A. B. of D. in
to wit. the County aforesaid, *Yeoman,*
*was on the Day of the Date hereof duly convicted
before me* E. M. *Esq; one of his Majesty's Justices
of the Peace for the said County, upon the Oath
of* * J. W. *of,* &c. *that he the said* A. B. *did on
the Day of this Instant* May, *at* D. *aforesaid, and*

* One Credible Witness,

within

within the Manor of the said J.W. *kill* † *one Hare not being qualified by the Law so to do, and not being truly imployed by him to take or kill any* Game *for his sole Use and Benefit ; by Reason whereof he the said* A. B. *hath forfeited* 5 l. *pursuant to the Statutes in that Case made and provided : These are therefore to require you forthwith to levy the said Sum of* 5 l. *on the Goods and Chattels of the said* A. B. *by* * *Distress and Sale thereof; and that you pay one Moiety thereof to the said* J. W. *who first informed me of the said Offence, and the other Moiety to the Overseers of the Poor of the Parish of* D. *where the said Offence was committed, for the Use of the Poor thereof.* Given, *&c.*

Note ; A Conviction upon the *Game* Acts muſt aver the Want of Qualifications parti-cularly, as Degree, Eſtate, *&c.* 2 Ld. *Raym.* 1415. See *Lucas*, 26, 27.

A Conviction for killing *Game*, not being qualified, was quaſhed, becauſe it was only ſaid that the Party was not *qualified*; but did not ſhew particularly, in what reſpect he was not qualified. *King* and *Marriot.*

Glandage, Maſtage ; the Seaſon of turning Hogs into the Woods in Maſt-time.

Greyhounds, In *Saxon* Lnizhunt. An Action was brought againſt the Defendant for killing a Brace of the Plaintiff's *Greyhounds*. The

---

† Or keep a Greyhound or Setting Dog, as the Caſe is.

* If no Diſtreſs, then to the Houſe of Correction for three Months.

De-

Defendant juftifies, for that the *Greyhounds* did chafe a Deer in his Park, and killed him there ; and to prevent further Harm, he took the faid *Greyhounds* and killed them. The Plaintiff replied, That the Deer was out of the Defendant's Park upon the Plaintiff's Land and feeding on his Grafs ; that he loofed the *Greyhounds* to chafe him off his Land ; that they purfued the Deer in the Park, and there killed him. To this the Defendant demurred, and upon Argument it was adjudged, that the Replication was naught, becaufe he does not fay, That he did his Endeavour to ftop the *Greyhounds* at the Park-fide, and prevent their Entrance therein : But then it was objected, that the Bar was naught ; for though it was unlawful to chafe in his Park, yet when the Defendant had taken the *Greyhounds* he ought not to have killed them : And for this was cited 2 *Roll. Abr.* 567. *Lewis's* Cafe ; againft which was cited 2 *Cro.* 44. *Wadhurft* againft *Damme.* Afterwards, upon Confideration of both thefe Books, Judgment was given for the Defendant. 3 *Lev.* 28.

A Declaration for Keeping and ufing *Greyhounds,* not being qualified. (5 *Ann. c.* 14. 8 *Geo.* 1. *c.* 29.)

Southampton, } J. D. *Gent. who as well for*
to wit, } *himfelf, as the Poor of the Parifh of* W. *in the County aforefaid, in this Behalf profecutes, complains of* B. J. *in the Cuftody of the Marfhal,* &c. *of a Plea, that he render to him*

him the said J. D. *and to the said Poor of the said Parish of* W. 5 l. *which the said* J. D. *and the said Poor of the said Parish he owes, and unjustly detains; for that, to wit, That whereas the said* B. *the* 20th *Day of* October *in the Year of the Reign, &c. and so forth, at the said Parish of* W. *in the County aforesaid, used two* Greyhounds *to kill and destroy the Game, against the Form of the Statute in that Case lately made and provided; he the said* B. *not being qualified so to do according to the Laws of this Realm; by which and by Force of the Statute in that Case lately made and provided, the Action accrued to the said* J. *as well for himself, as for the said Poor of the said Parish of* W. *in the County aforesaid, to have and receive from the said* B. *the aforesaid* 5 l. *yet the said* B. *although often requested, the said* 5 l. *to the said* J. *who as well, and so forth, hath not rendered, but the same to the said* J. *who as well, and so forth, to render hath hitherto altogether refused; wherefore the said* S. *who as well, and so forth, saith he is prejudiced, and hath Damage to the Value of* 10 l. *and for that, as well for himself as for the Poor of the said Parish of* W. *he brings his Suit.*

Grouse or Moor Game.

By **Stat.** 1 *Jac.* c. 27. f. 2. ' Every Per-
' son who shall shoot at, kill or destroy, with
' any Gun or Bow, any *Grouse*, Heath Cock,
' or *Moor Game*, shall, on Conviction before
' two Justices, by Confession, or Oath of two
' Witnesses, be committed to Gaol for three
' Months, unless upon Conviction he pay to
' the Churchwardens, for the Use of the Poor

20 s,

' 20 *s.* or, after one Month after his Commit-
' ment, become bound by Recognizance with
' two Sureties in 20 *l.* each, before two Juſtices,
' not to offend again in like Manner; the Re-
' cognizance to be returned to the next Seſſions.

By **Stat.** 9 *Ann. c.* 25. *ſ.* 3. ' If any Per-
' ſon whatſoever ſhall take or kill any *Moor,*
' *Heath Game,* or *Grouſe,* in the Night-time,
' he ſhall, on Conviction before one Juſtice, on
' Oath of one Witneſs, forfeit 5 *l.* Half to the
' Informer, and Half to the Poor, by Diſtreſs ;
' for Want of Diſtreſs to be ſent to the Houſe
' of Correction three Months for the firſt Offence,
' and for every other Offence four Months.' See
' *Stat.* 4 & 5 *W.* & *M. c.* 23. and 5 *Ann. c.* 14.
' Tit. **Game.**

Quarii, Signifies the principal Officers of
the Foreſt. 4 *Inſt.* 293.

Guns and Croſs-Bows. By **Stat.** 33.
Hen. 8. *c.* 6. ' None ſhall ſhoot in, or keep in
' his Houſe, any Croſs-bow, *Hand-gun,* Hagbut
' or Demi-hake, unleſs his Lands be of the
' Value of 100 *l. per Annum,* on Forfeiture of
' 10 *l.* for every Offence ; nor ſhall ſhoot in
' any *Hand-gun* under the Length of one
' Yard, nor Hagbut or Demi-hake of three
' Quarters of a Yard long, on the like Penalty ;
' and any Man, having Lands of 100 *l. per*
' *Annum,* may ſeize any ſuch *Gun* or Croſs-bow
' uſed contrary hereto ; but he muſt break them
' in twenty Days after, on Pain of 40 *s.* and
' none ſhall travel with a Croſs-bow bent or
' *Gun* charged, except in Time of War ; or
' ſhoot within a Quarter of a Mile of a City,
'   ' Borough

' Borough or Market-Town, except in Defence.
' of himfelf or his Houfe, or at a dead Mark,
' in Pain of 10*l.* and none fhall command his
' Servant to fhoot in a *Gun* or Crofs-bow, ex-
' cept as above, on the like Penalty ; the above
' Penalties to be divided between the King and
' the Profecutor.'

' But the Followers of Lords Spiritual and
' Temporal, Knights, Efquires, Gentlemen,
' Inhabitants of Cities, &c. and thofe that
' dwell two Furlongs diftant from a Town,
' may keep in their Houfes, and fhoot (at a
' dead Mark only) with *Guns* not under the
' above Lengths.'

' Perfons impowered by the King to take
' away *Guns, &c.* in Forefts, &c. may re-
' tain the fame ; and Smiths and Merchants,
' that make and fell *Guns,* may keep them in
' their Houfes, the feveral Lengths above be-
' ing duly obferved.'

' Any Perfon may convey the Party of-
' fending againft this Act before the next Ju-
' ftice of Peace, who may commit him to Prifon
' till the Penalty is fatisfied, which in this Cafe
' fhall be divided between the King and him
' who takes the Offenders.'

' Juftices in Seffions, and Stewards of Leets
' have Power to hear and determine thefe Of-
' fences ; and when the Conviction is in the
' Seffions, the whole Forfeiture fhall go to the
' King: When in a Leet, one Half is the King's,
' and the other fhall be divided between the Lord
' and the Profecutor.'

' If

' If a Jury wilfully conceal any Thing, the
' Juftices or Steward have Power to impanel
' another Jury, by whom, if the firft Jury be
' found guilty of Concealment, they fhall for-
' feit 20 *s.* a-piece, *viz.* to the King if in Sef-
' fions ; but if in a Leet, one-Half to the
' Lord, the other to the Profecutor.'

' Forfeitures arifing by this Act fhall be
' fued for by the King within one Year, and
' by a common Perfon within fix Months, other-
' wife they fhall be loft.'

' A Servant may by Command ufe his
' Mafter's Crofs-bow or *Gun,* fo as he fhoot
' at no Fowl, Deer or other Game : And
' any Owner of a Ship may keep a *Gun,* but only
' to ufe it in the Ship.'

By **Stat.** 3 *Jac.* 1. *c.* 13. *f.* 5. ' If any Per-
' fon not having 40 *l.* per *Annum* in Lands or
' Hereditaments, or not worth in Goods 200 *l.*
' fhall ufe any *Gun,* Bow or Crofs-bow, to kill
' [Deer or] Conies, or fhall keep any Ferrets,
' or Coney Dogs (except he have Grounds in-
' clofed for keeping of Conies, the Increafing
' of which fhall amount to 40 *s.* a Year to be
' let, and except Warreners in their Warrens) it
' fhall be lawful for any Perfon, having Lands
' worth 100 *l.* per *Annum,* to take fuch *Gun, &c.*
' from any fuch Perfon, and convert the fame to
' his own Ufe'.

By 22 & 23 *Car.* 2. *c.* 25. ' Perfons not
' having Lands, or fome other Eftate of In-
' heritance in their own or their Wives Right
' of 100 *l.* per *Annum,* or for Life or Leafe
' of 99 Years of 150 *l.* per *Annum,* other than
' the

' the Son and Heir of an Efquire, or other
' Perfon of higher. Degree, and Owners and
' Keepers of Forefts, Parks, Chafes, or Warrens
' ftocked with Deer or Conies for their neceſſary
' Uſe, in refpect of the faid Forefts, &c. are
' declared to be Perfons not allowed to keep any
' Guns, Bows, &c.'

Vide Stat. 5 *Ann.* Tit. **Dogs.**

The Form of a Conviction * upon the Statute
33 *H.* 8. before one Juſtice.

[Profecution by the King to be within a Year;
by any other Perfon within fix Months.]

Suffex, ⎱ **Be it remembered,** *That this 6th*
to wit. ⎰ *Day of* Febuary *inſtant, in the
seventh Year of the Reign of our Sovereign Lord*
George *the Second, by the Grace of God, now of*
Great Britain, France *and* Ireland, *King, Defender
of the Faith, and fo forth,* J. R. *of* H. *in the
County aforefaid, Labourer, came before me* J. C.
*Eſq.; the next Juſtice of our faid Lord the King,
affigned to keep his Peace in the County aforefaid;
and then and there upon his Oath faid and depofed,
That* W. P. *late of* H. *aforefaid, in the County
aforefaid, Yeoman, the firſt Day of* January *in the
faid seventh Year of the Reign, and fo forth, at* H.
aforefaid, in the County aforefaid, had and kept a
Hand-gun, *and then and there, with the* Hand-
gun *aforefaid, charged with Gun-powder and Hail-
Shot, unlawfully and unjuſtly did ſhoot, againſt the
Form of the Statute in that Cafe made and pro-*

* *See* Dalt. *c.* 47.

vidid;

vided ; the said W. P. not then having in his own
Right, or in Right of his Wife, or for the Use of the
said W. P. or any other Person or Persons having
to the Use of the said W. P. any Lands or Tenements
in Fee, Annuity or Office, of the yearly Value of
one hundred Pounds : And forasmuch as that the
aforesaid W. P. being taken and brought before
me the aforesaid next Justice, by the said J. R.
for the Offence aforesaid, and charged with the
said Offence in Manner aforesaid, could not deny
the same : **Therefore** it is considered by me the
aforesaid next Justice, That the said W. P. hath
forfeited the Sum of 10 l. according to the said Statute in that Case made and provided ; Half of
which said Sum of 10 l. is to be paid to the Use
of our said Lord the King, and the other Half to
be paid to the said J. R. he being the first Bringer
of the said W. P. before me the said next Justice
for the Offence aforesaid, according to the Direction
of the Statute aforesaid ; And that the aforesaid
W. P. be committed to the Gaol of the County
aforesaid, there to remain until he hath paid the said
10 l. to the Uses aforesaid, according to the Direction
of the said Statute.

No Replevin of Goods taken upon a Conviction,
Str. 1184. See **Replevin.**

A Declaration in Debt for shooting with a
Gun not being qualified. (Stat. 8 Geo. 1.)

Huntingdon,⎫ **A** J. late of S. in the said
  to wit, ⎬ **A.** County, Yeoman, was attached to answer to the Lord the King, and W. H.
who as well for the said Lord the King as for him-
    self

self in this Behalf profecutes, of a Plea, that he render unto the faid Lord the King and the faid W. who as well and fo forth, 10l. *of lawful Money of* Great Britain, *which to the faid Lord the King and the faid* W. *who as well, and fo forth, he owes and unjuftly detains, and fo forth ; by* H. H. *his Attorney, faith, That whereas the faid* A. *the fixth Day of* January *in the feventh Year of the Reign of the faid Lord the new King, not having in his own Right, or in Right of his Wife, or for the Ufe of the faid* A. *or any other Perfon or Perfons having to the Ufe of the faid* A. *any Lands or Tenements in Fee, Annuity or Office, of the yearly Value of one hundred Pounds, had and kept a certain* Gun, *and then and there loaded or charged the faid* Gun *with Gun-powder and Shot, and did fhoot therewith againft the Form of the Statute in that Cafe made and provided ; by which and by Force of the faid Statute the faid* A. *forfeited ten Pounds for the faid Offence ; whereby and by Force of the Statute in that Cafe made and provided, the Action accrued to the faid Lord the King and the faid* A. *who as well, and fo forth, to have and receive from the faid* A. *the faid* 10 l. *yet the faid* A. *although often requefted, the faid* 10 l. *to the faid Lord the King and the faid* W. *who as well, and fo forth, hath not rendered, but the fame to them hitherto to render hath altogether refufed, and ftill doth refufe ; Wherefore the faid* W. *who as well, and fo forth, faith, that he is prejudiced, and hath Damage to the Value of* 20 l. *and therefore as well for the faid Lord the King, as for himfelf, he brings his Suit.*

Law

3

Law Cases.

One *Cole* being brought before a Juftice of Peace upon a Warrant againft him for *fhooting in a Gun*; and upon Examination and Proof being convicted thereof, he was committed till he fhould pay 10 *l.* one Moiety to the Crown, the other to the Informer; and the Juftice having made a Record of the Conviction, it was certified into *B. R.* upon the Return of a *Habeas Corpus*; and adjudged, that if the Statute 33 *H.* 8. *c.* 6. is rightly purfued, no Court could difcharge the Offender without paying the Forfeiture. *W. Jones* 170.

A Conviction was certified into *B. R.* againft one for *fhooting in a Hand-gun*, not being qualified according to Statute 33 *H.* 8. by which Statute the Juftice of Peace hath Authority to commit the Offender upon due Examination and Proof; and now it was infifted for the Defendant, that the Proof of this Offence ought to be made by a Jury, and not by a Witnefs before a Juftice of Peace; but it was adjudged, that in this Cafe Proof might be made by Witneffes, and not to a Jury, and that no Writ of Error lies upon this Conviction. *The King* againft *Saunders*, 1 *Vent.* 53, 39. *Sid.* 491. S. C. 1 *Sand.* 262. S. C.

The Defendant was convicted before a Juftice of Peace for keeping a *Gun*, not having 100 *l. per Annum*, according to the Statute 33 *Hen.* 8. and now the Record of this Conviction being removed into *B. R.* it was objected, that the Words in the Indictment were, *non habuiffet* 100 *l.*

100 *l. per Annum* generally, but did not set forth
when; for he might have 100 *l. per Annum* when
he kept the *Gun*, though not at the Time when
he was convicted; but it was answered, that the
Word *habuisset* shall relate to all Time, and 'tis
as much as to say *nunquam habuisset*; and the
Indictment concluding *contra formam statuti*,
that Conclusion must explain any doubtful
Words; but it was adjudged, that this being
a Conviction before a Justice of Peace, the
Time when the Offence was committed should
be alledged with the utmost Certainty, *(viz.)*
that the Defendant on such a Day and in such
a Year had not 100 *l. per Annum*; and for this
Reason the Indictment was quashed. *The King*
against *Silcox*, 3 *Mod.* 281.

The Defendant was indicted upon the Statute
33 *H.* 8. for shooting in a *Hand-gun*, and killing two *Lepos*, (instead of *Lepores*;) it was objected that the Indictment was ill, because it did
not set forth, that the Defendant was not worth
100 *l. per Annum*; but this Objection was not
allowed, because if he was worth so much, he
might have shewed it in order to his Acquittal;
but this Indictment was quashed for these Rea-
sons, *(viz.)* because it set forth, that the Defendant killed two *Lepos*, when it should have been
Lepores; and for that the Caption was *ad Ses-
sionem pacis Domini Regis* [*at the Sessions of the
Peace of the Lord the King*], and did not say *nunc
Regis* [*now King*], *&c. The King*, against *Wolst.*
2 *Keb.* 582.

The Defendant was convicted upon the said
Statute 33 *H.* 8. for having a *Gun* in his House
whe

when the Words of the Statute are against keeping a *Gun* in his Houſe or elſe-where, and probably this *Gun* might be lent to the Defendant ; therefore this being upon a penal Statute, the Words thereof ought to be purſued, for which Reaſon this Conviction was quaſhed. *The King* againſt *Lueling, Shower's Rep.* 48.

It hath been a Queſtion, whether an Indictment will lie upon the Statute 33 *H.* 8. in the Seſſions for ſhooting in a *Gun* ; 'tis true, the Juſtices have Power by their Commiſſion to puniſh Offences againſt the Peace ; but ſhooting in a *Gun* is not ſuch an Offence, 'tis only the Defect of the Qualification of the Perſon which makes it criminal. *The King* againſt *Alſop,* 4 *Mod.* 49.

Note ; It was ſaid in *Bullock's* Caſe, that a ſingle Juſtice cannot convict upon the Statute 33 *H.* 8. unleſs the Offender is brought before him *inſtanter* [*inſtantly*] after the Offence committed. *The King* againſt *Bullock,* 4 *Mod.* 146.

Two Indictments, one was preferred againſt the Defendant for keeping a *Gun,* and the other for ſhooting in it ; but they were both quaſhed, becauſe the Diſability of the Perſon was not rightly ſet forth. *Hill.* 9 *W.* in *B. R.*

An Indictment ſet forth, that the Defendant had eight Nets and two *Guns,* with which he had deſtroyed the Game, on Motion to quaſh the ſame, two Exceptions were taken. Firſt, the Indictment does not mention he was not qualified. 2. 'Tis not indictable, ſince it was no Offence at Common Law. 2 *Salk.* 460.

King

King and *Whigg.* Where a new Penalty is given
for a Matter which at Common Law was an
indictable Offence, as for keeping Swine in a
City, which is a Nusance; then one may
either indict, or bring an Action on the Statute
for the Penalty; but where the Statute makes
the Offence, that Remedy must be taken which
the Statute gives. *Salk.* 45. Indictments will
not lie where there was no Offence at Common Law, because the Statute which has made
the Offence, has made it punishable in another
Manner. 1 *Show.* 398. Judgment for Defendant; the Name of the Case is *King* and
Fowlin.

The Plaintiff brought an Action of Trespass
against the Defendant for entering his (the Plaintiff's) House and taking away his *Gun*; the Defendant justified by Virtue of the Statute 22 &
23 *Car.* 2. [Vide **Qualification,** *p.*   and
Game-keeper, *p.* 130.] setting forth, that the
Lords of Manors and other Royalties may
depute Game-keepers, who by Virtue of such
Deputation may seize *Guns* within the Precincts
of their Manors, &c. and that such Game-keepers or any other Person may *by a Warrant from a Justice,* * search the Houses of
Persons suspected to keep *Guns,* and seize them
for the Use of the Lord of the Manor; that
Sir *E. W.* was seised in Fee of the Hundred of
Burton, and of a Court-Leet there, &c. and
that the Defendant, *by a Warrant of a Justice,*
entered into the Liberty of *W.* to search in the

* *Vide* the following Case.

3

Manors

Manors of *M.* and *W.* and within the Precincts of the Court-Leet and Hundred aforesaid, which were within the Liberty of *W.* and that Sir *E. W.* was Lord of the said Manor, and that the Plaintiff was not qualified to keep a *Gun*; and being suspected to keep one, the Defendant entered his (the Plaintiff's) House, which was *within the said* † *Hundred*, and within the Precincts of the Court-Leet and Liberty of *W.* where he (the Defendant) found the said *Gun*, and seized it, &c. and upon a Demurrer to this Justification it was held good, though there was no Occasion for the Defendant to set forth all this Matter, because he acted under a Warrant of a Justice of Peace, therefore he might have pleaded the General Issue; but if he had justified as a Game-keeper only, and without a Warrant, in such Case he must plead specially. *Bowkby* against *Williams*, *Lutw.* 1506.

Trespass for taking away a *Gun*. Defendant justifies as Game-keeper * duly made within ten Miles of *London: Cur.* The Plea is ill, not saying by whom he was made, nor that the Plaintiff was an unqualified Person by the Statute: And Defendant ought to have had a *Warrant from a Justice of the Peace*; and an Authority from the Lord of the Manor is not sufficient. *Trin.* 3 *W. & M. in B. R. Carpenter* and *Adams, Comb.* 183.

---

† It should be within the said Manor, because the *Gun* was seized to the Use of the Lord of the Manor.
* *Vide* 22 & 23 *Car.* 2. *c.* 25. *sect.* 2. Tit *Game-keeper, p.* 130.

Bluet.

Bluet, qui tam, &c. verſus *Needs C. B.*

DEclaration *verſus* Defendant, an Attorney of this Court, for 40 *l.* Debt; for that be at *Holcomb Regis in Com. Devon,* 28 *Nov.* 1733. did uſe a *Gun* to kill and deſtroy the Game, not being qualified ſo to do by the Laws of the Realm, whereby an Action accrued to Plaintiff to demand 5 *l.* Part of the ſaid 40 *l.*

Secondly, That 16th of *January* 1733. he did keep another *Gun,* not being qualified, *&c.* by which an Action accrued for other 5 *l.*

Thirdly, The ſame Day he expoſed to Sale ſix Hares, againſt the Form of the Statute, not being qualified in his own Right to kill Game, whereby an Action accrued to demand 30 *l.* Reſidue of ſaid 40 *l.*

Defendant pleads he owes nothing, and moves in Arreſt of Judgment.

FIRST, That the firſt Count is not good, ſince by the Statute 5 *Annæ, c.* 14. §. 4. it is Enacted, That any Perſons, not qualified to keep and uſe any Greyhounds, Setting-Dogs, Hays, Lurchers, Tunnels, or other Engine to kill and deſtroy the Game, ſhall forfeit 5 *l.* but a *Gun* is not mentioned in the ſaid Act; and therefore when by the Statute 8 *Geo.* 1. it is Enacted, That pecuniary Penalties may be recovered by Action of Debt, *&c.* before the End of the next Term after Offence, *&c.* yet Debt lies

lies not, unless the Offence be within the Statute 5 *Ann. c.* 14.

Secondly, It is not sufficient to say he was not qualified, without shewing he had not 100 *l.* a Year, or other Estate which makes a Qualification.

Thirdly, The Selling six Hares together is but one Offence, and by the Statute 9 *Annæ, c.* 25. which enacts such Penalties, as on Higlers, *&c.* by 5 *Annæ, c.* 14. is inflicted, *viz.* the Sum of 5 *l.* which ought not to be understood 5 *l.* for every Hare, Pheasant, *&c.* but for all sold at once.

But the Penalty on Higlers, *&c.* by 5 *Ann.* is 5 *l.* for every Hare, Pheasant, *&c.*

For Plaintiff: As to the first *Objection*, a *Gun* is an Engine to destroy Game. So as to the second *Objection*, We have exactly pursued the Words of the Act, and if Defendant had been qualified, he must shew it. *Dyer* 312. *Carth.* 124, 304.

As to the third *Objection*, that all is one Offence, the Statute 9 *Ann.* refers to the 5 *Ann.* which gives 5 *l.* for every Hare.

Per Cur. As to the first *Objection*, the Averment of his not being qualified is sufficient, since the Words of the Act are pursued; and the Defendant may come and shew his Qualification.

As to the second *Objection*, this is after Verdict, and it is a Matter of Evidence whether a *Gun* be an Engine to kill and destroy Game.

And as to the *Third*, the Statute 9 *Ann.* saith not he shall for every Offence pay 5 *l.* but shall

forfeit

forfeit the Penalty of the Statute 5 *Ann.* on Higlers, and which is 5 *l.* for every Hare.

Note; The Jury found 10 *l.* without shewing to which of the Offences it is to be applied. *Per Cur:* This being a Debt, the Jury may find Part of the Debt ; Judgment for the Plaintiff. *Comyns* 522 to 525.

Note ; If a Man stands in one County and shoots into two or three (as he may in some Places) he must be convicted by the Justice or Justices where the Offence was committed *i. e.* where he stood when he shot, not where the Object was which he shot at. *King* and *Alsop*, *Show.* 339.

The Defendant was convicted by the Justices at Sessions on 5 *Ann. c.* 14. *sect.* 4. that he unlawfully had and kept in his Custody a *Gun*, being an Instrument for the Destruction of the Game. Motion to quash the Conviction, because that simply Keeping a *Gun* was not within the Act. *Lee* Chief Justice: 'Tis true a *Gun* is mentioned amongst other Things in 22 & 23 *Car.* 2. *c.* 25. but in 5 *Ann. c.* 14. the Word *Gun* is omitted amongst the Instruments mentioned for the Destruction of Game ; since therefore the Instrument, upon the keeping of which this Conviction is grounded, is omitted, and at the End of the Act these Words are used, ' or other Instrument for the Destruction of the ' Game,' it must mean such as are originally and in themselves adapted for the Destruction of the Game. Lurchers and Greyhounds are expresly mentioned in the Act, so it need not be said they are kept for Destruction of the Game.

Probyn

Probyn Juſtice: The Defendant confeſſing he
kept this *Gun* for the Deſtruction of the Game,
will carry the Conviction no farther than the
Words of it extend, and no Penal Law ought
to be carried any farther than the Words of the
Statute, inaſmuch as every ſuch Law is an
Abridgment of a Man's natural Liberty; it
muſt be proved that the *Gun* was kept for the
actual Killing the Game; and this can be done
in no other Way than by ſhewing he did attempt
it, and frequently has intended ſo to do; as, by,
proving he run a Hare with his Grey-hound,
this would be ſufficient to bring a Man within
the Act. When the Court had quaſhed the
Conviction, a Gentleman then preſent ſaid, that
at the Time of making this Act, Lord *Mac-
cleſfield* deſired the Word *Gun* might be omitted
and not mentioned among the other Engines de-
ſigned for the Deſtruction of the Game, ſince
great Inconveniences would enſue, as none could
keep a *Gun* in his Houſe for his Safety. The
King and *Gardner, Trin.* 11 *Geo.* 2.——2 *Str.* 1098.
S. C. and *per Cur.* a *Gun* differs from *Nets* and
Dogs, which can only be kept for an ill Purpoſe;
and therefore they quaſhed the Conviction.
Andr. 255. *Seſſ.* C. V. 2. 204. — See *Dominus
Rex, v. Filer,* p.   this Work.

    Note; At a *Juſtice-Seat* held for the Foreſt of
Windſor, one *Wheatly* was fined 50 *s.* for carrying
a *Gun* in the Foreſt to kill the Deer. *Wheatly's
Caſe, W. Jones* 275.

Hampton-Court Chase. King *Hen.* 8.
intending to make a Foreſt about his Houſe at

Hampton-Court, affigned and limited feveral Grounds for that Purpofe, extending over the Lands of feveral Freeholders and Copy-holders within the Manors, Townfhips and Villages of *Eaft* and *Weft Mulfey*, *Walton*, *Efher*, *Weybridge*, and Part of *Chobham*; but finding he could not erect either Foreft or Chafe over other Men's Grounds, without the Confent of the refpective Owners of thofe Lands; therefore by an Indenture bearing Date 1 *October* in the 29th Year of his Reign, and made between him of the one Part, and Sir *Richard Page*, *Thomas Henage*, Efq; and feveral others, the Owners of the faid Lands, on the other Part, it was agreed between them, that the Lands thus intended for a Foreft fhould be called *Hampton-Court Chafe*; but that it fhould have the like Liberties, Jurifdictions and Pre-eminences, Laws, Statutes and Officers, as any other Foreft or Chafe in the Realm; and that all Offences done therein fhould be punifhed as if done in any Foreft or Chafe whatfoever; and by this Indenture the King did covenant with the faid Owners of the Lands, that they might fell and take their Woods, Groves, and Coppices at Pleafure, without any View of the Officers, and that they might make great Hedges and Fences about their Corn to keep out the Deer; and for a Recompence to them, that the third Part of the Fee-Farm Rent of every Freeholder fhould from thenceforth be abated, and the Moiety of the Fine of every Heir on his Admittance to a Copy-hold, *&c.* which Indenture being recited in an Act of Parliament made in
the

the 31ſt Year of his Reign, it was accordingly
enacted. 4 *Inſt.* 301.   By the ſame Act the
Manor of *Hampton-Court* was made an Honour,
by the Name and Title of the Honour of *Hampton-Court.*

𝕳𝖆𝖗𝖊.   The *Hare* is a Beaſt of Foreſt, and
alſo of Warren, and by the old Foreſters was
called the King of all Beaſts of Venary; but
there is little Variety of Terms concerning this
Beaſt, being called the firſt Year a *Leveret,* the
ſecond a *Hare,* and the third a *Great Hare.* The
Seaſon for hunting begins at *Michaelmas* and
ought to end about the latter End of *February.*

By 𝕾𝖙𝖆𝖙. 14 & 15 *Hen.* 8. *c.* 10. ' No Per-
' ſon, of what Eſtate, Degree, or Condition he
' be, ſhall trace, deſtroy or kill any *Hare* in the
' Snow, with any Dog, Bitch, Bow, nor other-
' wiſe, and Juſtices of Peace in Seſſions, and
' Stewards in Leets, have Power to inquire of
' ſuch Offenders, and ſhall aſſeſs upon every
' ſuch Offender 6 s. 8 d. which Penalty aſſeſſed
' in Seſſions ſhall go to the King; but in the
' Leet to the Lord thereof.'

And by 1 *J. c.* 27. *ſ.* 2. " Every Perſon who
" ſhall trace or courſe any *Hares* in the Snow,
" ſhall, on Conviction before *two* Juſtices, by
" *Confeſſion* or Oath of *two* Witneſſes, be com-
" mitted to Gaol for *three* Months, unleſs he
" pay to the Churchwardens for the Uſe of the
" Poor, 20 s. for every Hare; or after *one*
" Month after his Commitment, become bound
" by Recognizance with *two* Sureties in 20 *l.*
" a piece, before *two* Juſtices, not to offend
" again in like Manner.   And every Perſon

" who

" who fhall at any Time take or deftroy any
" Hares, with Harepipes, Cords, or any fuch
" Inftruments, or other Engines ; fhall forfeit
" for every Hare 20s. in like Manner.'

By 22 & 23 Car. 2. c. 25. f. 6. ' If any Per-
' fon fhall be found or apprehended fetting or
' ufing any Snares, Harepipes, or other like
' Engines, and fhall be thereof convicted, by
' Confeffion, or Oath of one Witnefs, before
' one Juftice, in one Month after the Offence ;
' he fhall give to the Party injured, fuch Da-
' mages, and in fuch Time, as the Juftice fhall
' appoint, and fhall pay down prefently to the
' Overfeers for the Ufe of the Poor, fuch Sum
' not exceeding 10s. as the Juftice fhall appoint;
' which if he fhall not do, the Juftice fhall
' commit him to the Houfe of Correction, not
' exceeding one Month.'

By Stat. 4 & 5 W. & M. c. 23. ' Con-
' ftables, Headboroughs and Tithingmen, by
' Warrant of a Juftice of Peace, may enter
' into and fearch, in fuch Manner, and with fuch
' Power as in Cafe where Goods are ftolen, or
' fufpected to be ftolen, the Houfes, Outhoufes,
' or other Places belonging to fuch Houfes of
' fufpected Perfons not qualified; and in Cafe
' any Hare, Partridge, Pheafant, Pigeon, Fifh,
' Fowl or other Game, fhall, upon fuch Search
' or otherwife, be found, the Offender fhall be
' carried before a Juftice ; and if he do not give
' a good Account how he came by them, or
' produce the Party of whom he bought the
' fame, or fome other credible Perfon to depofe
' upon Oath fuch Sale thereof, he fhall be con-
' victed

' victed of such Offence by the said Justice, and
' forfeit for every *Hare*, Partridge, Pheasant,
' Fish, Fowl, or other Game, any Sum not
' under 5 *s.* nor exceeding 20 *s.* to be divided
' betwixt the Informer and the Poor of the
' Parish where the Offence was committed, to
' be levied by Distress and Sale of his Goods,
' rendering the Overplus; and for want of Di-
' stress, the Offender shall be committed to the
' House of Correction for any Time not ex-
' ceeding a Month, nor less than ten Days,
' there to be whipped and kept to hard Labour.'
See *Stat.* 5 *Ann. c.* 14. *Tit.* Dogs. p. 63. ' And
' if any Person not qualified by Law do keep or
' use any Bows, Grey-hounds, Setting Dogs,
' Hays, Lurchers, Nets, Tunnels, Lowbells,
' Hare-pipes, Snares or other Instruments for
' Destruction of the Game, and shall be com-
' mitted as above, he shall be subject to the like
' Penalties and Pains as aforesaid; and if any
' Person so charged shall not before the same
' Justice give such Evidence of his Innocence
' as aforesaid, he shall be convicted thereof in
' like Manner as the Person first charged there-
' with is hereby directed to be, and so from Per-
' son to Person, till the first Offender be dis-
' covered.'

    ' Offenders punished by this Act, shall not
' incur the Penalty of any other Law for the same
' Offence.'

    ' Persons prosecuted at Law for any Thing
' done in Pursuance of this Act, may plead the
' General Issue, and give this Act, or any other
' special Matter in Evidence; and if the Ver-

' dict

' dict pass for the Defendant, or the Plaintiffs
" become Nonsuit, or suffer a Discontinuance,
" the Defendant shall recover treble Costs.'

By **Stat.** 9 *Ann. c.* 25. ' If any *Hare*, Phea-
' sant, Partridge, Moor, Heath Game or
' Grouse, be found in the Shop, House or
' Possession of any Person not qualified in his
' own Right to kill Game, or being intitled
' thereto under some Person qualified, the same
' shall be adjudged an Exposing to Sale, within
' the Meaning of 5 *Ann. c.* 14.' [See **Higler**].

' If any Person whatsoever shall take, kill or
'destroy an *Hare, &c.* in the Night-time, he
' shall on Conviction before *one* Justice, on
' Oath of *one* Witness, forfeit 5 *l.* Half to the
' Informer, and Half to the Poor, by Distress;
' for want of Distress, to be sent to the House of
' Correction for *three* Months for the *first* Of-
' fence, and for every *other* Offence *four* Months.'
Same *Stat.*

An Indictment * for tracing a *Hare* in the
Snow. [14 & 15 *H.* 8. *c.* 10. 1 *Jac.* 1.
c. 27.]

Southampton, } **T**H E *Jury, &c. upon their
to wit. } Oaths present, That J. T.
late of W. in the County aforesaid, *Yeoman,* the
third Day of September *in the seventh Year of the
the Reign, &c.* at, &c. *in the County aforesaid,*

* *Vide* the Cases of the *King* and *Fowlin*, p. 145. and
the *King* and *Buck*, p. 163.

one Hare *with a Dog did trace, and the same Hare then and there in the Snow with the same Dog did destroy and kill, contrary to the Form of the Statute in that Case made and provided, and against the Peace,* &c.

A Warrant to search for Game. [4 & 5 *W. & M. c.* 23.]

To the Constable of, *&c.*

Huntingdon, } **B**Y *Virtue of an Act of Par-*
to wit. } *liament in this Case made,*
These are to charge and command you, on Sight. hereof, to enter into and search (as for stolen Goods) the Houses, Out-houses, and all other Places belonging to such Person or Persons, within your Precincts, as are not qualified to kill the Game; and if on such Search you shall find any Hare, Partridge, *Phea-sant*, Pigeon, Fish, Fowl, *or any other Game, then you are forthwith to bring such Person or Persons, in whose Custody the same shall be found, not being lawfully qualified as aforesaid, before me or some other of his Majesty's Justices of the Peace for this County, to be proceeded against according to Law.* Given, *&c.*

If you shall find any Grey-hound, Setting-Dog, Coney-Dog, Ferrets, Nets, Snares, Guns, or any Instruments for Destruction of the Game, then by Virtue of an * Act of Parliament in this Case also made, you are to seize them to and for

* 22 & 23 *Car.* 2. *c.* 25.

the Ufe of the Lord of the Manor or Royalty where the fame fhall be found, and lay an Information before me, to the End that Profecution may be made according to Law. *Given*, &c.

A Warrant to levy the Penalty. [4 & 5 *W. & M. c. 23.*]

To the Conftable of, &c.

Huntingdon, to wit. } WHereas J. W. *of your Parifh, is brought by you before me, (being one of his Majefty's Juftices of the Peace for this County) for having in his Cuftody one* * *Hare which was dead, being found in his Poffeffion by you, on your Search, by Virtue of a Warrant under my Hand and Seal, the faid* J. W. *not being lawfully qualified to kill the Game; and upon my Examination of the faid* J. W. *concerning the Premiffes, he cannot give any good Account how he came by the fame, nor produce any credible Witnefs to prove of what Perfon he bought the faid* † *Hare, whereby he hath forfeited, for fuch* ‖ *Hare fo found upon him, the Sum of* 15 s. [*or any Sum not exceeding* 20 s. *nor under* 5 s.] *one Moiety to the Informer, and the other Moiety to the Poor of your Parifh, according to an Act of Parliament in that Cafe made in the fourth and fifth Years of the Reign of King* William *and Queen*

* Or two Pigeons (as the Cafe is) which were dead.
† Pigeons.
‖ For each Pigeon.
The Penalties for Fifh or Fowl to be levied in the fame Manner.

Mary.

Mary : *These are therefore to authorize and require
you, on Sight hereof to levy the said Sum of* 15 s.
by Distress and Sale of the Goods of the said J. W.
*for the Uses aforesaid, returning the Overplus ; and
what you do herein, you are to certify to me within
six days.* Given, &c.*

A Mittimus for want of Distress. [4 &
5 W. & M. c. 23.]

To the Constable of, &c. and to the
Keeper of, &c.

Huntingdon, }WHereas J. W. of your
  to wit. { Parish, is lawfully con-
victed before me, (being one of his Majesty's Justices
of the Peace for the said County) for having in his
Possession one Hare (or as the Case is) being killed,
he not being duly qualified to kill the Game ;
and whereas the said J. W. hath not sufficient
Distress, whereon to levy the Fine imposed on him
for this Offence : These are therefore to authorize
and require you, on Sight hereof, to convey the said
J. W. to the House of Correction aforesaid, and
deliver him to the aforesaid Keeper of the same (together with this Precept) : Requiring also you the
said Keeper to receive him into your said House, and
there detain him to be whipped and kept to hard
Labour for fourteen Days, [or one Month, but not
less than ten Days]. Given, &c.

Note ; The Law as to Pigeons, Fish and Fowl,
is not altered by 5 *Annæ*.

An

An Information * againſt a Perſon for killing a Hare, &c. on 5 *Ann. c.* 14.

THE *Information of* A. B. *of,* &c. *before*
C. D. *Eſq ; one of his Majeſty's Juſtices*
of the Peace for the ſaid County, on the —— *Day*
of —— *who ſaith, that on the* —— *Day of* ——
E. F. *of* —— *did kill and deſtroy a* Hare *in the*
Pariſh *of* —— *with a Greyhound (or as the Caſe*
is) the ſaid E. F. *not being lawfully qualified to*
kill *the Game.*

A. B.

-Taken the Day and Year above-
ſaid, before me C. D.

An Information * for killing a *Hare* in the
Night, on the 9 *Ann. c.* 25.

The Information of *H. C.* of, &c. taken
before *A. T.* Eſq; one of his Majeſty's
Juſtices of the Peace for the County of
Huntingdon, on the ſeventh Day of
October 1735.

THE *ſaid Informant, upon his corporal Oath,*
ſaith, That W. G. *of,* &c. *did in the Night*
which was between the firſt and ſecond Days of
this inſtant October, *kill and deſtroy one* Hare *in*

* An *Indictment* lies not for killing a *Hare.* See *poſtea,*
p. 163.

a. *Field.*

a Field called C. *in the Parish of* S. *in the County aforesaid, contrary to the Statute in that Case made and provided.*

Affidavit made by a credible Person who
saw the *Hare* killed.

R. K. *of,* &c. *maketh Oath, That he this Deponent saw the said* W. G. *in the Information
named, kill and destroy one* Hare, *as in the Information mentioned; and this Deponent further saith, that
the said Information touching the same, given by*
H. C. *aforesaid, and every Part thereof, is true.*
　　　　　　　　　　　R. K.

Sworn the Day and Year above-
　said before me *A. T.*

Law Cases.

If a Man hunt and kill a *Hare* in the Forest,
the Forester may apprehend him, because it is
a Trespass in the Venison in the King's Forest:
For Proof whereof, it appeareth in the *Assizes
of the Forest of* Pickering, *fo.* 13. That two
Men were indicted, *viz.* one *Bulmer,* for striking
a *Hare* in her Form; and another Man for
taking a *Hare* in the *Forest:* One of them was
committed and fined for the said Offence, and
was bound to his good Behaviour in the Forest;
and the other was outlawed. *Manwood* 175.

Chief Justice *Holt* delivered it for Law in
Sutton's Case, that where a Man starts a *Hare*
　　　　　　　　　　　　　　　　　　in

in another Man's Grounds, and kills it there,
'tis the *Hare* of the Owner of the Ground, becaufe he hath a local Property in the *Hare*; but
if it is hunted into the Ground of another and
killed there, in fuch Cafe 'tis the *Hare* of the
Hunter. *Sutton* againft *Moody*, 2 *Salk* 55. 1
Ld. *Raym.* 251.

Trefpafs, for that he entered into his Warren,
nd took 100 *Hares*, and doth not fay, *his*, yet it
s good. 3 *H.* 6. *fol.* 58. *Kitchen* 118.

A Conviction *fuper pramiffis* for three Penalties
of 5 *l.* each for killing three *Hares*, where it appears it was done the fame Time, is bad, for
the * Statute does not give 5 *l.* for every *Hare*,
it being but one Offence, for all was done the
fame Day. *Marriot* verfus. *Shaw & al. Mich.* 4.
Geo. Comyns 274.

On a Conviction, Exception was taken, that
the Perfon was charged with fo many 5 *l.* as he
had killed *Hares* in the *fame* Day. *Cur.* was
of Opinion, that the Offence for which the Statute * gave the Forfeiture, was the keeping
Dogs and Engines, and not killing the *Hares*.
If a Man not qualified goes a Hunting, and kills
never fo many *Hares* on the *fame* Day, he would
forfeit but one 5*l.* for it is but one Offence;
but if a Man keeps Dogs, and goes a hunting
feveral Days, and kills *Hares*, if it was thus laid,
that he, fuch a Day kept Dogs and killed, and
then again fuch a Day, by laying thus feverally,
the Offence is fevered, and he fhall forfeit 5 *l.*
for each Offence. *Lucas*'s Rep. 26.

* 5 *Ann. c.* 14.

The

The Defendant was indicted for killing an *Hare*; and upon Motion the Indictment was quashed, because the Stat. 5 *Ann c.* 14. which makes this an Offence, appoints a particular Method of punishing it in a summary Way, before a Juftice of Peace. *Mich.* 12 *Geo.* 1. *Rex v. Buck. M. S. Rep.* — 1 *Str.* 679. S. C. fays *Hil.* 12. *Geo.* 1.

Hart, In *Saxon* Heort, Is the moft noble and worthieft of the Beafts of Venary, and is called the firft Year a *Hind-Calf* or *Calf*, the fecond a *Brocket*, the third a *Spayad*, the fourth a *Staggard*, the fifth a *Stag*, the fixth a *Hart*; and if afterwards he is hunted by the King, and efcapes alive, he is called a *Hart-Royal*; and if in hunting he is driven out of the Foreft, fo far that he is not likely to return of himself, and the King giveth over hunting him then, becaufe he had made fuch Sport, he caufeth a Proclamation to be made in all the Towns and Villages near the Place, to which he was purfued and hunted, that no Perfon fhould kill, hurt or hunt him, and appoints certain Forefters to look after him till he returns to the Foreft, and afterwards he is called a *Hart-Royal-proclaimed*. The Time of Grace or Seafon of a *Hart* begins at *Midfummer* and lafteth till *Holy-Rood-Day.* *Manwood* 180, 190. See *Hind*.

Hawk and **Hawking**; A *Hawk* in *Saxon* is called Hapoc, and is a Bird of Prey, which when reclaimed affords a noble Recreation.

By **Stat.** 34 *E.* 3. *c.* 22. ' A *Hawk* taken ' up fhall be delivered to the Sheriff, who after ' Proclamation made in the good Towns of
the

' the County, fhall deliver it (if challenged) to
' the right Owner.'

' If the *Hawk* was taken up by a mean Man,
' and not challenged afterwards within four
' Months, the Sheriff fhall retain the *Hawk*,
' fatisfying the Perfon for taking it up ; but
' if taken up by a Man of an Eftate, who might
' keep a *Hawk*, the Sheriff fhall reftore it to
' him, upon anfwering the Charge of keeping
' the *Hawk*.'

. By * **Stat.** 37 *Ed.* 3. *c.* 19. ' He who
' fteals and carries away a *Hawk*, or conceals
' it after Proclamation made by the Sheriff, not
' obferving the aforefaid **Stat.** 34 *Ed.* 3. fhall
' be a Felon. Clergy allowed.'

My Lord *Coke* in his 3 *Inft.* tells us, that the
aforefaid Statute 37 *Ed.* 3. extends only to *long-
winged Hawks*, and not to *Gofhawks* ; and that
it is not material, whether they have *Vervels* on
or not, fo as they are really reclaimed ; but
before that Statute was made, it was Robbery
to take either a *long-winged or fhort-winged Hawk*
from the Perch, or from the Party ; but it was
not Felony to find and conceal them, before this
Statute. 3 *Inft.* 27.

By **Stat.** 11 *Hen.* 7. *c.* 17. ' No Man fhall
' bear any *Hawk* of the Breed of *England* called
' a *Nyeffe, Gofhawk, Taffel, Laner, Laneret,* or
' *Faulcon,* on pain of forfeiting his *Hawk* to the
' King ; and if he bring any of them over Sea,
' or out of *Scotland,* he fhall bring a Certificate

---

* *N. B.* This Statute, tho' in Print, is not of Record in
the Roll of Parliament. 4 *Inft.* 51.

' thereof

' thereof from the Officer of the Port or War-
' den of the March, on the like Pain of for-
' feiting the fame to the King. And the Perfon
'. that bringeth fuch *Hawk* to the King, fhall
' have a reafonable Reward of the King, or
' elfe for his Labour.'

' None fhall take, kill or fright away any of
' the *Hawks* above-mentioned from the Coverts
' where they ufe to breed, in Pain of 10 *l.* to
' be recovered before the Juftices of the Peace,
' and divided between the King and Profecutor'.
Same *Stat.*

By 𝖘𝖙𝖆𝖙. 5 *El. c.* 21. *f.* 3. ' If any Per-
' fon fhall take away any *Hawks* or their Eggs,
' by any Means unlawfully, out of the Woods
' or Grounds of any Perfon, and be thereof
' convicted at the Affizes or Seffions, on Indict-
' ment, Bill or Information, at the Suit of the
' King or of the Party, he fhall be imprifoned
' three Months and fhall pay Treble Damages;
' and after the three Months are expired, fhall
' find Sureties for his good Abearing for feven
' Years, or remain in Prifon till he doth.'

A Man may have a Writ of Trefpafs for
taking his young * *Hawks.*

---

* Yet for taking a *Hawk* (reclaimed) he fhall not have
Trefpafs, but Trover and Converfion. *Quære.* 2 *Lev.*
201. 1 *Salk.* 667, &*c.* And the Count ought to be,
that he is reclaimed; and it is not fufficient to fay he was
poffeffed of him as of his proper Goods. *Dyer* 306. Sir
Mat. Hale's Commentary on *Fitzherb.* 196.

The

The Form of the Writ.

THE *King to the Sheriff,* &c. *If* A; &c. *then put by Sureties and safe Pledges* B. *so that he be before us on Tuesday next after the Morrow of* All-Souls, *wheresoever we then are in* England, [if returnable in the Common Pleas, then thus,] *before our Justices at* Westminster, *on the Morrow of* All-Souls, *to shew wherefore with Force and Arms the Wood of him the said* A. *at* N. *be entered, and three of his young* Hawks *of great Price, lately in the same Wood in a Net hatched, he took and carried away, and other Enormities did, to the great Damage of the said* A. *and against our Peace: And have you there the Names of the Pledges and this Writ.* Witness, &c.

N. B. By this Writ it appears, that the Property of the *Hawks* are in him who hath the Land, by the Word *(his)* in the Writ *Fitzherb. New Nat. Brev.* 197.

The Place where *Hawks,* &c. build their Nests and hatch their young, is called an Ayerie, and is the proper Term ; and by *Chart. de Foresta, c.* 13. every Freeman may have his Ayerie of *Hawks,* Eagles and Herons, and the Honey found in his Woods within the Forest.

Law Cases.

In Trespass for striking and killing *accipitrem suum* [*his* Hawk], upon Not guilty pleaded, the Plaintiff had a Verdict; but it was moved in Arrest of Judgment, that the Declaration was ill, because the Plaintiff did not set forth what Sort of *Hawk* it was, (*viz*) whether a *Goshawk* or a *Lanner, &c.* for the Word *accipitrem* in the Declaration is the *Genus,* and therefore the Plaintiff ought to shew of what *Species* the *Hawk* was; besides he did not alledge that the *Hawk* was *reclaimed,* for it being a Bird of Prey, and *feræ naturæ,* no Man can have a Property in it, unless it is *reclaimed;* but adjudged, that the Declaration was good, it being *in Trespass, in which a Man may declare upon his Possession,* without shewing what Sort of *Hawk* it is; neither is it necessary in this Action to shew that the *Hawk* was *reclaimed,* as 'tis in *Trover,* where the Plaintiff must shew a Property in the Thing he demands: As for Instance; *Trover, &c.* for a *Ramish Hawk;* upon Not guilty pleaded the Plaintiff had likewise a Verdict in this Action; and it was moved in Arrest of Judgment, that this Declaration was not good, because the Plaintiff had declared for a *Ramish Hawk;* which is a *Hawk* living *inter Ramos* [*amongst the Boughs*], and by Consequence *feræ naturæ;* and when it flies away, it hath not *animum revertendi,* [*the Sense of returning*]; and therefore *occupanti conceditur,* [*is not allowed to be in Possession*], which is this Defendant's Case; for which Reason the
Plaintiff

Plaintiff fhould have fet forth in his Declaration,
that the *Hawk* was reclaimed ; and it was adjudged accordingly. *Vincent* againft *Difney, Cro.
Car.* 13. *Lifter* againft *Hone, Cro. Car.* 390. *March*
12. S. C.

By Stat. 23 *Eliz. c.* 10. *Hawking* in ftanding
Corn, or before it be fhocked, is prohibited
under Pain of 40 *s.* to the Owner of the Corn,
to be recovered by the Owner in any Court of
Record.

Heath. In *Henry* II.'s Time, the Inhabitants
of this Part of the Foreft in *Surrey* were fined
100 Marks for burning of *Heath*, for it fpoileth
the Layer of the Deer and difturbs them. *W.
Jones* 276.

Heath-Cock. By Stat. 4 & 5 *W. & M.
c.* 23. ' For the better preferving the *Red* and
' *Black Game* of *Groufe*, commonly called
' *Heath-cock* and *Heath-Polts*, no Perfon fhall
' deftroy the Cover.' See **Groufe.**

Hedges. One was prefented for fuffering
three Rood of Wood to be fpoiled with Cattle : He came and fhewed, that the Fence
through which the Spoil came, belonged to another Man to make, and the Spoil was in his
Default. But Mr. *Attorney* faid, That it being
within the Foreft, he whofe Wood is in Danger
to be fpoiled, ought to requeft the other to make
the *Hedges* ; and if he refufe then he muft do
it himfelf, and have an Action on the Cafe
againft the other that ought to have done it.
W. Jones 277.

Heron. By Stat. 19 *Hen.* 7. *c.* 11. ' No
' Perfon, except out of his own Ground, fhall
' take

' flee, take, or cauſe to be taken, by means of
' Craft or Engine, any *Herons*, unleſs it be
' with Hawing or a Long-bow, on Pain of 6*s*.
' 8*d*. to him that will ſue for the ſame, by Action
' of Debt, or otherwiſe ; and any two Juſtices of
' Peace in Seſſions may examine the Offenders,
' and commit them to Priſon till they have
' found Sureties for the Payment of the Forfei-
' ture to the King ; and the ſaid Juſtices are to
' have the Tenth, of the Forfeiture.'

' And no Perſon, without his own Ground,
' ſhall take any young *Herons*, out of the Neſt,
' on Pain of 10*s*. in like Manner for every
' young *Heron*.' Same *Stat*.

For more concerning *Heron*, ſee *Stat*. 25.
H. 8. *c*. 11. Tit. **Eggs**. p. 80. And *Stat*. 1. *Jac*.
1. *c*. 27. ſ. 2. Tit. **Pheaſant**. p.

Higler. By **Stat**. 5 *Ann*. *c*. 14. ſ. 2. ' If
' any *Higler*, Chapman, Carrier, Inn-keeper,
' Victualler or Alehouſe-keeper, ſhall have in
' his Cuſtody or Poſſeſſion, any Hare, Pheaſant,
' Partridge, Moor, Heath-Game or Grouſe,
' or ſhall buy, ſell, or offer to ſell, any Hare,
' *&c*. (unleſs ſuch Game in the Hands of
' ſuch Carrier be ſent up by ſome Perſon
' qualified to kill the Game) he ſhall be carried
' before ſome Juſtice of the Peace where
' the Offence is committed, and upon View
' or Oath, being convicted of the ſame, ſhall
' forfeit for every Hare, Pheaſant, *&c*. 5 *L*.
' one Half to the Informer, and the other, to
' the Poor of the Pariſh where the Offence was
' committed, to be levied by Diſtreſs, by War-
' rant of the Juſtice before whom convicted ;

I ' and

' and for Want of Diſtreſs, to be committed
' to the Houſe of Correction, for the firſt Of-
' fence, for three Months without Bail ; for
' every other Offence four Months.'

   ' And no *Certiorari* ſhall be allowed to remove
' the Conviction or other Proceedings, unleſs
' the Party convicted ſhall, before the Allowance
' thereof, become bound to the Proſecutor in
' 50 *l.* with ſuch Sureties as the Juſtice ſhall
' think fit, to pay full Coſts within 14 Days
' after the Conviction confirmed, or *Procedendo*
' granted. And in Default thereof, the Juſtice
' ſhall proceed in Execution of the Conviction,
' in ſuch Manner as if no *Certiorari* had been
' awarded.'

   ' And if any Hare, Pheaſant, Partridge,
' Moor, Heath-Game, or Grouſe, ſhall be *found
' in the Shop* (*) Houſe, or Poſſeſſion of any
' Poulterer, Saleſman, Fiſhmonger, Cook or
' Paſtry-Cook, or any other Perſon not quali-
' fied in his own Right to kill Game, or intitled
' thereunto, under ſome Perſon ſo qualified,
' ſhall be deemed an Expoſing thereof to Sale.'
9 *Ann. c.* 25. *ſ.* 2. 28 *Geo.* 2. *c.* 12.

   ' Any Perſon who ſhall deſtroy, ſell or buy
' any ſuch Hare, Pheaſant, Moor, Heath-Game
' or Grouſe, and ſhall within three Months make
' Diſcovery of any *Higler,* Chapman, Carrier
' Inn or Alehouſe-keeper, or Victualler, that
' hath bought, ſold, or offered to buy or ſell,
' or had in their Poſſeſſion, any Hare, *&c.*

---

   * This muſt be underſtood of Proof that it was found.
Sos 6. *Mod.* 57.

' fo as any one fhall be convicted of fuch Of-
' fence, the Difcoverer fhall be difcharged of the
' Pains and Penalties hereby enacted for killing
' or felling fuch Game, and fhall receive the
' fame Benefit as other Informers.' 5 *Ann. c.* 14.

' The Juftices within their refpective Liber-
' ties, and Lords of Manors within their re-
' fpective Manors, may take away any fuch
' Hare, Pheafant, &c. from fuch *Higler, &c.*
' and Perfons not qualified to kill the fame,
' if found in their Cuftody.' 5 *Ann. c.* 14.

A Warrant to levy the Penalty againft a
Higler for having a Hare in his Cuftody.
(5 *Ann. c.* 14.)

To the Conftable, &c. and the Keeper
of the Houfe of Correction, &c.

Huntingdon, W HEREAS T. A. of
to-wit. H. *in the faid County,*
Higler, hath on the Day of the Date hereof been
duly convicted before me T. F. Efq; one of his
Majefty's Juftices of the Peace for the faid County,
upon the Oath of A. A. of, &c. *for that the faid*
T. A. *had, on the third Day of Auguft laft, in*
his Cuftody, at H. aforefaid, one Hare, contrary
to the Statute in that Cafe made and provided; by
Reafon whereof he hath forfeited the Sum of 5 l.
Thefe are therefore to require you to levy the faid
Sum of 5 l. *by Diftrefs and Sale of the Goods of*
the faid T. A. *rendering to him the Overplus, if*
any fuch fhall happen to be, the Charge of diftrain-

ing

ing being first deducted; and you forthwith pay one Moiety thereof to the said A. A. who first informed me of the said Offence, and the other Moiety to the Poor of the Parish of H. aforesaid, where the same was committed; And *for Want of such Distress, that then you carry the said* T. A. *to the House of Correction, at, &c. and deliver him to the Keeper thereof, together with this Precept; who is hereby commanded to receive him into his Custody, and keep him in the House of Correction for the Space of three Months next ensuing the Date hereof, without Bail or Mainprize, this being his first Offence of this Nature:* And *hereof fail not,* &c. Given, *&c.*

The like Warrant, *mutatis mutandis,* for buying, selling or offering to Sale an Hare, *&c.*

Hind, In *Saxon* Hind, Is the Female of the *Hart,* and is called the first Year a *Calf,* the second a *Brocket's Sister,* and the third a *Hind.* The Season begins on *Holy-Rood-Day,* and lasteth till *Candlemas.*

Homine replegiando. If a Man be taken by the Officers of the Forest, then he shall have this Writ unto the Keeper [Warden] of the Forest.

The Form of the Writ.

THE *King to our well beloved and faithful* W. *of* B. *Warden of our Forests on this Side the* Trent, *or his Deputy in the Forest of* S. *We command you, That if* A. *and* B. *taken and detained in in our Forest of S. for Trespass of Venison by them committed, for which they are indicted, as it is said, find you, to wit, each of them twelve honest and and lawful Men of your Bailiwick, who will be bound to have them before our Justices at the next Eyre of our Forest in the County of N. to answer the Trespass aforesaid; if according to the Assise of the Forest they are replevisable, then in the mean Time deliver them the said A. and B. to bail to the twelve Men as aforesaid: And have you there the Names of the twelve Men, and this Writ, Witness, &c.*

If the Warden will not bail him, he shall have an *Alias* and *Pluries* against the Warden, directed unto the Sheriff, to attach him to answer before the King in his Bench, and shew wherefore he has not replevied him, *&c.* And in the same Writ it shall be contained, that he call to him the Verderors, to deliver him, who is so taken, in the Presence of the Verderors by good Bail, and that the Sheriff do deliver the Names of the Bail unto the same Verderors, to answer before the Justices in the next Eyre. And no Man shall be taken or imprisoned for Vert. or Venison, if he be not found in the Manner, or indicted; in which Case he shall be set to bail by the Warden *ex Officio,* or otherwise by Writing as aforesaid. *Fitzherb. New Nat. Brev.* 145. *Hawk. Pleas of the Crown,* 2 Book 97.

Horn Geld, A Tax within the Bounds of a Forest, for all Manner of horned Beasts.

I 3

Due

Hue and Cry, *i. e.* to cry out aloud. When a Forester, or any other Officer of the Foreft, fhall find any Perfons do or intending to do any Hurt or Damage to the Foreft, and they fly for the fame, they are forthwith to make an *Outcry* unto the Inhabitants and next Dwellers in the Foreft where fuch Perfons were feen, requiring them in the King's Name to aid and affift them to purfue fuch Offenders from Town to Town, and from Village to Village, Place and Place, within the Limits and Bounds of the Foreft, until they are taken. *Manwood* 182.

This *Hue and Cry* of the Foreft, is properly to be made by the Forefter himfelf, becaufe he is ufually a Perfon known in that Place, and the more likely to be followed; yet any other Officer or Minifter of the Foreft may make it; as appears by the *Affizes and Ordinances of the Foreft. Artic.* 11. ' If any fee any Mifdoers ' within the Bounds of the Foreft to carry ' away any Deer, he fhall do what he may to take ' him; and if he cannot, he fhall levy *Hue* ' *and Cry*, and if he do not fo, he fhall ftill remain ' in the King's Mercy.' *Ibid.* 182, 409.

If after fuch *Hue and Cry* made, any Perfon is negligent or refufe to purfue the Offenders, then the Default of fuch Perfon or Perfons, Townfhip or Village, fo offending, fhall be prefented by the Forefter of the fame Baili-wick at the next Court of *Swainmote*, or *Ju-ftice-Seat*, which fhall firft happen; and if after fuch Prefentment, the Offenders fhall be duly convicted according to the Laws of the Foreft, they

they fhall be fined. *Ibid.* 182, 183, 184.
Itin. Lanc. fo. 7.

Hue and Cry is not to be made for every
Trefpafs and Offence done in the Foreft, but only
for fuch as are done in hunting and deftroying
the wild Beafts of the Foreft, as appears by the
above recited *Affifes of the Foreft. Artic.* 11. ' If
' any fee any Mifdoers within the Bounds of
' the Foreft to carry away any Deer', in fuch
Cafe he is to make *Hue and Cry*; *viz.* after thofe
who are Hunters and Takers of Venifon and
not after fuch as commit Trefpafs in Vert.

But fome are of Opinion, that *Hue and Cry*
is limited to be within the Bounds of the Foreft;
for by the fame *Affifes, Artic.* 10. ' If any Man
' take a Deer in the Foreft, without a Warrant,
' his Body fhall be arrefted wherefoever he be
' found within the Bounds of the Foreft.' *Manwood* 216, 409.

If after fuch *Hue and Cry* made, and the People
come to the Place where the Offenders are, if
they refift and will not yield; or if they fly; and
any Perfon who came in Affiftance to the Forefter, or other Officer, fhall happen to kill one
or more of them *in the Bounds of the Foreft,*
either in apprehending or taking them or any
of them, he fhall not be arraign'd for the fame
before the King and his Juftices, or before any
of the King's Bailiffs, or any other within any
Franchife or without; neither fhall he for fo
doing lofe either Life or Limb, or fuffer any
other Punifhment, but fhall enjoy the King's
Peace as before. *Manwood* 183. *Hawkins's*

Pleas

Pleas of the Crown, 1 Book 71. Crom. 30. b. Dyer 326. pl. 3. Vide *Table*.

Hunting, Is a Recreation and Pleasure, which is common for any Man to use in his own Grounds. Sed Vide *Table*.

By Stat. 1 *H.* 7. *c.* 7. * ' If any shall *hunt* ' within the Forests, Parks or Warrens in the ' Night-time, or disguised, one of the King's ' Counsel; or a Justice of Peace, to whom In- ' formation thereof shall be made, shall by his ' Warrant cause the Offender to be brought ' before himself, or some other Counsellor or ' Justice of Peace, to be examined; where if he ' conceal the Fact, such *Hunting* shall be deemed ' Felony; but being confessed, the Offence is ' only finable at the next General Sessions. And ' here a Rescous of the Execution of any such ' Warrant shall be also deemed Felony.'

My Lord *Coke*, in his Comment on this Statute, says, That 'tis a general Law, and extends to all Persons, of what Estate or Degree soever, and as well to Women as to Men; and that to *hunt disguised in the Day-time* is equally punishable as *hunting in the Night*, because the Offender cannot be known; but this Statute doth not extend to Hunting in *Chases*, nor to *Forests, Parks* or *Warrens*, which are not really so, but only so reputed. 3 Inst. 76.

* *Note,* The *Stat.* 9 *Geo.* 2. *c.* 22. commonly called the Black Act, whilst it continues in Force, renders this *Stat.* of 1 *H.* 7. *c.* 7. of little Use: But it is to be observed, that if said *Stat.* of 9 *Geo.* 2. should be suffered to expire, the Offence will fall back again upon the *Stat.* 1 *H.* 7. *c.* 7.

The

The fame great Lawyer in his 4th *Inft,* 309. fays, That albeit *Spiritual Perfons* are prohibited by the Canon Law to *hunt,* yet by the Common Law they may *hunt* for their Recreation, in Order to make them fitter to perform their Office and Duty.

A Subject who is Owner of a Foreft may grant Warrants to *hunt* there, but no Man can give Licence to *hunt* in the King's Forefts, but himfelf or his Chief Juftice in Eyre, being within his Jurifdiction, or thofe who by fome Grant from the King have a fpecial Authority fo to do. *Manwood* 189.

When a Man hath a Warrant to kill and carry away the Thing *hunted* and killed, in this Cafe he hath a Property in it, and his Warrant is called a Warrant of Profit, and he may *hunt* with what Company he will.

But where he hath no Property in the Thing *hunted* or killed, 'tis only a Licence of Pleafure, and he cannot *hunt* with any more than himfelf. *Ibid.*

He who hath a Warrant to *hunt, &c.* muft purfue his Authority very ftrictly, for if he doth not, he is a Trefpaffer *ab initio,* and punifhable. *Manwood* 186.

By 𝕾𝖙𝖆𝖙. 23 *Eliz. cap.* 10. ' *Hunting* is pro-
' hibited in ftanding Corn.' See Tit. 𝕯𝖔𝖌𝖘.

A Warrant

A Warrant or Summons on 23 *Eliz.* c. 10.
for *hunting* in standing Corn.

To the Constable, &c.

Suſſex, } WHereas Complaint hath been this
to wit. } Day, made unto me D. A. Eſq;
[one of his Majeſty's Juſtices of the Peace of the ſaid
County,] That R. B. of the Pariſh of, &c. Gent.
did, on the eighth Day of June laſt paſt, hunt with
Spaniels in the Ground of T. M. and without his
Conſent, there being then Corn ſtanding, growing
and eared in the ſame Ground, by Reaſon whereof
the ſaid R. B. hath forfeited the Sum of 40s. to
the ſaid R. M. the Owner of the ſaid Ground and
Corn: Theſe are therefore in his Majeſty's Name
to command you forthwith, upon Sight hereof, to
warn the ſaid R. B. perſonally to come before me or
ſome other Juſtice of the Peace of this County, to
be examined concerning the Premiſſes. Given, &c.

If the Offender doth not appear on the Return of this Warrant, then inſtead of theſe
Words, [to be examined, &c.] ſay.

To give Bond with Sureties for his Appear-
ance at the next General Seſſions of the Peace to be
holden for this County, to anſwer the Premiſſes;
and if he ſhall refuſe ſo to do, that then you ſafely
convey him to the Gaol of, &c. and deliver him to
the Keeper thereof: Commanding *you the ſaid*
Keeper *to receive the ſaid* R. B. *into your Cuſtody, and*
him

*him there safely to keep until he shall find Sureties;
as aforesaid.* Given, *&c.*

Note; One Juftice hath Power to examine
and to bind over to the Seffions where this Offence
is to be tried upon an Information, if the Offence
be not before heard and determined by Juftices
of Affize, Steward of Leets, *&c.*

Law Cafes.

Trefpafs for *entering his Clofe, and treading
down his Grafs and Corn,* and *hunting* there, the
Defendant being an *inferior Tradefman, (viz.)* a
Clothier; and the Plaintiff concluded his Declaration *contra pacem, &c. & contra formam ſtatuti
inde edit' & provis'*; upon Not guilty pleaded the
Plaintiff had a Verdict, and it was moved in
Arreft of Judgment, that the Words *contra
formam ſtatuti* go to the Whole Declaration,
whereas *the Entring his Clofe, and Treading down
his Grafs and Corn,* are not contrary to any Statute, but only the *Hunting*; and when that is
done by an inferior Tradefman, the Statute 4
& 5 *Will.* increafes the Forfeiture to 5 *l.* or to
any other Sum not exceeding 20 *s.* and befides,
it gives the Party grieved an Action of Trefpafs,
in which he fhall recover his Damages and *full
Cofts*; but adjudged, that where a Statute increafes the Penalty, or deprives a Man of that
Liberty, which he had by the Common Law;
if the Plaintiff will declare upon fuch a Statute,
he muft bring his Cafe within it, and then conclude *contra formam ſtatuti*, otherwife his Decla-

ration

ration will be ill; and this was *Penhallo's* Cafe.
3 *Cro.* 231. 4 *Leon.* 49. But where there is
no Statute in the Cafe, if the Plaintiff conclude
contra formam statuti, it shall not make his
Declaration ill; for 'tis only Surplusage, and
that was *Ward's* Cafe, 1 *Vent.* 102. 'Tis true,
in the principal Cafe *Hunting* is only within the
Statute; and though in a grammatical Construction the Words *contra formam statuti* will go
to the other Trespasses, which are not prohibited by any Statute; yet in a legal Construction,
those Words shall be applied only to *Hunting,*
which was really within the Statute: and as to
the Rest, they shall be rejected as Surplusage.
Bennet against *Talbot,* 1 *Salk.* 212.

Trespass for breaking his (the Plaintiff's)
Close, and entering and *hunting* there on such
a Day, *continuando* the Trespass as to the *Hunting*
at divers Days and Times, from the Day of the
Trespass, &c. to such a Day ; the Defendant
pleaded Not guilty, upon which they were at
Issue, and the Plaintiff had a Verdict; it was
moved in Arrest of Judgment, that *Hunting* is
a Recreation which could not be laid with a
Continuando, because both Men and Dogs must
have some Rest from that Sport ; 'tis true, there
are several Facts which are permanent in their
Nature, and those properly lie in Continuance;
but there are other Trespasses which terminate
in themselves, and cannot be continued, as killing a Mastiff, &c. But adjudged, that *Hunting* is not an Act which terminates in itself, and
therefore it may be laid with a *Continuando* at
divers

divers Days and Times, between fuch a Day,
&c. *Monkton* againſt *Paſhley*, 2 *Salk.* 638.
See the *Table.*

As Hunting *in alieno folo* is a Treſpaſs at
Common Law and actionable, and as there is
no Act which enables *any Man* (tho' qualified)
to hunt, &c. in another's Ground, I would ad-
viſe the Poſſeſſor of Lands to write out two
Copies of the following Notice, and to cauſe
one Copy thereof to be ſerved on the Perſon he
ſuſpects will come upon his Premiſſes to kill
Game, by a Perſon who can read and write,
and to keep the other Copy himſelf, a Memo-
randum being firſt indorſed thereon, and ſub-
ſcribed by the Perſon who ſerved the Copy in
the Words following, viz. *On the   Day of*
1761, delivered to the within named A. B. *a*
true Copy of the within written Notice. Witneſs
my Hand,

E. F.

The Form of a Notice to be given by the
Occupier of Lands to forbid Perſons (even
though qualified) to hunt, &c. upon his
Premiſſes.

Mr. A. B.

TAKE *Notice, That I do hereby forbid you,*
at any Time or Times whatſoever after your
Receipt hereof, to enter into or upon any of the
Cloſes, Lands, or Premiſſes, in my Poſſeſſion, herein-
after

after particularly mentioned, viz. one Close called
———— all which said Premisses are situate and
lying within the Manor of ——, in the Parish of
——, in the County of ——, or into or upon any
other of the Lands and Tenements within the said
Manor, Parish, and County, now in my Possession,
and not above particularly set forth; or into or
upon any of them, or any Part thereof, either to
hunt, course, search for or kill Game there, or on
any other Account or Pretence whatsoever, so long as
the same or any Part thereof shall remain in my
Possession: And I do hereby give you Notice, that
if at any Time after your Receipt hereof, you do
enter into or upon any of the said Lands, Tenements,
or Premisses above-mentioned, or any Part thereof,
either to hunt, course, search for or kill Game there,
or on any other Account or Pretence whatsoever,
during the Time the same, or any Part thereof, shall
remain and be in my Possession, that I shall consider
you as a wilful * Trespasser, and I shall immediately
thereupon prosecute you at Law for so doing. Given
under my Hand this —— Day of ——, 1761.

To Mr. *A. B.*   C. D.
   at ————

Inclosures in Forests. If a Chief Justice
in *Eyre* will grant a Licence to a Man to *inclose*
his Ground in the Forest, paying a certain
Rent, and such Licence is made *sedente curiâ*,

---

* This may induce the Jury (in an Action of Trespass)
to give such Damages as will intitle the Plaintiff to his
full Costs.

fitting the Court, it is good for ever, but not otherwise; for if it is not granted in Court, it may be pulled down again. *W. Jones Rep.* 277. But such *Inclofure* muſt be with low Hedges, which may not diſturb the Game. *Manwood* 199.

Arable Land may be *inclofed*, but not with high Hedges, though Woods and Coverts in the Foreſt may be *inclofed* with high Hedges and Ditches, to preſerve them from Hurt and Cropping by Cattle, until they are paſt all Danger. *Manwood* 200.

Upon a Preſentment againſt *John Taylor* for *Inlofing* a common Lane, he was fined 10 *s.* and to lay out the Lane: Mr. Attorney ſaid, the Way for the King's *Hunting* ought to be as free as the Highway for Men's travelling. *W. Jones* 269.

Infant. If an *Infant* is impleaded before the Chief Juſtice in *Eyre* for a Treſpaſs done in a Foreſt, he may appear in proper Perſon, and ſhew that he is under Age, and pray the Chief Juſtice that *J. P.* may be aſſigned for his Guardian; or if he doth not appear in Perſon, but the ſaid *J. P.* for him, and ſheweth he is an *Infant*, and prayeth he may be admitted his Guardian, the Court will admit him accordingly. *Manwood* 17.

If an *Infant* hath choſen his Guardian who is afterwards ſick, or will not appear before the *Juſtice-Seat*; yet if the *Infant* appears and prayeth *J. S.* may be admitted for him as *Prochein Amy*, he will alſo be admitted according to that Prayer. *Ibid.*

Judgment.

Judgment. If the Juftice in *Eyre* give erroneous *Judgment*, the Party grieved may have a Writ of Error out of Chancery returnable in the King's Bench, and there Juftice fhall be done. 4 *Inft.* 297.

Jury. By **Stat.** 7 *Ric.* 2. *c.* 3. ' No Manner' of *Jury* fhall be from henceforth compelled by any Officer of the Foreft, or other Perfon whatfoever to travel from Place to Place out of the Places where their Charge was given to them againft their Gree, nor by Malice, or by Menace, nor other Durefs, conftrained to give their Verdict of a Trefpafs done in the Foreft, otherwife than their Confcience will clearly inform them; but they fhall give their Verdicts upon their Charge, in the Place where the Charge is given.' *N. B.* This Act extendeth to Forefts only. 4 *Inft.* 314. Vide *Table.*

Juftice-Seat, or *the Eyre of the Foreft,* is a *Court of Record,* and though the Trefpaffes of Offenders are prefented at the Court of Attachments, and afterwards thofe Offenders are upon fuch Prefentments indicted at the Court of Swainmote, according to the Statute 1 *Ed.* 3. *c.* 8. and the Statute *de Ordinatione Forestæ,* yet thofe Courts cannot give Judgment, or affefs any Fine, for that muft be done at the *Juftice-Seat,* and therefore the Rolls of fuch Offences, in both thofe Courts, are to be fealed with the Seals of the Verderors, who are to keep them until the *Juftice-Seat,* and then they are to prefent them to the Chief Juftice in Eyre;

This

This Court may be proclaimed to be held within the Foreſt on ſuch a Day; and at leaſt forty Days before the Sitting thereof, 'tis uſual to ſend out two Writs of Summons, one directed to the Sheriff of the County, and the other directed *Cuſtodi foreſtæ Domini Regis, &c. vel ejus locum tenenti in eadem, &c.* which laſt Writ conſiſts of two Parts; firſt to ſummon all the Officers of the Foreſt, and that they bring with them all the Records, &c. and ſecondly, all Perſons who claim any Liberties or Franchiſes within the Foreſt, and to ſhew by what Authority they claim the ſame. 4 *Inſt.* 291.

After forty Days Notice given by the Sheriff by Proclamation, of holding the Court of *Juſtice-Seat*, and after the Chief Juſtice in *Eyre*, and thoſe in Commiſſion with him, are come to the Place appointed, then the firſt Commiſſion muſt be read, and the Officers called, and the Freeholders and all other Perſons who were ſummoned to appear; then there muſt be a ſubſtantial Jury of twenty-four, twenty or eighteen, choſen out of thoſe Freeholders and others there preſent, who muſt be ſworn truly to inquire and true Preſentment make of all ſuch Matters and Things as ſhall be given them in Charge. *Manwood* 65.

For the Charge, ſee *Manwood* 65.

After the Court is ſat, the Chief Juſtice may adjourn it to any Place within the County, and he may likewiſe take Recognizances any where; and a Preſentment or an Indictment found by the Jury (but not in the Swainmote)

may

may be traversed, becaufe only *found by one Jury.*

The Proceedings are *de hora in horam*, and the Defendant muft plead prefently. *Wood's Inft.* 497.

Note; If a *Juftice-Seat* be difcontinued by the not Coming of the Chief Juftice, it may be revived by the King's Writ. *Manwood* 78.

Keeper *of the Foreft*, * Is an Officer who has the principal Government of all Things belonging to the Foreft, and the Check of all the other Officers, called alfo the Chief Warden of the Foreft; when the Chief Juftice in *Eyre* of the Foreft thinks fit to hold his Juftice-Seat, he fends out his general Summons to the *Keeper* forty Days before, to warn the Officers, &c. to appear. See **Warden.**

Kipper time, A Space of Time between the Feftival of the Invention of the Holy Crofs, *May* 3. and *Twelfth-Day*; during which Salmon-fifhing in the River *Thames* from *Gravefend* to *Henley* was forbidden by *Rot. Parl.* 50 *Ed.* 3.

King. The King having a continual Care for the Prefervation of the Realm, and for the Peace and Quiet of his Subjects, he had there-fore, amongft many Privileges, this Preroga-tive, *viz.* To have his Place of Recreation wherefoever he would appoint. *Manwood* 148,

* Account lieth againft him for the Deer, for he hath Poffeffion as a Bailiff. *10 H.* 7. *fo.* 30. *Kitchin* 119.

203. But fee **Hampton-Court Chafe**, whereby it appears that the *King* cannot erect either Foreft or Chafe over other Mens Grounds, without Confent. The *King* may grant a Foreft to a Subject. *Manwood* 155, 156. See the *Table*.

Lawn, A great Plain in a Park, or between two Woods.

Laws *of the Foreft*. The *Laws of the Foreft* are *general*, becaufe they refpect all Forefts alike, and they are likewife *particular*, becaufe they relate to Forefts and to no other Places. *Manwood* 205.

Before the making of *Charta de Foreftâ* there was no certain *Law* to punifh Offences committed in Forefts; for at firft the King caufed fuch Offenders to be punifhed in fuch Manner as he thought fit, till King *Canutus*, and other Kings, made Canons and Conftitutions to preferve the *Vert* and *Venifon*. Thefe Conftitutions afterwards, by Continuance of Time, were taken for *Laws*. *Ibid.* 206.

Leap, An Engine, made of Twigs, to catch Fifh in.

Libera Chafea habenda, Is a judicial Writ granted to a Perfon for a *Free Chafe* belonging to his Manor; after Proof made by Inquiry of a Jury, that the fame of Right belongs to him. *Jac. Law-Dict,* fub Tit,

Ling. See **Game.**

Bail a Cuftody, and Mainprife only Security.

Mainprife, Signifies the Taking a Man into friendly Cuftody; and *Manwood* makes this
Difference

Difference between *Mainprife* and *Bail*: He that
is *mainprifed,* is faid to be at large, after the
Day he is let to *Mainprife* until the Day of his
Appearance, and under no Poffibility of being
confined by his *Mainpernors*; but where a Man
is let to *bail,* he is always accounted by Law to
be in their Ward for the Time; and they may,
if they will, keep him in Prifon all that Time;
fo that *Mainprife* is more large than *Bail,* for
every *Bail* is *Mainprife,* but every *Mainprife* is
not *Bail. Wood's Inft.* 581. *Manwood* 32, 33.

Manner. A Forefter or other Officer muft
not arreft or imprifon the Body of any Offender
without due Indictment, except he take him
with the Manner, that is, for Venifon, either
Dog-draw, Stable-ftand, Back-bare or *Bloody-hand*;
and for Vert, cutting it and carrying it away;
nor fhall conftrain any to make Obligation of
Ranfom againft his Will, and the Affize of the
Foreft, in Pain to pay the Party grieved double
Damages, and Fine and Ranfom to the King.
1 *Ed.* 3. *c.* 8. 7 *R.* 2. *c.* 4.

If any Forefter or Keeper fhall take any one
in the Manner, then he may carry him to
Prifon, from whence he fhall not be delivered,
without a fpecial Warrant from the King or the
Chief Juftice in *Eyre* of the Foreft. *Manwood* 192.

The Punifhment for being taken *in the Manner* is, by a judicial Sentence at the *Juftice-Seat,*
to be fined at the Difcretion of the Lord Chief
Juftice, committed till he pays the Fine, and
then and there to be bound to his good Behaviour

viour in the Foreſt for ever afterwards. *Ibid.* 193.

Dog-Draw, Is where a Man hath wounded a wild Beaſt, and is found with a Hound or other *Dog.* drawing after him to recover the Beaſt ſo wounded.

Stable-Stand, Is where one is found at his *ſtanding* ready to ſhoot any Deer, or *ſtanding* cloſe by a Tree with Grey-hounds in his Leaſh, ready to let ſlip.

Back-Bare, Is where a Man hath killed a wild Beaſt in the Foreſt, and is found carrying him away.

Bloody-Hand, Is where one is found in a Foreſt in a ſuſpicious *Manner,* and is Bloody. *Manwood* 193.

Mares. By **Stat.** 27 *Hen.* 8. *c.* 6. ‘ Every ‘ one, having Inheritance or Frehold in a Park ‘ kept for Deer which is a Mile about, or his ‘ Farmer, ſhall keep two *Mares* apt and able to ‘ bear Foals, each of them being thirteen Hands ‘ high from the loweſt Part of the Hoof to the ‘ higheſt Part of the Shoulder, and each con- ‘ taining four Inches, in Pain of 40 *s.* for every ‘ Month they want them : And if the Park be ‘ four Miles about they ſhall keep four ſuch ‘ *Mares,* upon the like Pain.’

‘ If any of the *Mares* die, they have three ‘ Months given them to provide another, with- ‘ out Danger of incurring the ſaid Penalty.’

‘ They ſhall not ſuffer their *Mares* to be ‘ leapt by any Stone-Horſe under fourteen ‘ Hands high, in Pain of 40 *s.*’

‘ The

' The ſaid Forfeitures are to be divided be-
' twixt the King and the Proſecutor.'

' This Act ſhall not extend to *Weſtmorland,*
' *Cumberland, Northumberland,* nor Biſhoprick
' of *Durham,* nor to the Parks wherein the
' Inhabitants of the Town next adjoining have
' Common.'

' Spiritual Perſons may ſell the Increaſe and
' Breed of their *Mares,* notwithſtanding this
' Act.'

And by 32 *H.* 8. *c.* 13. (in order to preſerve
the Breeding of ſtrong Horſes) no Stone-Horſe
above two Years old, and under fifteen Hands
(every Hand four Inches) to be put into Foreſts
where *Mares* are kept, upon Pain of forfeiting
the Horſe.

𝔚arren, A Kind of wild Cat, and is a Beaſt
of Chaſe. *Manwood* 50.

𝔚aſt, In *Sax.* mæɾt, is the Fruit of Wild-
Trees; as Oak, Beech, *&c.*

𝔚aſt-time, Is the Seaſon when *Maſt* is
ripe.

𝔚ill. A Man may not build a *New Mill*
in the Foreſt without Leave. *Manwood* 297.

𝔚ower. By the *Aſſiſes* and *Cuſtoms* of the
Foreſts, ' No *Mower* ſhall bring with him a
' great Maſtiff to drive away the Deer of our
' Lord the King, but little Dogs to look to
' Things without the Coverts.'

𝔚urder. The Lord *Dacres,* and *Manſell*
and others in his Company, came unlawfully
to hunt in a Foreſt, and being reſiſted, one of the
Company, when the Lord *Dacres* was a great
Way off, and not preſent, killed a Man; and it

was

was adjudged *Murder* in him and all the Reſt. *Keil. Rep.* 87. *Moor* 86.

𝕸𝖆𝖑𝖊𝖋𝖆𝖈𝖙𝖔𝖗. See 𝕽𝖊𝖈𝖊𝖎𝖛𝖊𝖗.

𝕹𝖊𝖙𝖘. By 𝕾𝖙𝖆𝖙. 1. *Jac.* 1. *c.* 27. ' Every
' Perſon (not qualified) convicted by his own
' Confeſſion, or Oath of two Witneſſes before
' two Juſtices, to keep a *Net* to kill Deer,
' Hare, Pheaſant or Partridge, ſhall be com-
' mitted for a Month without Bail, unleſs he
' immediately pay, to the Uſe of the Poor,
' where the Offence was committed, or where
' he was apprehended, 40 *s.* for every *Net.*'

By 𝕾𝖙𝖆𝖙. 7 *Jac.* 1. *c.* 11. ' Every Con-
' ſtable or Headborough, upon a Warrant under
' the Hands of two Juſtices, may ſearch the
' Houſes of Perſons ſuſpected to have any Set-
' ting-Dogs or *Nets*, for taking Pheaſants or
' Partridges, and may kill and cut in Pieces
' at Pleaſure the Dogs and *Nets* there found, as
' Things forfeited to the ſaid Officers.'

By 𝕾𝖙𝖆𝖙. 4 & 5 *W.* & *M. c.* 23. ' No
' Perſon ſhall keep a *Net*, Angle, Leap, Piches,
' for taking Fiſh, other than the Maker or
' Seller thereof, or Owner or Occupier of any
' River or Fiſhery ; and that ſuch Owner, &*c.*
' and ſuch whom he ſhall authoriſe, may ſeize
' and keep ſuch *Net*, &*c.* to their own Uſe,
' which ſhall be uſed or found in the Poſſeſſion
' of any Perſon whatſoever, fiſhing in any
' River or Fiſhery without the Conſent of the
' Owner or Occupier ; and any Perſon, by a
' Warrant from one Juſtice, may ſearch the
' Houſes and other Places of Perſons prohi-
' bited,

' bited, and fufpected to have in their Cuftody
' any *Nets*, or other fuch Engines, and either
' to deftroy them, or feize and keep them to his
' own Ufe.'

By **Stat.** 4 & 5 *Ann. c.* 21. ' No Perfon
' whatfoever fhall keep any *Net*, Angle, &*c.*
' other than fuch as are allowed fo to do by 4
' & 5 *W. & M. c.* 23.'

A Warrant to fearch for *Nets* and Setting
Dogs. [7 *Jac.* 1. *cap.* 11.]

To the Conftable of, &*c.*

Surry,⎬ **B**Y *Virtue of an Act of Parliament*
to wit,⎬ *made in the feventh Year of the
Reign of King* James *the Firft: Thefe are (in his
Majefty's Name) to authorife and command you
to enter into and fearch the Houfe or Houfes of any
Perfon or Perfons (not being qualified within your
Precincts, fufpected to have Setting Dogs or Nets,
(for the taking of Pheafants and Partridges) and
that wherefoever you find any fuch Setting Dogs or
Nets, the fame you take, carry away and detain, kill,
deftroy and cut in Pieces, as Things prohibited by
the Act aforefaid, and forfeited to you, and fhall
find out and take the fame as aforefaid: Hereof
fail not at your Peril.* Given, &*c.*

A Warrant

A Warrant againſt one keeping fiſhing *Nets*, and to ſearch for them. [4 & 5 *W. & M. cap.* 23.]

To the Conſtable, &c.

Norfolk, to wit. } **W**Hereas *Complaint hath been made unto me, that the Fiſh in,* &c. *hath lately been deſtroyed by ſome idle, diſorderly Perſons, not qualified by Law, either as having a free Fiſhery, or being Owners thereof, or otherwiſe lawfully authorized to fiſh in navigable Rivers; and that ſeveral* Nets, Leaps, Piches, *and other Inſtruments and Engines are kept in the Pariſh of,* &c. *for the Deſtruction of Fiſh by Perſons who are not Makers or Sellers thereof, contrary to the Statute in that Caſe made and provided:* Theſe *are therefore to require you forthwith to enter into and ſearch the Houſes, Out-houſes, and other ſuſpected Places of Perſons within your Pariſh, or of ſuch who you are informed have any* Nets *or other Inſtruments for Deſtruction of Fiſh, and to ſeize the ſame where you ſhall find any ſuch, and likewiſe to bring the Perſon, in whoſe Houſe it ſhall be found, before me or ſome other Juſtice of the Peace for this County, to anſwer the Premiſſes.* And hereof fail not, &c.

Law Caſes.

An Information was brought againſt the Defendant upon the *Stat.* 2 *H.* 6. *c.* 15. for faſten-

ing

ing *Nets* upon the River *Thames* to Boats *Day and Night*, *so long as the Tide did serve*, and did not set forth, that it was continually *Day and Night*; but adjudged, that the Word *continually* in this *Statute* shall be taken to mean so long as the *Nets* fastened may take Fish; and so long as the Time of fishing continueth. 12 *Rep.* 89.

Trespass was brought against the Defendant for cutting the Plaintiff's *Nets* and Oars; who pleaded, that he was seised of a several *Fishery* in, &c. and that the Plaintiff with others endeavoured to row on the Water, and to catch Fish there with their *Nets*; and thereupon to preserve his (the Defendant's) Fishing, he cut the *Nets*, &c. and upon a Demurrer to this Plea, the Plaintiff had Judgment; for the Defendant might have seized the *Nets* Damage-feasant, and detained them, but cannot justify the Cutting them; which he may now do by Virtue of an Act of Parliament. *Reynell* against *Champernoon*, *Cro. Car.* 228.

The Defendant was indicted for fishing with a *Net* not exceeding two Inches and an Half in the Mesh; but this Indictment was quashed, because it should have been exceeding two Inches and an Half. *The King* against *Hawkins*, 2 *Keb.* 635.

In *Warren*'s Case it was adjudged, that every Subject hath a Right or Liberty to fish with lawful *Nets* in any navigable River; and the King cannot deprive him of that Liberty, for he hath only a Right to Royal Fish. *Warren* against *Matthews*, *Modern Cases* 75.

Night.

Night. See Forest.

Non-user. In all Cases where Liberty is granted of any Thing in a Forest, if the Grantee doth not use the same continually, and it appeareth so upon Inquiry, then the Liberty is to be seized, for *Non-user* is a good Cause of Seizure; as appears in the Case of the Abbot of *Rivall*. *Itin. Pickering fo.* 15, 17, 18. *Manwood* 93. But the *Non-user* of Parks or Warrens, is neither a Cause of Seizure or Forfeiture. *Manwood* 236, see 208.

Nusance of the Forest. Whatsoever tends to the Hurt or Destruction of the Forest, or of the *Vert* or *Venison*, or which tends to the Breach of those Laws made for the Preservation of them, the same is a *Nusance* of the Forest, and may be comprehended under these three Heads. 1. *Common Nusance*, 2. *Special Nusance*, 3. *General Nusance*.

Of the *Common Nusance*; this Sort of *Nusance* is a general Hurt, as well to the Inhabitants, as to the Beasts of the Forest; as suffering a Bridge to go to decay, so that People are forced to go through the Forest, both to the Trouble of themselves, and the Disquiet of the Deer; the erecting a Mill; stopping a Water-course, &c. *Manwood* 207, 208.

Of the *Special Nusance*; this tends chiefly to the Hurt of the wild Beasts of the Forest, and comprehends all Manner of Hunters and Trespassers, which in any ways offend against the *Venison* or the Wild Beasts, as by Hunting or in any other Manner, to take and destroy them, or intending so to do. *Ibid.* 208.

Of

Of the *General Nuſance* ; this Kind tends to the Hurt of the whole Foreſt, and as it may happen to the wild Beaſts, it comprehends all Manner of Treſpaſſes, which tend to the Waſte, Hurt or Deſtruction of the *Vert* ; the Conſequence whereof is the Driving the Deer out of the Foreſt to other Coverts, which is a Hurt to them ; for whatſoever tends to the Hurt of the *Vert* and *Veniſon*, tendeth to the general Hurt of the Foreſt itſelf. And this *Nuſance* comprehends likewiſe all Surcharges of the Commons, Aſſarts, Purpreſtures, &c. *Ibid.* 208.

The Regarders of the Foreſt are to inquire into all the *Nuſances*, and to make their Preſentments and Certificates to the Verderors at the next *Swainmote* to be holden for the Foreſt, that the Offenders may be tried according to the Ordinances of the Foreſt : After ſuch Offences are tried, the Proceedings are to be ſealed up and kept by the Verderors, until the Coming of the Chief Juſtice in *Eyre*, and then cannot be traverſed : At the Coming of the Chief Juſtice, all ſuch who are convicted of any *Common Nuſance* in the Foreſt, are to be committed, fined and bound to amend it by a certain Day. Such as are convicted of a *Special Nuſance* are to be committed, ranſomed, and bound to the good Behaviour of the Foreſt ; and ſuch as are convicted of a *General Nuſance* are to be committed, fined, and bound to the Good Behaviour of the Foreſt. *Manwood* 209, 210, 211.

𝕺𝖋𝖋𝖎𝖈𝖊𝖗. By **𝕾𝖙𝖆𝖙.** 12 *Geo.* 1. *c.* 3. ' If ' any Officer or Soldier ſhall, without Leave of ' the Lord of the Manor under his Hand and ' Seal,

' Seal, take, kill or deftroy any Hare, Coney,
' Pheafant, Partridge, Pigeon, or other Sort of
' Fowls, Poultry or Fifh, or his Majefty's
' Game, and be convicted thereof, on the Oath
' of one or more Witneffes, before one Juftice
' of Peace; every *Officer* fhall for every fuch
' Offence forfeit 5 *l.* to the Poor of the Place
' where, &c. and every Commander in Chief,
' for every fuch Offence committed by a Soldier
' under his Command, fhall forfeit 20 *s.* to be
' diftributed in like Manner; and if on fuch
' Conviction, and Demand made by the Con-
' ftable or Overfeers of the Poor, fuch *Officer*
' fhall not in two Days pay the faid refpective
' Penalties, he fhall forfeit his Commiffion;
' which is hereby declared void.'

Note ; This is for the better Prefervation of
the Game in or near fuch Place where *Officers* or
Soldiers are quartered.

Outlawry. Offenders in Forefts may be
profecuted by Way of *Outlawry*, viz. If a Man
be indicted for any Offence done there, who lives
in another County, and out of the Foreft, fo
that he cannot be taken by the Forefters; in fuch
Cafe the Offender may be *outlawed*, and the
Proceedings againft him are the fame as at
Common Law; and by Virtue of that *Outlawry*
his Goods and Chattels are forfeited to the
King, and fo the Profits of his Lands found on
Inquifition. *Manwood* 223, 224. See the *Table*.

If a Man is *outlawed* for an Offence either in
the *Vert* or *Venifon*; and afterward taken by a
Capias Utlagatum, he fhall be committed without Bail, to remain in Prifon until delivered

K 3

by a special Warrant from the King, or from the Chief Justice in *Eyre*, or Chief Warden of the Forest. *Ibid* 224.

Pannage. See *Table*.

Park, (From *Parquer* to inclose, and in *Saxon* Deopralo, Is a great Quantity of Ground inclosed and privileged for wild Beasts of Chase, by the King's Grant or by Prescription, and it is not * lawful for any Man to erect a *Park*, Chase or Warren, without a Licence under the Great Seal ; for the Common Law gave no Encouragement to Matters of Pleasure (wherein most Men do exceed) because they brought not Profit to the Common-wealth. † The Beasts of the *Park* properly extend to the Buck, Doe, Fox, Martern and Roe, ‡ but in a common and legal Sense, to all Beasts of the Forest. ‖ A *Park* must be inclosed, for if it lies open, it is a good Cause of Seizure into the King's Hands as a Thing forfeited ; and the Owner cannot have an Action against those that hunt in his *Park*, if it lies open.

To a *lawful Park* three Things are required. 1. A Liberty, either by Grant or Prescription ; 2. Inclosure, by Pale, Wall or Hedge ; and 3. Beasts of a *Park*. 2 *Inst.* 199.

There are *Parks* in Use and Reputation erected without lawful Warrant, and such nominal *Parks*, having been used as *Parks* for a long

* 1 *Inst.* 199. † 1 *Inst.* 233. a. ‡ Neither *Martern* nor *Roe* now in *England*, *Manw.* 50. ‖ *Wood's Inst.* 207.

Time,

Time, the Law doth * allow that the Owner may
have an Action for killing his Deer therein ;
but whether they are *Parks* or not, in the Eye
of the Law, yet they are Grounds inclosed,
where Deer are usually kept ; and therefore Offenders therein are punishable by the *Stat.* 3 &
4 *W. & M. c.* 10. and others. See, **Deer.**

Parks as well as Chases are subject to the
Common Law ; and are not to be guided by
the Forest Laws. 4 *Inst.* 314.

A Man may have a *Park* in the Forest by
Grant or Prescription ; but then it must be so
inclosed, that the Beasts of the Forest cannot
enter ; for if there is any Deer-leap, or it is not
kept inclosed, 'tis a Forfeiture thereof. *Manwood* 210, 226.

Parks being laid open to Forests for forty
Years may yet be inclosed again ; and they may
kill any Deer which come into those *Parks* : So
though Inclosures have been continued forty
Years, if they were not before, they may be
destroyed and laid open. 2 *Rep.* 155. *Manwood* 200.

By **Stat.** *Westm.* 1. *c.* 20. ' Trespassers in
' *Parks* or Ponds shall give treble Damages to
' the Party grieved, suffer three Years Imprison-
' ment, be fined at the King's Pleasure, and give
' Surety never to offend in the like Kind again ;
' and if they cannot find Surety, they shall ab-
' jure the Realm, or being Fugitive shall be
' outlawed.'

---

* *Wood's Inst.* 207.

By **Stat.** 3 & 4 *W. & M. c.* 10. ' If any
' Perfon fhall in the Night-time pull down or
' deftroy, or caufe to be pulled down or de-
' ftroyed, the Pales or Walls of any *Park,* Foreft,
' Chafe, Purlieu, Paddock, Wood, or other
' Ground inc———, where red or fallow Deer
' are kept, and thereof convicted by the Oath
' of one Witnefs, before a Juftice of Peace,
' he fhall by fuch Juftice's Warrant fuffer Im-
' prifonment for three Months without Bail or
' Mainprife.' '

By **Stat.** 5 *Geo.* 1, *c.* 15. *f.* 6. ' Perfons
' convicted by Confeffion, or Oath of one Wit-
' nefs, before a Juftice of Peace, of pulling
' down or deftroying the Pales or Walls of
' any Parks, Foreft, *&c.* where any Red or
' Fallow Deer fhall be then kept, without the
' Confent of the Owner or Perfon chiefly in-
' trufted with the Cuftody thereof; fhall be
' fubject to the Penalties inflicted by 3 & 4
' *W. & M. c.* 10. for killing a Deer.' See
' **Deer,** and *Table.*

A Grant of a *Park* and Free Warren.

GEORGE the Second, *by the Grace of God,*
of Great Britain, France, and Ireland,
King, Defender of the Faith, &c. **To all** *to*
whom thefe prefent Letters Patent fhall come,
Greeting: **Know ye,** *that we of our fpecial Grace,*
and of our certain Knowledge and meer Motion,
have *given and granted,* **and** *by thefe Prefents*
do give and grant, for us, our Heirs and Succeffors,
unto our well beloved Subject R. C. *of,* &c. *the*
Liberty

*Liberty of one Park for wild Beasts, and also Free
Warren in all his Demesne Lands of and within
his Manor or Lordship of* U. *with all Liberties
which to such Park or Warren do belong or appertain :* To have, *hold, enjoy and exercise the said
Liberty of* Park *and Warren to the said* R. C.
*his Heirs and Assigns in all his Demesne Lands afore-
said.* Provided *that the same Lands be not
within the Bounds of our Forest of,* &c. *so that
no Man can enter into the said Lands to hunt, or
to take any Thing in them, which to a* Park *or
Warren belongeth, without the Licence and good
Will of the said* R. C. *and his Heirs, under the
Pain of forfeiting to us ten Pounds. Though or
for that there is no express Mention of the true yearly
Value, or any Certainty of the Premisses, or any of
them, or of any Grant or Grants heretofore to the
said* R. C. *by us, or by any of our Progenitors appeareth to be made, or any Statute, Act, Ordinance,
or Provision to the contrary published, made, provided, or any other Cause or Matter to the contrary
notwithstanding.* In Witness *whereof we have
caused these our Letters to be made Patent.* Witness *ourself at* Westminster *the fourth Day of*
May, *in the sixth Year of our Reign.*

A Mittimus

A Mittimus for the pulling down and the deſtroying Pales of a *Park*, in the Night-time; according to 3 & 4 *W*. & *M*. *c*. 10.

To the Conſtable of, &c. and to the
Keeper of the Common Gaol, &c.

Bedford, ⎱ **W**Hereas *Complaint hath been*
to wit. ⎰ *made unto me, that* W. K.
of your Pariſh, of, &c. *did, on the third Day of*
June laſt paſt in the Night-time of the ſaid Day,
pull down and deſtroy ſeveral Pales of the Park *of*
Sir R. F. *Bart. in the County aforeſaid, contrary*
to the Statute in that Caſe made and provided: And
whereas the ſaid W. K. *hath been duly convicted*
before me this preſent Day, upon Oath, of the ſaid
Offence: Theſe are therefore *to charge and com-*
mand you to apprehend the ſaid W. K. *and convey*
him to the Gaol aforeſaid, and to deliver him to the
Keeper thereof, together with this Warrant: Commanding *you the ſaid Keeper to take him into your*
Cuſtody, and him ſafely to keep in the ſaid Gaol
for the Space of three Months without Bail.
Given, &c.

A Warrant

A Warrant to levy 30 *l.* for pulling down the Pales of a *Park*, according to 5 *Geo.* 1. *c.* 15.

To the Conftable, &c.

Bedford, to wit, } **WW**Hereas N. B. *of, &c. hath this prefent Day been duly convicted before me, that he, on the fixth Day of* Auguft *laft paft, did pull down* [or caufe to be pulled down,] *three Pales of the Park of* H. M. *of, &c. in which Park red and fallow Deer are ufually kept ; and that the faid* N. B. *committed the faid Offence, contrary to the Statute in that Cafe made and provided, and without the Confent of the Owner, or the Perfon chiefly intrufted with the Cuftody of the faid* Park, *by Reafon whereof he hath forfeited* * 30 l. *Thefe are therefore to require you forthwith to levy the faid* 30 l. *fo forfeited, as aforefaid, by Diftrefs and Sale of the Goods and Chattels of the faid* N. B. *and that you pay and difpofe one third Part thereof to* H. J. *who firft informed of the faid Offence ; and that you diftribute another third Part thereof to and amongft the Poor of the Parifh of* H. *where the Offence was committed ; and that you pay the other third Part to the aforefaid* H. M. *being Owner of the faid* Park ; *and if it fhall happen that the faid* N. B. *fhall not have any Goods or Chattels within your Parifh, fufficient to fatisfy the faid Forfaiture of* 30 l. *that then you certify me*

---

* The Penalty, inflicted by 3 & 4 *W.* & *M. c.* 10. for killing a Deer.

K 6 *thereof,*

thereof, that such further Order may be taken therein as is pursuant to the said Statute. And hereof *fail not,* &c.

Commitment for Want of Diftrefs. [5 *Geo.* 1. *c.* 15.]

To the Conftable; &c. and to the Keeper of the Gaol of, &c.

Bedford, } WHereas *you the said Conftable*
to wit. } W *of,* &c. *was lately required by Warrant under my Hand and Seal to levy the Sum of* 30 l. *by Diftrefs and Sale of the Goods of* N. B. *of,* &c. *by him forfeited, for an Offence which he committed againſt the Form of the Statute,* &c. *made, intituled,* An Act, &c. *And whereas I have been certified by you, That you cannot find a fufficient Diftrefs to be taken of the Goods and Chattels of the said* N. B. *for the Offence aforesaid:* Thefe are therefore, *in his Majefty's Name, to require you to apprehend the said* N. B. *and to convey him fafely to the Gaol of the said County, and deliver him to the Keeper thereof, together with this my Warrant for your fo doing:* Requiring *alfo you the said Keeper to take into your Cuftody the said* N. B. *and him fafely to keep for the Space of one whole Year next enfuing, and that then you deliver him to the Chief Officer of,* &c. *being the Town next adjoining to the Place where the Offence was committed, or fome of the Under Officers, together with this Precept, who are required to fet the said* N. B. *in the Pillory, in the said Town on fome*

Market-

Day for the Space of one Hour : And hereof *fail
not, as you will feverally anfwer the contrary at
your refpeEtive Perils.* Given *under my Hand and
Seal,* &c.

Law Cafes.

When the Owner of a *Park* dies, his Heir
at Law fhall have the Deer, becaufe without
them the *Park* which is his Inheritance, is no
Park. 7 *Rep.* 17.

In Trefpafs for entring into a *Park,* Warren, *&c.* it is no Plea to fay it is no *Park* or
Warren, but he muft plead *Not guilty,* and give
the fpecial Matter in Evidence. 10 *H.* 6. 16. 19
H. 8. 9. And therefore it is held clearly, that
if one has a Warren, if he inclofe or impark
without the King's Licence, and another hunts
there, and he bring Trefpafs *de Parco fraEto,*
the other may Plead *Not guilty,* and give this
Matter in Evidence. Sir *Matthew Hale's* Notes
on *Fitzherb.* 197.

One *Roger Wormale,* and *Rowland Triftram*
and *Thomas Banks,* two of his Companions,
entered *Hyde-Park* with Arms to kill and fteal
the Deer in the *Night-Time;* but being oppofed by the Keeper and his Servants they ran
away ; but being purfued, one of them was
wounded by a Shot, whereupon they all came
back, and *Wormale* killed one of the Keeper's
Servants ; for which they being apprehended
were all found guilty of Murder ; becaufe they
all came into the *Park* to do a premeditated and
an unlawful Act, and the Event fhewed their
Malice

Malice extended to kill any Perfon that fhould oppofe them, they being all armed for that Purpofe. *Palm.* 35. 2 *Roll. Rep.* 120.

Anno 15 *Ed.* 3. The Earl of *Lancafter*, who was Lord of a Foreft, granted to *John Harrington* that he might make a *Park* there; it was adjudged, that if the Grantee inclofe it fo flightly that the Beafts of the Foreft might get in, this was a Forfeiture, and the Lord might enter fuch *Park*, and take the Deer, *The King* againft Sir *John Byron*, *Bridgm*. 26.

See **Difpark** and *Table*.

Park-bote, Signifies to be quit of inclofing a Park, or any Part thereof. 4 *Inft.* 308.

Parker, Is one that hath the Cuftody or Keeping of a Park.

A Grant of the Office of *Parkerfhip* of a Park.

KNow all Men, &c. *That I* B. M. *Efq; Lord of the Manor of* M. *have given and granted,* and *by thefe Prefents do give and grant to my faithful Servant* J. J. *the Cuftody or Office of Keeper of my Park of* M. *in the County of* G. To have and to hold, *occupy and enjoy, the faid Cuftody or Office of Keeper of my faid Park by himfelf or Deputy) for whom he fhall be anfwerable to me,) for and during the natural Life of the faid* J. J. *with the Wages of one Shilling and Fourpence for every Day yearly, during his Life, to be paid to him by the Receiver, Bailiff or Farmer of the faid Manor of* M. *out of the Rents and Profits*

of

of the said Manor, at the Feasts of, &c. by even and equal Portions; AND also one Suit of Livery, such as my Parkers are wont to have, at the Feast of, &c. AND I DO hereby will and command the Receivers, Bailiffs and Farmers of my said Manor of M. both now and hereafter to be, that he or they, out of the Rents and Profits of my said Manor of M. do pay or cause to be paid unto the said J. J. or his Assigns, the aforesaid Wages of one Shilling and Four-pence for every Day at the Feasts aforesaid, by equal Portions, from Year to Year, during the Life of the said J. J. KNOW ye also, that I have moreover given and granted, and by these Presents do give and grant unto the said J. J. Pasture for two Horses, and six Kine, within the Park aforesaid, during his Life as aforesaid, to be depastured, together with free Egress and Regress in and out of the said Park, without any Contradiction whatsoever. IN WITNESS, &c.

Law Cases.

If a Man grant by his Deed to another the Office of *Parkership* of a Park, to have and occupy the same Office for Term of his Life, the Estate which he hath in the Office, is upon Condition in Law, to wit, that the *Parker* shall well and lawfully keep the Park, and shall do that which to such Office belongeth to do, or otherwise it shall be lawful to the Grantor and his Heirs to oust him, and grant it to another if he will; but this Condition must be understood with a Distinction; for if the *Parker* doth not attend on the Park one or two Days,

this

this is no Forfeiture of the Office of *Parkerſhip*; but if in his Default any Deer be killed, and ſo a Damage to the Lord ; that is a Forfeiture. For note this ; *Non-uſer of itſelf, without ſome ſpecial Damage, is no Forfeiture of private Offices ; but Non-uſer of publick Offices, which concern the Adminiſtration of Juſtice, or the Common-wealth, is of itſelf a Cauſe of Forfeiture* Lit. 378. 1 Inſt. 233. a.

If a *Keeper* kill any Deer without Warrant, or fell or cut any Trees, Woods or Underwoods, and convert them to his own Uſe, it is a For-feiture of his Office ; for the Deſtruction of *Vert* is, by a Mean, Deſtruction of *Veniſon* ; ſo it is if he put down the Lodge, or any Houſe within the Park for putting of Hay into it for feeding of the Deer, or ſuch like, it is a For-feiture. 1 *Inſt.* 233. *b. Benl.* 16. 4 *Leon.* 120. 1 *Anderſ.* 29. 9 *Rep.* 50, 95.

An Ejectment lies not of a Park, 1 *Cro.* 591. which is but a Liberty, as a Piſcary, but muſt be by the Number of Acres. 2 *Keb.* 460. *Pemble* and *Ster.*

If a Gentleman licenſe another to chaſe in his Park, ſuch a Perſon cannot bring others with him to hunt there without particular Words in the Licence, and a *Parker* or Keeper may not licenſe any one to hunt in his Maſter's Park.

Partridge, Is a Fowl of Warren ; and the *Statutes* which relate to *Partridges*, are the ſame that concern *Pheaſants*, to which Head *I refer the Reader.*

A Warrant

A Warrant of Summons againſt one for deſtroying *Partridge* out of Seaſon. [7 *Jac.* 1. *c.* 11.]

To the Conſtable, *&c.*

Surry,}WHereas Complaint hath been made
to wit.} unto us A. F. and T. F. *Eſquires*,
*two of his Majeſty's Juſtices, &c. that A. P. of,
&c. did at ſeveral Times with Nets, &c. kill and
deſtroy ſeveral Partridges in, &c. between the
Days, &c. being the Time prohibited by Law for
doing thereof : Theſe are therefore to require you
to apprehend the ſaid A. P. and to bring him before
us, or ſome other of his Majeſty's Juſtices of the
Peace for this County, to anſwer the Premiſſes,
and be dealt with according to Law. Given, &c.*

Declaration for entering the Plaintiff's Free Warren, and taking away his *Partridges*.

Suſſex,}J K. *complains of* W. Y. *in the Cuſ-*
to wit.} *tody of the Marſhal, and ſo forth, for
that the ſaid W. the fifteenth Day of September,
in the ſeventh Year of the Reign of the Lord the
now King, &c. with Force and Arms, the Free
Warren of him the ſaid J. at S. in the ſaid County,
broke, and in the ſame, againſt the Will, Licence
and Conſent of the ſaid J. entered, and then and
there took and carried away thirty Partridges, and
other Enormities to him did, againſt the Peace of
the ſaid Lord the now King, and to the Damage*
of

of the said J. *fifteen Pounds ; and therefore he brings his Suit.*

Note ; Partridges and Pheafants yield no Tithe of Eggs or young; though they are tame and kept in a Place inclofed. *Wood's Inft.* 169. See **Pheafant.**

Pedage, Is Money given for paffing through a Foreft.

Peers. By **Charta Forestæ,** *cap.* 11. ' Whatfoever Archbifhop, Bifhop, Earl or ' Baron, coming to us at our Commandment, ' paffing by our Foreft, it fhall be lawful for ' them to take and kill one or two of our Deer, ' by View of our Forefter, if he be prefent, ' or elfe he fhall caufe one to blow an Horn ' for him, that he feem not to fteal our Deer ; '' and likewife they fhall do returning from us, ' as it is aforefaid.'

Concerning this, it is to be obferved, that before the Making this Charter, *Peers* could not hunt in the King's Forefts without Warrant fo to do ; neither can they now, but when they are fent for to the Court by the King's Command, and in their Return home ; and even then, four Things are to be ftrictly obferved, *viz.* 1. That he be either *Lord Spiritual* or *Temporal.* 2. That he be fent for by the King. 3. That it be done by the View of the Forefter, if prefent. 4. If he be abfent, that a Horn be blown for him. See *Table.*

Perambulation. The Subject may demand a Writ of *Perambulation* of Right, which the King in Juftice cannot deny ; and when a *Per-*
-*ambulation*

ambulation is duly made, returned into *Chancery*, and proclaimed in the County, the same is peremptory and binding against the Subject : And if it was not duly made, the Subject cannot of Right Claim or demand another, but the King may grant another *ex gratia*, and after the same is executed, it will take away the Force of the first. *Manwood* 45.

Form of a *Perambulation*.

THE *Perambulation of the Forest of* Waltham *in the County of the* Essex, *made at* Chelmsford *on* Friday *the Morrow of the* Ascension *of our Lord, in the* 28th *Year of the Reign,* &c. *before* R. H, W. T. S. G. *Justices of our Lord the King, to make the said Perambulation, by the Oath of* R. S, H. B. J. H. S. W. &c. *who upon their Oath say, that;* &c. [Here set down the Metes and Bounds of the Forest, shewing what is within the Forest, and what is out of the Forest,] *according to the Tenor of the great Charter of the Forest. In Witness whereof we the said Jury have hereunto set our Hands and Seals the Day and Year above-written.*

Pheasant.

The *Pheasant* is a Fowl of Warren.

By Stat. 11 *Hen.* 7. c. 17. * ' None shall ' take *Pheasants* or Partridges with Engines in

---

* *Note;* The Act says, no Manner of Person or Persons, of what Estate, Degree or Condition soever, shall, &c.

another's

' another's Ground without Licence, in Pain
' of 10 _l._ to be divided betwixt the Owner or
' Poffeffor of the Ground and the Profecutor,
' to be recovered by Action of Debt, &c.

By **Stat.** 23 _Eliz._ _cap._ 10, ' None fhall
' kill or take any _Pheafants_ or Partridges, with
' any Net or Engine in the Night-time, on Pain
' to forfeit for every _Pheafant_ 20 _s._ and for
' every _Partridge_ 10 _s._ which if the Offender
' pay not within ten Days, he fhall fuffer one
' Month's Imprifonment, and enter into Bond
' (for two Years only) with good Sureties,
' before fome Juftice of Peace, not to offend
' in the like.'

' The Forfeiture fhall be recovered in any
' Court of Record, by Action of Debt, &c.
' and divided betwixt the Lord of the Liberty
' or Manor where the Offence is committed,
' and the Profecutor; but in Cafe the Lord
' fhall difpenfe with the Offender, the Poor
' of the Parifh are to have his Moiety, to be
' recovered by any of the Churchwardens.'

' Juftices of Affife and Seffions, and Stewards
' of _Leets_, have Power to hear and determine
' thefe Offences; and one Juftice of Peace
' may examine fuch Offender, and bind him
' over with good Sureties to anfwer it at the
' next General Seffions, if the Offence be
' not before determined at the Affizes, or in
' a _Leet._'

' This Act fhall not reftrain Fowlers, which
' unwillingly take _Pheafants_ or _Partridges_, and
' forthwith let them go at large.'

And

And by **Stat.** 9 *Ann. c.* 25. ' If any Perfon
' whatfoever fhall take or kill any *Pheafant* or
' Partridge in the Night-time; he fhall, on
' Conviction, before one Juftice, on Oath of
' one Witnefs, forfeit 5 *l.* Half to the Informer,
' and Half to the Poor, by Diftrefs; for Want
' of Diftrefs, to be fent to the Houfe of Cor-
' rection, for three Months for the firft Offence,
' and for every other Offence four Months.'

By **Stat.** 1 *Jac.* 1. *c.* 27. §. 2. ' Every
' Perfon convicted by his own Confeffion, or
' by two Witneffes upon Oath, before two
' or more Juftices of Peace, to have killed or
' taken any *Pheafant*, Partridge, Pigeon, Duck,
' Heron, Hare, or other Game, fhall by the
' faid Juftices be committed to Gaol three
' Months, unlefs he immediately pay to the
' Churchwarden for the Ufe of the Poor where
' the Offence was committed, or he apprehend-
' ed, 20 *s.* for every *Fowl* or *Hare* fo killed;
' and after one Month's Commitment, fhall
' before two or more Juftices of Peace be
' bound with two fufficient Sureties in 20 *l.*
' a-piece, with Condition never to offend in the
' like again. The Recognizance to be returned
' to the Seffions.

' None fhall fell, or buy to fell again, any
' Deer, Hare, *Pheafant* or Partridge, (except
' *Pheafants* or Partridges reared and brought
' up in Houfes or brought from beyond Sea,)
' on Pain to forfeit for every Deer 40 *s.* Hare
' 10 *s. Pheafant* 20 *s.* and Partridge 10 *s.* to
' be divided betwixt the Profecutor and the

Poor

' of the Parish where the Offence is committed.'
Same *Stat.*

' Juſtices of Aſſiſe and Seſſions, and two or
' more Juſtices out of Seſſions, have Power to
' hear and determine theſe Offences.' Same
Stat.

' This Act ſhall not reſtrain one licenſed
' in open Seſſions to kill Hawkſmeat, but then
' he muſt become bound by Recognizance in
' 20 *l.* not to kill any Game prohibited by this
' Law; nor to ſhoot within 600 Paces of an
' Hernery, 100 Paces of a Pigeon-houſe, or
' in a Park, Foreſt or Chaſe, whereof his
' Maſter is not Owner.'

By **Stat.** 7 *Jac.* 1 *c.* 11. ' Every Perſon
' convicted by his own Confeſſion, or by two
' Witneſſes upon Oath, before two or more
' Juſtices of Peace, in ſix Months after the
' Offence, to have hawked at or deſtroyed any
' *Pheaſant* or *Partridge* betwixt the firſt of
' *July* and the laſt of *Auguſt*, ſhall ſuffer one
' Month's Impriſonment, without Bail, unleſs
' he forthwith pay to the Uſe of the Poor where
' the Offence was committed, or he apprehend-
' ed, 40 *s.* for every Time ſo hawking, and 20 *s.*
' for every *Pheaſant* or Partridge ſo deſtroyed
' or taken.'

' If any Perſon of a mean Condition ſhall
' be convicted by his own Confeſſion, or by
' one Witneſs upon Oath before two or more
' Juſtices of Peace, to have killed or taken
' any *Pheaſant* or Partridge with Dogs, Nets
' or Engines, ſhe ſhall by the ſaid Juſtices be
' committed to Priſon without Bail, unleſs he
　　　　　　　　　　　　　' forthwith

' forthwith pay, to the Use of the Poor where
' the Offence was committed, 20 s. for every
' *Pheasant* or Partridge so killed or taken; and
' also become bound, before one or more Ju-
' stices of Peace, in a Recognizance of 20 l.
' never to offend in the like Kind again.' Same
Statute.

' Every free Warrener, Lord of a Manor,
' or Freeholder, seised in his own, or his Wife's
' Right, of 40 l. a Year Estate of Inheritance,
' or Lives Estate of 80 l. or worth in Goods
' 400 l. may take *Pheasants* and Partridges (in
' the Day-time only) in his own Free Warren,
' Manor, or Freehold, betwixt *Michaelmas* and
' *Christmas* yearly.' Same *Statute.*

It is to be observed, that the Killing of Partridges and *Pheasants*, is prohibited in almost
all Manner of Ways, except Hawking only;
and that Hawking at them is only prohibited
in two Summer Months when the Corn is growing, and the Brood is very young.

For the other *Statutes* relating to *Pheasants*,
see *The Table.*

Law Cases.

A Man was indicted on *Statute* 23 *El. c.* 10.
for taking *Partridges cum Retis*; but it was
quashed, for it should be *cum Retibus* (with
Nets) 3 *Bulst.* 178. The *King* and *Rivett*.

In Trespass for taking *Phasianos suos*, in such
a Place; upon Not guilty pleaded, the Plaintiff had a Verdict; and afterwards it was moved
in Arrest of Judgment, that this Declaration
was

was ill, becaufe the Plaintiff had declared for
taking *Phafianos fuos*, whereas *Pheafants* are Birds
feræ naturæ; and therefore the Plaintiff cannot
have fuch a Property in them, as to call them
fuos; but the Judgment was affirmed, becaufe
after a Verdict it fhall be intended that thefe
Pheafants were dead; and then the Plaintiff
might have a Property in them. *Ufher* againft
Bufhnell, Raym. 16. *Sid.* 39.

Pond. By **Stat.** *Weftm.* 1. *cap.* 20. ' Tref-
' paffers in *Ponds* fhall give treble Damages to
' the Party grieved, fuffer three Years Impri-
' fonment, be fined at the King's Pleafure, and
' give Surety never to offend again in the like
' Nature; and if they cannot find Sureties;
' they fhall abjure the Realm, or flying, they
' fhall be outlawed.'

By **Stat.** 5 *Eliz. c.* 21. ' *Ponds* by Day
' or Night unlawfully broken down; or de-
' ftroying the Head of any *Pond*, Moat or Dam,
' Stew or Pit where Fifh are put, or wrong-
' fully fifhing in them, to the Intent to deftroy,
' kill, take or fteal any Fifh, againft the Con-
' fent of the Owner or Poffeffor, or not having
' lawful Authority fo to do, and being con-
' victed at the Suit of the King or the Party
' grieved, fhall be imprifoned for three Months,
' and pay him treble Damages, and give Secu-
' rity for his good Behaviour for feven Years,
' or remain in Prifon without Bail or Mainprife,
' till he do find Security.'

' The Party grieved fhall in Seffions, or any
' Court of Record, recover treble Damages
' againft the Delinquent, and on Satisfaction
' fhall

' shall have Liberty to procure his Releafe of
' the Behaviour.'

By **Stat.** 9 *Geo.* 1. *c.* 21. ' Any Perfon
' armed and difguifed, and Breaking down the
' Head of a *Fifh-pond*, whereby the Fifh fhall
' be loft, or fhall refcue fuch Offender, or pro-
' cure another to join with him in fuch unlawful
' Act, is guilty of Felony without Benefit of
' Clergy.' See *Table.*

* **Prescription.** The Form of a *Prefcription* in the Foreft, differs from a *Prefcription* at
Common Law ; for a Claim, that he and his
Anceftors *tempore quo,* is good, without faying,
that he and his Anceftors, and all thofe whofe
Eftate he hath in certain Lands. *Manwood*
232.

Though a Man may *prefcribe* to hunt wild
Beafts in his own Land, yet a *Prefcription* is not
good to hunt the King's wild Beafts, though
they are in his own Land, *viz.* thofe which
efcape out of the Foreft into the Purlieus. *Ibid.*
293. Vide *Table.*

Presentment. Every *Prefentment* for an Offence done in the Foreft, in *Vert* or *Venifon*, muft
be certain in Refpect of the *Perfon, Place,
Thing, Inftruments, Manner of the Act, Value of
the* Vert.

1. In Refpect of the *Perfon*; it muft fet forth
the Name and Surname, and the Place where
he dwelleth.

---

* *Prefcription,* Is a Title acq .ired by Ufe and Time,
and allowed by Law.

2. In Refpect of the *Place*; it muft fet forth, that it was done in fuch a Place within the Foreft, that it may appear the Fact was committed therein.

3. In Refpect of the *Thing*; it muft fet forth, that the Offender killed a *Buck* or *Doe*, or as the Cafe is.

4. In Refpect of the *Inftruments*; it muft fet forth, that the Offender entered the Foreft with a *Crofs-bow*, *Long-bow*, *Gun*, &c. and did there kill a Deer.

5. The Manner of the *Act*, and the Value of the *Vert*, muft be fet forth as the Facts are.

There is fome Variance between the Form of an Entry of a *Prefentment* in the *Swainmote*, and in the Court of *Attachments*; for in the *Swainmote* the Words are, *It is prefented by the Forefters and the twelve Jurors, and convicted by the Verderors*, &c. but in the Court of *Attachments* thus, *It is prefented by A. B. Forefter*, &c.

Prefentments made in Court of *Attachments* before the *Verderors*, and inrolled by them in the Rolls of the Foreft, muft be thence tranfmitted to the Court of *Swainmote*, and the Offender may traverfe fuch *Prefentment* before it comes to the *Swainmote*, but not after; and a *Prefentment* in the *Swainmote* is not traverfable. *Manwood* 237, 238. Vide *Table*.

Principals. In Trefpaffes in Forefts all are *Principals*. 4 *Inft.* 314. *Manwood* 214.

Property, Is either abfolute or qualified, and a Man may have an abfolute *Property* in feveral Things, which are not *feræ naturæ*, as in *Ducks*, *Poultry*, *Geefe*, &c. but he cannot have

have fuch *Property* in Things which are *feræ na-*
turæ, as *Wild Fowl*, (viz.) *Partridge*, *Pheafants*,
&c. and wild Beafts, fuch as *Conies*, *Hares*, &c.
or *Fifh* in the Sea or in Rivers; but he may have
an abfolute *Property* in other Things of a bafe
Nature, fuch as *Grey-hounds*, *Hounds*, *Maftiffs*,
Spaniels, &c. and for fuch Things, if taken
away, an Indictment will lie for a Trefpafs, or
the Party grieved may have an Action of Trefpafs, *&c.* and recover Damages. However a
Man may have a qualified *Property* in Things
which are *feræ naturæ*, which *Property* is poffeffory, and only for a certain Time, and may
be obtained by Induftry, (viz.) by taking fuch
Creatures, and making them tame; and in fuch
Cafe a Man may have a poffeffory *Property* in
them, fo long as they continue tame, and do
not regain their natural Liberty. Likewife a
qualified *Property* may be gained in Things
feræ naturæ, by Reafon of *Impotency and Place*,
as of young Hawks or young Pigeons in their
Nefts bred in my Ground; for which I may
have an Action of Trefpafs, if taken when they
cannot fly. A qualified *Property* may alfo be
gained in fuch Things, by Reafon of a Privilege
in a Park or Warren, as Deer, Conies, *&c.*
Fifh in a Trunk, or Pigeons in a Dove-houfe;
but none of thefe Things can be properly called
fuos, becaufe no Perfon hath an *abfolute Property*
in them, and therefore Felony cannot be committed by taking them away, unlefs reduced to
be tame; though whilft they are wild, they do
really belong to the Owner of the Park or Warren. 7 *Rep.* 17, 18. 11 *Rep.* 50. *Wood's Inft.* 314.

Cro. Car. 553. *March* 48. ' Sed vide **Deer,
Conies, Fish,** &c. .

Proto-Forester, Was one whom our ancient Kings used to make Chief of *Windsor Forest,* to hear Causes of Death or Maim, or of
Slaughter of the King's Deer in the Forest.

Purlieu, From *Pur, i. e.* clear, intire, and
exempt; and *Lieu, i. e.* a Place : So that it is
a Place intire or exempt from the Forest, though
adjoining to the Forest, meered and bounded
with unremoveable Marks and Boundaries, and
known by Matter of Record only, and signifies those Grounds, which *Hen.* 2. *Ric.* 1. or
King *John* added to their ancient Forests over
other Mens Grounds, and were disafforested by
Force of the Statute of *Chart. Forest. c.* 1 & 3.
and the * Perambulations and Grants thereupon:
By this Disafforestation the Owners of the
Grounds within the *Purlieu* may at their Will
and Pleasure, fell, cut down, eradicate, and
stub up all the Timber, Woods and Under-
woods, convert their Pastures, Meadows and
other Grounds to arable, inclose them in with
any Kind of Inclosure, build and erect new
Edifices upon the same or any Part thereof, and
to dispose and use the same after the Disafforestation, as if they never had been afforested. 4 *Inst.*
303. *Manwood* 242, 301.

* By the Perambulation the *Purlieu* is made, for the
Purlieu and the Perambulation are distinct Things, and the
right Name of the Place disafforested is *Purlieu.* 4 *Inst.*
303.

Notwith-

Notwithstanding the *Purlieu* is exempt from the Forest, yet the *Purlieu-man* is in some Cases restrained; for he must not hunt in his own *Purlieu* in the *Night*, nor on a *Sunday*, nor in the *Fence Month*, nor oftener than *three Days in a Week*; nor with any other Company, than his own Servants; nor forty Days *before* and *after* the *King's Hunting*; he must not *forestal* or hunt Deer out of Season: All which has been taken for Law ever since *Purlieus* were first made. *Manwood* 297, 298, 299.

Offences committed in the *Purlieus*, contrary to the Laws aforesaid, are accounted Offences of the Forest, because they are Injuries done to the wild Beasts there; and such Offences are to be presented by the *Rangers* at the next Court of *Attachments*, to be holden for the Forest adjoining to the *Purlieu*, or else at the next *Swainmote* or *Justice-Seat*, which shall first happen to be kept, that such Trespassers and Offenders in the *Purlieu* may be punished according to the Quality of the Offence, after a lawful Trial at the *Swainmote*; after such Trial had and Conviction of them, they are to be bound with good Sureties to the good Behaviour of the Forest, until the next *Justice-Seat*, and then they are to appear there, and to be punished according to the Direction of the Lord Chief Justice in *Eyre*, either by Imprisonment, Fine or Ransom. *Ibid.* 300.

If a *Purlieu-man's* Dog fastens on the Deer before he recovers the Boundaries of the Forest, and by Force and Strength of the Beast is drawn into the Forest, and there kills the Beast, the

Purlieu-

Purlieu-man may enter by Reaſon of the firſt Property which he had *ratione ſoli*, and by the Purſuit and Poſſeſſion which he had by the faſtening of his Dog, and may take and carry the Deer away. *Ibid.* 294. Vide *Table.*

Purlieu-men, Are thoſe who have Grounds in the *Purlieus* of a Foreſt, and if duly quali- fied according to Law, [See **Qualification,**] they may hunt in their own Grounds. *Manwood* 293.

Purpreſſures, In the King's Foreſts are of four Sorts. 1. *Purpreſtures againſt the King* ; as where a Man doth new erect or build any Dwell- ing, or other Houſe in the Foreſt without Li- cence. 2. *Againſt the King and Publick* ; as where a Man builds a new Houſe or Mill on the King's Highway, or Waſte in the Foreſt. 3. *Againſt the King and a common Perſon* ; as where a Man hath Land incloſed, lying in a Foreſt, and adjoining to the Waſte of a Lord of a Manor, and the Owner incroacheth on that Waſte, by removing a Hedge and taking in Part of it, and ſo wrongfully inlarging his own Ground. 4. *Againſt a common Perſon only* ; as where a Man hath an ancient Dwelling-houſe, or other Houſe in the Foreſt, and by inlarging it he in- croacheth upon the Lands of his Neighbour. *Manwood* 304, 308.

Where a Man doth wrongfully incroach any Thing to himſelf in a Foreſt, either upon the King or any other Perſon, or doth take upon himſelf any Juriſdiction or Franchiſe there, without lawful Warrant, are *Purpreſtures.* *Ibid.* 209.

The

The Puniſhment of thoſe who commit *Pur-preſtures* is of two Kinds. 1. *Purpreſtures on the King's Land,* is to be committed without Bail until he paid a Fine to the King, which Fine is arbitrary, at the Will of the Chief Juſtice, and the Place on which the *Purpreſture* was made, is to be ſurrendered to the King. 2. *On his own Lands,* is for the *firſt Offence* to be committed until he be delivered by ſix Pledges; for the *ſecond,* until he be delivered by twelve; and for the *third,* to be committed till he pay a Fine to the King, in which Caſe he is not bailable, but at the Diſcretion of the Lord Chief Juſtice in Eyre. *Ibid.* 210.

It is neceſſary, that in all Indictments or Preſentments for *Purpreſtures,* there be a ſufficient Certainty in theſe following Particulars. 1ſt, *Who* made the *Purpreſture*; in what Manner and when the ſame was done. 2d, *Where* the Ground lies in which it was made; in whoſe Tenure it is, and what Quantity the ſame doth contain, and what is the yearly Value thereof. 3d, *Whether* the *Purpreſture* was made on the Soil and Inheritance of the King, or of a common Perſon. 4th, *In* whoſe Fee the ſame is; in what Pariſh, and who hath the Inheritance. See *Table.*

Putura, is a Cuſtom claimed by Keepers in Foreſts, and ſometime by Bailiffs of Hundreds, to take Man's-meat, Horſe-meat and Dog's-meat, of the Tenants and Inhabitants, within the Perambulation of the Foreſt or Hundred. 4 *Inſt.* 307.

Quaſſ.

Quail, The *Quail* is a Fowl of Warren.
1 *Inst.* 233. *a.*

Qualification. By **Stat.** 13 *Rich.* 2. ' A
' Layman muſt have 40 *s. per Annum*; and a
' Prieſt 10 *l. per Annum*; otherwiſe he ſhall not
' keep or have any *Grey-hound, Hound, Dog,*
' *Ferret, Net* or *Engine* to deſtroy *Deer, Hares,*
' *Conies* or any other Gentleman's Game.'

By **Stat.** 1 *Jac.* 1. *c.* 27. ' A Man muſt
' have 10 *l. per Annum Inheritance,* or a *Leaſe for*
' *Life* of 30 *l. per Ann. or be worth* 200 *l. in*
' *Goods,* or be the Son of a Baron or Knight,
' or Heir apparent of an Eſquire, otherwiſe
' he ſhall not keep a *Grey-hound, Dog* or *Net,*
' to kill *Deer, Hare, Pheaſant* or *Partridge.*'

By **Stat.** 7 *Jac.* 1. *cap.* 11. ' Any Man,
' who is Lord of a Manor, or who hath a free
' Warren, or an Inheritance of 40 *l. per Annum,*
' or Freehold of 80 *l. per Annum, or Goods worth*
' 400 *l.* may either by himſelf, or his Servants
' by his Licence, take *Pheaſants* or *Partridges*
' in the Day-time, *within their own Grounds or*
' *Precincts,* betwixt *Michaelmas* and *Chriſtmas,*
' and at no other Time.'

By **Stat.** 22 *&* 23 *Car.* 2. *c.* 25. ' Perſons
' not having Lands, or ſome other Eſtate of
' *Inheritance,* of 100 *l. per Ann. in their own or*
' *their Wife's Right, or for Life, or a Leaſe for*
' *ninety-nine Years of* 150 *l. per Ann. other than*
' *the Son and Heir of an Eſquire, or other Perſon*
' *of ſome higher Degree,* or Lord of a Manor, or
' Owners and Keepers of Parks, Chaſes, or
' Free Warrens ſtocked with Deer or Conies,
' ſhall not keep *Bows, Engines, Ferrets, Grey-*
' *hounds,*

' *hounds, Guns, Hare-pipes, Lowbels, Lurchers,*
' *Nets, Setting Dogs, Snares* or *Trammels* for
' taking *Conies, Hares, Pheafants, Partridges* or
' other Game.'

Note; Tho' a Gun is mentioned (*int' al'*) in
the above Statute, yet in the Statute of 5 *Ann.* the
Word *Gun* is omitted among the Inftruments
mentioned for the Deftruction of the Game ;
therefore I apprehend a Man may keep a Gun
in his Houfe for his Safety ; and that keeping
a Gun barely without *ufing*, or *Intention laid*, is
not within the Statute 5 *Ann. c.* 4. *fect.* 4.

Rail, Is a Fowl of Warren. 1 *Inft.* 233.

Ranger. A *Ranger* is made by the King's
Letters Patent, who alloweth every one of them
a yearly Fee of 20 *l.* or 30 *l.* payable out of the
Exchequer, and a Fee-Deer, both red and fallow,
out of the Foreft ; his Office confifts in ranging
and walking about the *Purlieus*, to drive the wild
Beafts fafely into the Forefts ; and prefenting
all Offenders and unlawful Hunters, and what
Trefpaffes they have done in the *Purlieus*, in
their Walks.

And to the Intent that every *Ranger* fhould
be the more careful to execute his Office, he
muft be fworn, and the Form of his Oath is as
followeth.

The Oath of a *Ranger*.

Y O U *fhall well and truly execute the Office of*
a Ranger *in the Purlieus of* W. *upon the*
Borders of the King's Forefts of W. *you fhall re*

L 5 *that*

*chaſe and with your Hounds drive back again the wild Beaſts of the Foreſt, as often as they ſhall range out of the ſame Foreſt into your Purlieus: You ſhall truly preſent all unlawful Hunting and Hunters of wild Beaſts of Venary and Chaſe, as well within the * Pourallees, as within the Foreſt, and thoſe and all other Offences you ſhall preſent at the next Court of Attachments or Swainmote which ſhall firſt happen.*

So help you God.

Note; In this Oath is contained the whole Office and Duty of a *Ranger*.

Ranſome, Is a Sum of Money paid for the Pardoning ſome great Offence, and ſetting the Offender at Liberty who was under Impriſonment.

Rape of the Foreſt, *(Raptus Foreſtæ)* Is Treſpaſs committed in the Foreſt by Violence.

Reafforeſted, Is where a Foreſt which had been diſafforeſted, is again made a Foreſt.

Receiver. Whoſoever *receiveth* within the Foreſt any Malefactor either in hunting or killing, knowing him to be ſuch a Malefactor, or any Fleſh of the King's Veniſon, knowing it to be the King's, is in this Caſe a principal Treſpaſſer; but if the Receipt be out of the Foreſt, he cannot be puniſhed by the Laws of the Foreſt. 4 *Inſt,* 317.

Reclaim, Signifies to make tame.

* Perambulations.

Reeve.

Reeve. The *Reeve* of every Town in the Foreft, and four Men with him, muft appear upon the firft Sitting of the Juftice-Seat, or the whole Vill fhall be amerced; but if after Appearance and an Adjournment they or any of them make Default, then he or thofe who made fuch Default, fhall be amerced. *W. Jones* 279. *Manwood* 15, 18.

Regarder, Is an Officer of the King's Foreft, and is either made by the King's Letters Patent, by the Chief Juftice in *Eyre*, or by the King's Writ to the Sheriff; but all the *Regarders* muft be fworn by the Sheriff, in the County-Court, by Authority of a Writ to him directed, before they can make the Regard of the Foreft. *Manwood* 216, 219, 220.

The Oath of a *Regarder*, (containing his Office and Duty.)

Y O U *fhall well and truly ferve our Sovereign Lord the King in the Office of* Regarder *of the Foreft of* W. *you fhall make Regard of the fame Foreft in fuch Manner as the fame hath been accuftomed to be made; you fhall range throughout the whole Foreft, and through every Bailiwick of the fame, as the Forefter there fhall lead you to view the fame Foreft: And if the Forefters will not or do not know how to lead you to make the Regard or Range of the Foreft, or that they will conceal from you any Thing that is forfeited to the King, you yourfelves fhall not let for any Thing, but you fhall fee the fame Forfeiture, and caufe the fame to be inrolled in your Roll; you shall inquire of all Wastes, Purprestures and Assarts of the Forest, and also of the Concealments of any Offence or Trespass in the Forest, either in Vert or Venison, by any Officers of the same Forest: And all these Things you shall to the utmost of your Power do.*

So help you God.

There muſt be twelve *Regarders*, otherwiſe there cannot be any Regard made in the Foreſt; for if any under that Number ſhould make a Certificate of their Inquiſition, 'tis not a ſufficient Charge againſt the Offender, for if eleven are agreed on a Verdict, 'tis not good if one diſagree, and they muſt *ſee, view* and *inquire* the Certainty of every Offence given them in Charge; and when they find any Offences done, they are to write the ſame fairly on a Roll, and bring it either to the *Court of Attachments*, or *Swainmote*; at the firſt of which Courts all ſuch Matters as are ſo found by the *Regarders*, they are to certify under their Hands and Seals, and preſent the ſame under their Hands and Seals to the Chief Juſtice in *Eyre* at the next *Eyre*; and ſuch Regard ought to be made every third Year. *Manwood* 317, 320, 321, 324, 328.

Note; A Man cannot be a *Regarder* for any Foreſt but for the King's only. *Manwood* 324.

All Woods and Lands, which are Part of the Foreſt, are within the *Regard*; and all which are within the Bounds, and yet no Part of the Foreſt, are out of the *Regard. Ibid.* 43, 330. See the *Table.*

Replevin.

𝕽eplebin. If a Man hath a Park within the Bounds of any Foreſt, which is not incloſed according to the Aſſiſe of the Foreſt, &c. it ſhall be ſeized into the King's Hands; and then the Party ſhall have a ſpecial Writ of *Replevin*, to *replevy* the Park out of the King's Hands. *New Nat. Brev.* 154.

The Form of a *Replevin* of a Park within the King's Foreſt, ſeized for not being incloſed.

GEORGE, &c. *To our faithful and well beloved* J. C. *Warden*, &c. *or his Deputy in the Foreſt of* W. *Greeting : We command you, that foraſmuch as the Park of* A. B. *which is within the Meets of our Foreſt aforeſaid, is ſeized, as it is ſaid, into our Hands, for that it was not incloſed according to the Aſſiſe of the Foreſt ; if according to the Aſſiſe of the Foreſt it is replaviable, cauſe Replevin to be made thereof to the ſaid* A. B. *until the Coming of our Juſtice of our Foreſt into the County aforeſaid.* Witneſs, &c.

Cur. ordered an Attachment (unleſs Cauſe) againſt the Town Clerk of *Guildford*, and a Defendant, convicted on the Game Act, for granting and ſuing out a *Replevin* of Goods diſtrained for the Penalty. But on ſhewing Cauſe the next Term, when *Eyre* J. only was preſent, he diſcharged the Rule, becauſe it was only a Contempt to the inferior Juriſdiction of the Juſtices; and in that Caſe the *King's Bench* never interpoſes.

3

poses. *T.* 9 *G.* 1. The *King* v. *Burchett.* 1 *Str.* 567.

Cur. granted an Attachment against the Under Sheriff of *Cumberland,* for granting a *Replevin* of Goods distrained on a Conviction for Deer Stealing. *E.* 16 *Geo.* 2. *Dominus Rex* v. *Monkhouse.* 2 *Str.* 1184.

Riding-Forester. His Duty is to lead the King in his Hunting, *W.* *Jones* 277.

Roe, Was a Beast of Chase, of which there are few or none in *England.*

Rolls. Sir *Richard Harrison* and Sir *Charles Howard* being Verderors, were, for delivering up their *Rolls* in Paper, whereas they ought to be ingrossed in Parchment, fined 20 *l.* a-piece. *W.* *Jones* 167. *Manwood* 331, 334.

Scotale, Is where any Officer of the Forest keeps an Alehouse, and by *Colour of his Office* causeth Men to come to that Alehouse in the Forest, to spend their Money ; and this, as also *Extortion* by *Colour of his Office,* is prohibited by **Charta Forestæ,** *c.* 7. *Viz.* ' No Forester ' or Beadle from henceforth shall make *Scotale,* ' or gather Garb, or Oats, or any Corn, or ' Lamb, or Pig ; nor shall make any Gather- ' ing, but upon the Sight and upon the Oath ' of the twelve Regarders, when they shall make ' their Regard.' The Offence is to be inquired by twelve Jurors at the *Swainmote*; and if the Officer is attainted, he is to be punished and turned out of his Office. *Manwood* 168, 169, 334.

The

The Prohibition in *Charta Foreſtæ* aforeſaid implies, That in ſome Caſes *Scotales* may be lawful, *viz.* If they are found and preſented upon the View of the Regarders, and upon their Oaths, when they make the Regard of the Foreſt, that ſuch *Scotales* had a lawful Beginning, which muſt be either by *Tenure, Grant* or *Preſcription*; ſo that it may appear the Thing was lawfully done, by Right and good Title, and not newly and wrongfully exacted on the People by *Colour of the Office* of any ſuch Officer. *Ibid.* 169, 170, 171, 335.

𝔖𝔢𝔞𝔯-𝔴𝔬𝔬𝔡, Dead Boughs cut off from Trees in a Foreſt.

𝔖𝔱𝔞𝔣𝔣-𝔥𝔢𝔯𝔡𝔦𝔫𝔤. The Miniſters of the Foreſt are to inquire, whether thoſe who claim a Right of Common in a Foreſt, do uſe *Staff-herding, i. e.* Whether they uſe to have one to follow their Cattle; for that is not allowable of common Right, becauſe by that Means the Deer are frighted, which would otherwiſe feed with the Cattle; beſides he who looks after the Cattle will drive them into the beſt Paſture, and ſo the Deer will have only what is left: Therefore if any Man hath Right of Common, and under Colour thereof uſeth *Staff-herding*, his Common ought to be ſeized till he hath paid a Fine for the Abuſe. *W. Jones* 282. *Dean and Chapter of Salisbury's* Caſe.

𝔖𝔱𝔞𝔩𝔨𝔦𝔫𝔤. By 𝔖𝔱𝔞𝔱. 19 *Hen.* 7. *c.* 11. ‘ No Perſon ſhall *ſtalk*, or cauſe any other to ‘ *ſtalk*, with any Buſh or Beaſt to any Deer in ‘ a Park, Chaſe or Foreſt, or without, except ‘ in his own Grounds, without Licence of the ‘ Owner,

' Owner, Mafter of the Game, or Keeper of the
' Foreft, Chafe or Park, on Pain of Forfeiture
' for every Time 10 *l.* to any Perfon who will
' fue for the fame by Action of Debt; and two
' Juftices of Peace in Seffions may examine the
' Offenders, and commit them to Prifon till
' they have fatisfied the Forfeiture, whereof
' the faid Juftices are to have the tenth Part.'

Steward. The *Steward* is a judicial Officer
of the Foreft, and muft be one learned in thofe
Laws; he is to join with the Verderors, and
direct them in their Proceedings, and to give
the Charge at the *Swainmote.* 4 *Inft.* 310. *Man-*
wood 34, 340, 411. See the *Table.*

Stickler, An Officer formerly who cut Wood
for the Priory of *Edcrofe*, within the King's Park
at *Clarendon.*

Surcharger, Is one who having Common
in a Foreft *furcharges* the fame, *i. e.* puts more
Cattle to depafture than he ought; in fuch Cafe,
upon Complaint of the Officers of the Foreft,
that the fame is fo much *furcharged,* that there
is not fufficient Pafture left for the Deer, a
Commiffion may be directed out of *Chancery* to
the King's Lieutenant of the Foreft, and the
Verderors and Chief Forefters there; commanding them to inquire by the Oath of good and
lawful Men, what Number of Acres the Place
doth contain, wherein the *Surcharge* is fuppofed
to be made; and what Number of Beafts are
commoning therein, and whofe they are; and
what Parifhes, Villages and Hamlets ought of
Right to have any Common there; and how
many Meffuages and Cottages there ai in each

of

of them; and how many Acres of Land do belong to every Houfe: And then by computing how many Beafts may common in the fame, leaving fufficient Pafture for the Deer, they fhall rate and apportion every Man what Number of Beafts and of what Sort he may keep. *Manwood* 96.

A *Surcharger* of a Foreft fhall be indicted and fined for the fame to the King, and imprifoned till paid. *Ibid.* 97.

Swainmote, A Compound of two *Saxon* Words, Spain, *i. e. Country-Swain*, and *mote*, *i. e.* a *Court*, is a Court of * Record preparative to the Juftice-Seat held before the Verderors as Judges by the Steward of the *Swainmote* thrice in the Year, *viz.* the fifteenth Day after St. *Michael*, about the Feaft of St. *Martin*, and fifteen Days before the Feaft of St. *John Baptift.*

At this Court all the † Forefters, (who are to prefent their Attachments), and other Officers are obliged to appear, and fo are the Freeholders within the Foreft to be upon the Inqueft or Jury, who are to ‖ inquire of all thofe who own Suit to the *Swainmote*; of Affarts, Purpreftures, of taking away or removing Bounds; of making Mines or Claypits; of Mills, Houfes, &c. if there are more Forefters or Walkers within the Foreft than ufual, of Oppreffions and Extortions by Officers; of furcharging Common;

* *Wood's Inft.* 496. 4 *Inft.* 289. † *Manwood* 339. ‖ *Wood's Inft.* 496. *Manwood* 340, 341, 342, 343. *Crompt. Jur.* 180, 181, 182, 183.

of

of burning Heath or Fern; and of all other Abuſes and Treſpaſſes in Vert and Veniſon.

If at the *Swainmote* the Preſentment of the Foreſters is found true by the Jury concerning *Vert* or *Veniſon*, then the Offender ſtandeth convicted, and cannot * traverſe the Indictment.

Obſerve; This Court may inquire and convict, † but cannot give Judgment: Therefore a *Swainmote* without a Juſtice-Seat is of no Force. Vide *Table*.

Swan, Is a Royal Bird, and by **Stat.** 22 *Ed.* 4. *c.* 6. ' None (but the King's Son) ' ſhall have any Mark or Game of *Swans* of his ' own, or to his Uſe, except he have Lands ' and Tenements of Freehold worth five Marks ' *per Annum*, beſides ‖ Repriſes; in Pain to ' have them ſeized by any having Lands of that ' Value, to be divided betwixt the King and the ' Seizor.'

Law Caſes.

The Reſolution in the Caſe of *Swans*, in 7 *Coke Rep.* 16. is, That all *Swans* ſwimming in a common River, which have gained their natural Liberty, may be ſeized for the King's Uſe, becauſe they are *Volatilia regalia*; but yet a Subject may have a Property in them, if ſwimming in his own River; and that if they get into a common River, he may retake them upon

---

* 4 *Inſt.* 290.   *Manwood* 340.   *Wood's Inſt.* 497.
† 4 *Inſt.* 290.   2 *Bulſt.* 298.   ‖ Theſe are Duties or Deductions which are yearly paid out of Lands.

a freſh

a fresh Purfuit. That *Cygnets* fhall be equally divided between the Owners of the *Swans*; but that upon the River *Thames*, the Owner of the Lands next the River where the *Swans* have their Nefts fhall have the third Part of the *Cygnets* by Cuftom. That a Man may prefcribe to have *wild Swans*, but not as it was done in this Cafe; for the Defendant ought to have fet forth, that the *Abbot and Convent*, *&c.* and all *thofe whofe Effate they had*, *&c.* ufed to enjoy all the Profits of *Swans*, *&c.*

Stealing *Swans* marked and pinioned, or unmarked, if kept in a Mote, Pond, or private River, and reduced to Tamenefs, is Felony. *Hawkins Pl. Co.* 1 B. 94. Like of young *Cygnets. Co.* 7. 27.

Note; No Fowl can be a Stray, but a *Swan.* 4 *Inft.* 280. See *p.* 80 & 81.

Tithes: A Foreft (though in a Parifh) fhall pay no *Tithes* while in the Hands of the King; but otherwife, if in the Hands of a Subject, or be difafforefted. 1 *Roll. Abr.* 655. 3 *Cro.* 94.

A Park pays *Tithe* of Deer and Herbage by Cuftom; if converted into Tillage, it fhall pay *Tithe* in Kind. *Wood's Inft.* 169. See Page 199.

Trists, Is an Immunity, whereby a Man is freed from Attendance on the Lord of a Foreft when he is difpofed to chafe within the Foreft; and by this Privilege, he fhall not be compelled to hold a Dog to follow the Chafe, or ftand at any Place appointed, which otherwife he is obliged to on Pain of Amerciament. *Jacob's Law Dict.* fub *Tit.*

Tunnels. By **Stat.** 4 & 5 *W.* & *M. cap.* 23. ' If any Perfon, not qualified by Law, do
' keep any Bows, Greyhounds, Setting-dogs,
' Ferrets, Coney-dogs, Hays, Lurchers, Nets,
' *Tunnels*, Low-bells, Harepipes, Snares, or
' other Inftruments for Deftruction of Game,
' and cannot give a good Account to a Juftice,
' before whom he is brought, how he came
' thereby, or produce the Party of whom he
' bought them in fome convenient Time, or
' fome credible Perfon to depofe upon Oath of
' the Sale thereof, he fhall be convicted by the
' faid Juftice, and forfeit not under 5 *s.* nor above
' 20 *s.* to be divided between the Informer and
' the Poor of the Parifh where the Offence was
' committed, to be levied by Diftrefs and Sale,
' &c. and for Want of Diftrefs to be committed
' to the Houfe of Correction not exceeding one
' Month, nor lefs than ten Days, there to be
' whipt and kept to hard Labour. And if any
' Perfon fhall not before the fame Juftice give
' fuch Evidence of his Innocency as aforefaid,
' he fhall be convicted thereof in like Manner
' as the Perfon firft charged therewith is hereby
' directed to be convicted; and fo from Perfon
' to Perfon, till the firft Offender fhall be dif-
' covered.' See *p.* 145 & 147.

Tradefman. See **Apprentice.**

Tenifon, Is one of the greateft Ornaments of the Foreft, and is a Word of Art, proper only to Beafts of Foreft or Chafe; and Lord *Coke* in
his

his 4 *Inst.* 316. says, That whatsoever Beast of the Forest is for the Food of Man, is *Venison,* and whatsoever Beast of the Forest is not for Food of Man, is no *Venison.* See *Table.*

Verderor, Is a judicial Officer of the King's Forest; and he is to observe and keep the Assises or Laws of the Forest, and to view, receive and inrol the Attachments and Presentments of all Manner of Trespasses of the Forest in *Vert* and *Venison,* and to do equal Right and Justice as well to the Poor as to Rich.

Upon a Certificate made to the King in his Court of *Chancery,* That *T. B.* one of the *Verderors* of the Forest of *D.* is dead, there is granted a Writ *de Viridario Eligendo,* directed to the Sheriff of the County where the Forest is, thereby commanding him, in his full County, to choose another, *Manwood* 349. in the same Manner as Coroners. *New Nat. Br.* 366.

The Form of the Writ.

GEORGE the Second, &*c.* *To our Sheriff of* Gloucester, *Greeting. Because T. B. late one of our Verderors of our Forest of D. is dead, as we are informed, therefore we command you, if so it is, that then in your full County, with the Assent of the same County, you cause to be elected one other* Verderor *in the Place of the said* T. B. *who will upon his Oath take the same, as is customary, to do, observe and execute, what belongs to the Office of* Verderor *in the Forest aforesaid; nevertheless cause to be elected him who is best knowing and able to execute that Office, and*

let

let his Name be known to us. Witnefs, *&c.*
F. N. B. 164, 166.

When he is elected, the Sheriff muft fwear
him as follows :

The Form of the Oath, and which points to him out his Office and Duty.

*Y*O*U fhall well and truly ferve our Sovereign
Lord the King in the Office of a* Verderor
in the Foreft of D. *you fhall, to the uttermoft of your
Power, do the beft you can for the Profit of the King,
fo far as it doth appertain for you to do ; you fhall
preferve the antient Rights and Franchifes of the
Crown ; you fhall not conceal from his Majefty any
Right and Privileges, nor any Offence in Vert or
Venifon, nor any other Thing : You fhall not with-
draw or abridge any Default, but fhall endeavour
yourfelf to manifeft and redrefs the fame, and if you
cannot do that of yourfelf, you fhall give Knowledge
thereof to the King, or his Juftice of the Foreft.
You fhall deal indifferently with all the King's Liege
People : You fhall execute the Laws of the Foreft,
and do equal Right and Juftice, as well unto the
Poor as to the Rich, in that appertaineth to your
Office : You fhall not opprefs any Perfon by Colour
thereof, for any Reward, Favour or Malice ; all
thefe Things you fhall, to the utmoft of your Power,
obferve and keep.*

So help you God.

The

The Perfon thus chofen ought to be an Efquire, or Gentleman of good Eftate, and learned in the Foreft Laws ; and becaufe he is chofen in fome Manner as a Coroner ; fo in fome Refpects his Office is alike, for as a Coroner is to make Inqueft *upon the View of the Body*, and upon the Oath of twelve Men, how and in what Manner the Perfon was killed ; fo a *Verderor*, upon Notice given, is to view the Deer, which are killed or hurt, and to take an Inquifition *by four of the next Villages to the Foreft*, how and by whom they were killed ; which Inquifition fhall be written in the Roll, the Finder fhall be put by fix Pledges, and the Flefh fhall be fent to a Spittle-Houfe, if by the Teftimony of the *Verderors* and Country there be any nigh ; but if there be no fuch Houfe nigh, the Flefh fhall be given to the Poor and Lame ; the Head and Skin fhall be given to the next Town, and the Arrow, if there be any found, fhall be prefented to the *Verderor*, and inrolled in his Roll. *Note* ; If the Deer is fit to be eaten by the better fort of People, 'tis then to be difpofed of at the Pleafure of the Juftice of the Foreft. *Manwood* 350. *The Affifes of the Foreft* 7. *Manwood* 4. 9.

There are ufually in every Foreft four *Verderors* ; they are liable to be removed for Tranfgreffions, but if the Suggeftion is falfe, on Certificate thereof, and Commiffion out of Chancery, the Sheriff by Writ is to reftore him. *Manwood* 352. *Fitz. New Nat. Brev.* 383.

By *Affifes and Cuftoms of the Foreft*, c. 21.
‘ When *Verderors* have taken an Inqueft, one
‘ fhall

' fhall fet to his Seal, and the other keep the
' Roll; and fo from Time to Time till the
' coming of the Juftice : Then the firft Day
' he and all the Minifters fhall prefent the Roll,
' or elfe they fhall be amerced, and Mainpri-
' fors that Day fhall be preferred for the Foreft,
' or elfe they fhall incur a Seizure.'

If a *Verderor* dies, his Heir is to bring in the
Roll of his Anceftor's Time. 4 *Inft.* 312. See
Rolls.

If the *Verderor* alien his Land or die feifed,
and no Man bringeth in the Rolls, then the Land
fhall be feized by the Sheriff, which the *Verderor*
had, until the Rolls be brought in : And if the
Rolls be loft, then till he make his Fine, and
have his *Oufter le Main,* i. e. a Livery of his
Lands out of the King's Hands. *Ibid.* See the
Table.

Uert. *Green-Hue,* Is one of the principal Ornaments of the Foreft, (and *Venifon* is the other)
and is every Tree, Under-wood, Bufh, and fuch
like growing in a Foreft, and bearing green *
Leaves, which may cover or feed the Deer,
and is of three Sorts, *viz. Over-Vert,* which is
great Woods and Trees, as well thofe which
bear no Fruit as thofe which do. *Nether-Vert,*
which is properly all Manner of Under-woods,
Bufhes, Thorns, &c. and *Special Vert,* which
may be either *Over* or *Nether Vert,* or both if it
bears Fruit, for nothing is accounted *Special
Vert,* but fuch which beareth Fruit to feed the

---

* *Vert* comprehends every Thing which bears *Green*
Leaves in the Foreft. *Manwood.* 146.

Deer,

Deer, unlefs it is in the King's Demefne Woods and then every Tree which grows therein, whether great or fmall Wood, or whether it beareth Fruit or not, is accounted *Special Vert*, and is privileged in a particular Manner; and therefore the Offenders in this Kind of *Vert*, which is the *King-Vert*, are more feverely punifhed than thofe who offend in the *Vert of other Men*; for whofoever cuts this *Vert* and carries them away with Cart and Horfes, *&c.* both Cart and Horfes, *&c.* are forfeited to the King, and the Offender fhall be fined to the Value of the Wood. 4 *Inft.* 317. *Manwood* 354, 355, 356, 357, 358.

The *Vert of common Perfons* is the *Over-Vert*, *Nether-Vert* and *Special Vert*, that are not in the King's Woods; and by the *Affifes and Cuftoms of the Foreft, cap.* 1. ' If any Forefter ' fhall find any Man attachable for *Vert* in the ' Foreft, firft he fhall attach him by two ' Pledges, if they be to be found; if not, he ' fhall be brought to the next Town where ' they may be found; and if he be afterwards ' found, he fhall attach him by four Pledges; ' and if the third Time, he fhall be prefented ' before the Verderors, and be put by eight ' Pledges; and after the third Attachment, his ' Body fhall be attached and retained, that he ' may remember what Thing *Vert* is.' *Manwood* 359, 407.

If any Man offend in cutting down *Vert* in the Foreft, and dieth after it is prefented; yet the King fhall be anfwered for this Trefpafs, either by the Heirs of the Deceafed, or by the

Tenant of his Land. *Aſſiſe Pickering, fo.* 22. *Manwood* 306.

Viſne. A *Viſne* may come from a Foreſt, and ſo it may from a Park, but not from a Walk in a Foreſt. *Hawk. P. C.* 2 *Book,* 183.

Vivary, Signifieth a Place in Land or Water, where living Things are kept; and moſt commonly in Law ſignifieth Park, Warren, Piſcary, &c. 2 *Inſt.* 100.

Walkers, Foreſt Officers appointed to walk about a certain Space of Ground committed to their Care.

Warden of the Foreſt. The *Chief Warden of a Foreſt* is an Officer of great Authority, and next to the Chief Juſtice in *Eyre,* in order to bail and diſcharge Offenders out of Cuſtody, who are impriſoned or indicted for Offences in the Foreſt; but he is not a judicial Officer, becauſe he may make a Deputy by the Foreſt Law; and where-ever there is a *Caſtle* in a Foreſt, the *Conſtable of that Caſtle* is always *Chief Warden,* as the Conſtable of *Windſor* Caſtle is always *Chief Warden* of that Foreſt. 4 *Inſt.* 313.

By **Stat.** 1 *Ed.* 3. *Stat.* 1. *c.* 1. ' If any
' Perſon is taken in the very Act, and impri-
' ſoned or indicted for the *Vert* or *Veniſon*; the
' Chief *Warden* of the Foreſt ſhall let him to
' Mainpriſe until the Eyre, without taking any
' Thing for his Deliverance; which if he refuſe
' to do, then the Party grieved ſhall have a
' Writ out of the Chancery, of old ordained for
' Perſons indicted to be bailed till the Eyre; and
' that

‘ that if upon the Service of ſuch Writ, the
‘ *Warden* will not deliver the Perſon indicted
‘ to *Mainpriſe*, then he ſhall have another Writ
‘ out of the Chancery, directed to the Sheriff
‘ of the County, &c. to attach the *Warden* to
‘ anſwer his Default before the King at a cer-
‘ tain Day; and then the Sheriff (having called
‘ the Verderors to him) ſhall deliver the Perſon
‘ indicted by good Mainpriſe, in the Preſence
‘ of the ſaid Verderors, and ſhall deliver the
‘ Names of the Mainpernors to the ſame Ver-
‘ derors, to anſwer in the Eyre before the Juſ-
‘ tices. And if the Chief Warden be thereof
‘ attainted, he ſhall be awarded to pay treble
‘ Damages to the Party grieved, and be com-
‘ mitted to Priſon, and be ranſomed at the
‘ King’s Will.’

‘ And from henceforth it ſhall be written to
‘ him as to the Chief *Warden of the Foreſt*, be-
‘ cauſe he may not be Juſtice, nor have any
‘ Record but in the Eyre.’

If the *Warden* of the Foreſt die, and his Heir
or Tertenant bring not in the Rolls, &c. his
Heir or Tertenant ſhall anſwer for the ſame.
4 *Inſt.* 313.

Warrant. See **Hunting.**

Warren. A * Warren is a Franchiſe or
Liberty by Grant of the King, or by Preſcription,
for the Preſervation of Beaſts, and Fowls of
Warren only. † Beaſts, as Hares, Conies, &c.
Fowls, as Partridge, Pheaſant, Quail, Rail,
Wood-cock; or Water-Fowl, as Mallard, Hern,

* *Manwood* 362, 363.　† 1 *Inſt.* 233. *a.*

M 2　　　　　&c.

&c. * A Chafe, Park or *Warren* are collateral
Inheritances, and not iffuing out of the Soil as
Common doth. † A Free *Warren* may lie open,
there being no Neceffity of inclofing it ; and one
may have a *Warren* in another's Land ; for the
Grantee may, alien the Land and referve the
Franchife. ‡ But no one can make a *Warren*
appropriate thofe Creatures that are *feræ Naturæ*,
without the King's Licence.

Note; An Ejectment doth not lie of a Warren.
1 *Keb.* 506.

By **Stat.** 9 *Geo.* 1 *c.* 22. *f.* 1 ' If any Perfon,
' armed and difguifed, fhall appear in any
' *Warren*, or Place where Hares are ufually
' kept, or unlawfully rob any fuch *Warren*;
' or (*whether armed or difguifed or not*) fhall
' refcue any Perfon in Cuftody for either of the
' faid Offences, or procure any to join with him
' in fuch unlawful Act; fhall be guilty of Felony
' without Benefit of Clergy.'

A Warrant for unlawfully entering any
Warren. [22 & 23 *Car.* 2. *c.* 25. Vide
Tit. *Hares*].

Somerfet, ⎫ **W**Hereas an *Information is laid*
to wit. ⎰ *before me,* (*being one of his*
Majefty's Juftices of Peace for this County) *by*
W. L. *of,* &c. *Warrener, that* J. D. *of,* &c. *did*
wrongfully enter into his Warren *or Ground, law-*

* 4 *Inft.* 318.   † *Wood's Inft.* 208.   ‡ 2 *Inft.* 199.
11 *Rep.* 87.

fully

*fully used or kept for Breeding or Keeping of Conies,
and did then and there chase, take or kill Conies,
against the Will of the Owner or Occupier thereof,
not having any Title or lawful Authority so to do:
These are therefore to require you, on Sight hereof,
to bring the said* J. D. *before me, to shew Cause
why the Penalty of the Act of Parliament should
not be levied on him for his Offence.* Given, &c.

A Warrant to levy the Penalty.

To the Constable of, &c. and to the
Keeper of, &c.

Somerset, ⎰ *WHereas* J. D. *of,* &c. *is law-
to wit.* ⎱ *fully convicted before me, (being
one of his Majesty's Justices of the Peace for this
County) by the Oath of one Witness, of his wrongfully entering into the* Warren of W. L. *lying in the
Parish of* S. *in this County, on,* &c. *and then and
there did chase, take or kill Conies, against the Will
of the said Owner or Occupier thereof, the said* J.
D. *not having Title or lawful Authority so to do:
Therefore I do hereby order, that the said* J. D.
shall presently pay to the said W. L. *the Sum of,*
&c. *being treble Costs and Damages: And you are
hereby required to convey the said* J. D. *to the Gaol
at,* &c. *for the said County, and deliver him to the
Keeper thereof: And you the said Keeper are hereby
commanded to keep him the said* J. D. *in safe Custody for the Space of three Months.* Given, &c.

Le

Law Cafes.

Where a Man is feifed of a Manor, in which he had a *Warren,* and made a Feoffment of the faid Manor *cum pertinentiis*; it was held, that the *Warren* did not pafs, becaufe 'tis a collateral Inheritance, and doth not iffue out of the Soil; but this Cafe is denied to be Law, for it hath been fince adjudged, that by a Grant of a Manor *cum pertinentiis,* the *Warren* will pafs. *Bro. Abr.* Tit. *Warren.* 4 *Inft.* 318.

T. S. had a *Warren* in another Man's Land, and afterwards he granted the faid *Warren* to *E. G.* Adjudged, *that by the Grant of the* Warren *the Soil did not pafs,* probably for the Reafon mentioned in the laft Cafe, *(viz.)* becaufe a *Warren* is a collateral Inheritance, and doth not iffue out of the Soil. 3 *Bulft.* 82. *Cro. Eliz.* 547. S. C.

So where one Man was Lord of the Manor of *H.* in which Manor another Man had a *Warren* belonging to the Manor of *D.* and afterwards both thefe Manors came into one Hand, by the Purchafe of the Manor of *D.* Adjudged, that by the Union of the Land and the *Warren,* that the *Warren* was not extinct but ftill remained. Lord *Mounfon*'s Cafe, *Cro. Car.* 4 *Inft.* 318. So adjudged in the Cafe of a *Chafe.*

If a Man fprings a Pheafant on his own Land, and his Hawk flies at it, and purfues it into the *Warren* of *T. S.* the Owner of the Hawk cannot juftify the Entry into the *Warren,* and taking both the Hawk and Pheafant; but 'tis otherwife

if

if the Soil was not a *Warren.* 2 *Roll. Abr.*
567.

Sir *Richard Harriſon* claimed a *Warren* by Preſcription in *Windſor* Foreſt, and the Attorney
General *Noy*, at a Juſtice-Seat held for the
Foreſt, affirmed that the Claim was not good,
unleſs it had been *allowed in Eyre*; and therefore
he being preſented for the *Warren* was fined 10 *s.*
and it was ordered that the *Warren* ſhould be
deſtroyed. Sir *Rich. Harriſon*'s Caſe, *W. Jones*'s
Rep. 280. Vide Tit. **Conies.**

Waſte, Signifies a Spoil and Deſtruction in
the Covert and Paſtures of the Foreſt.

If a Man on his own Inheritance fell or cut
down any Wood, which grows ſcattering, or
any thick Covert in the Foreſt without Licence
of the Chief Juſtice in *Eyre* or View of the
Foreſters, 'tis *Waſte. Manwood* 366.

There is a Difference between *Deſtruction* and
Waſte in a Foreſt; for every *Deſtruction* of the
Covert is *Waſte*, and perpetually ſo; but every
Waſte is not *Deſtruction*; for a Man may fell his
Woods and deſtroy the Covert for a Time, and
by preſerving the Fences, the ſame may be Co-
vert again. *Ibid.* 366.

If a Man hath a Licence to fell Woods which
are Coverts in a Foreſt, and he felleth them, but
doth not make Fences to preſerve the Sprouts,
ſo that they are eaten and deſtroyed by the Cattle,
that they never grow again, this is *Waſte* and
Deſtruction; and ſo it is if he fell them at
unſeaſonable Times and they die. *Ibid.* 367.

He who commits *Waſte*, either by felling
Trees or deſtroying any Covert or Wood, is

to be fined by the Chief Juſtice in *Eyre,* and the whole Wood or Place ſo *waſted* ſhall be ſeized to the Uſe of the King; and ſo it ſhall remain till the Owner hath paid the Fine; and if the Offender dies before any Preſentment be made of the Offence, yet the Heir ſhall be fined, and the Land ſeized till he pays the Fine; and the like Law is when the *Waſte* is done by plowing any Meadow. *Anno* 8 *Ed.* 3. *Aſſiſe Pickering, fo.* 22. *Manwood* 368.

The Fine in theſe Caſes is neither certain nor altogether arbitrary, becauſe the Number of Acres contained in the Place *waſted* is mentioned in the Indictment or Preſentment, and uſually the Chief Juſtice in *Eyre* doth aſſeſs the Fine according to the Number of thoſe Acres; and not only according to the Number, but the Value of ſuch Acres *waſted* is likewiſe ſet forth in the Indictment; in which Indictment theſe Things are ſpecially to be conſidered. 1. Who made the *Waſte.* 2. What Manner of *Waſte* is done. 3. When it was done. 4. Where the Ground is, in which it was done. 5. In whoſe Tenure it was at that Time. 6. What Number of Acres it doth contain. 7. What every Acre is worth to be ſold. 8. Whether it be *Waſte* or *Deſtruction,* or both. 9. In whoſe Fee it is, and in what Pariſh. 10. Whoſe Inheritance it is. *Manwood* 369.

If the King pardons Tranſgreſſions in a Foreſt, this doth not pardon the *Waſte.* Sir *Walter Tichburne*'s Caſe, *Iter Windſor. W. Jones's Rep.* 279.

Weat.

𝔚𝔢𝔞𝔯. By 𝔖𝔱𝔞𝔱. 11 *Hen.* 7. *cap.* 5. ' Every
' Man may pull down the *Wears* and Engines
' in the Haven of *Southampton*, between *Calfhord*
' and *Redbridge* ; and whofoever levieth any
' other there fhall forfeit 100 *l.* to the King.
' Vide *Table.*'

𝔚𝔦𝔩𝔡-𝔇𝔲𝔠𝔨, &c. By 𝔖𝔱𝔞𝔱. 9 *Ann. c.* 25.,
f. 4. ' If any Perfon whatfoever between 1 *July,*
' and 1 *September* * in any Year, fhall by Hays,
' Tunnels or other Nets, drive and take any
' *Wild-Duck,* Teal, Widgeon or any other
' Fowl, commonly called Water-Fowl, in any
' Place of Refort for Wild-Fowl, in the Moult-
' ing Seafon, the Offender being convicted there-
' of before one Juftice of the Peace for the
' County where the Offence fhall be committed,
' and by the Oath of one credible Witnefs,
' he fhall forfeit 5 *s.* for every fuch Fowl, one
' Moiety to the Informer, the other to the Poor
' of the Parifh where the Offence was done, to
' be levied by a Warrant of the Juftice before
' whom the Offender was convicted, by Sale
' and Diftrefs of his Goods, rendering the Over-
' plus above the Penalty and Charges of Dif-
' ftrefs ; and for Want of Diftrefs, to be com-
' mitted to the Houfe of Correction for any
' Time not exceeding one Month, nor lefs than
' fourteen Days, there to be whipt and kept to
' hard Labour ; and the Juftice fhall caufe fuch
' Hays and Nets to be feized and immediately,
' to be deftroyed in his Prefence.'

* See *Stat.* 10 *Geo.* 2: *c.* 32. *p.*

M 5   But

But the said Act of 9 *Ann.* being found by
Experience to be ineffectual, by Reason that the
Wild-Fowl have not done moulting by the first
of *September*, so that great Numbers were yearly
destroyed, contrary to the Meaning of the said
Act ; therefore,

By **Stat.** 10 *Geo.* 2. *c.* 32. ' If any Person
' shall in any Year between 1 *July* and 1 *October*,
' by Hays, *&c.* or other Nets, drive and
' take any *Wild-Duck*, Teal, Widgeon, or any
' other Water-Fowl in any Marshes, Fens, or
' other Places of Resort for Wild-Fowl, and
' shall be thereof convicted in such Manner as
' in the said Act 9 *Anna* is prescribed, shall be
' liable to the same Penalties and Punishment as
' by the said Act is directed.'

Winter-Heyning, A Season which is excepted from the Liberty of Commoning in the Forest
of *Dean.*

Wood. By **Stat.** 1 *Ed.* 3. *c.* 2. ' Every
' Man having * *Woods* in the Forest might take
' House-bote and Hay-bote in his *Woods*, (which
' he had in the old Forests) without being at-
' tached for the same by the Officers of the Fo-
' rest, so that it be done by the *View of the Fo-*
' *resters.*'

By **Stat.** 22 *Ed.* 4. *c.* 7. ' Where a Man
' hath *Woods* in his own Ground within the old

---

* 'Tis necessary that there should be *Woods* in every
Forest, as well to shelter as at some Times to feed the Deer ;
and where the Trees grow scattering and at such a Distance
that they do not touch one another, such Places are properly called *Woods.* See **Covert.**

6

' Forests,

' Forefts, and fhall cut them down by the
' King's Licence where the *Foreft Purlieu* or
' *Chafe* belongs to the King, or without Licence
' where they belong to the Subject, he may
' inclofe the Soil for feven Years next after fuch
' cutting down.'

Law Cafes.

A Seizure being made of the Lord *Lovelace's*
Wood, for a Fine of 13 *s.* 4 *d.* the fame was
ftaid at the Juftice-Seat ; but his Claim of a
Privilege to fell *Wood* in the Foreft, without
Licence or View of the Forefters, was not allowed ; though in 4 *Inft.* 298. a *Prefcription* to
fell and fell *Wood* without View was held good ;
but at a Juftice-Seat held for the Foreft of *Wind-*
for, that was held to be no Law. *W. Jones's*
Rep. 270.

For in *Whitlock's* Cafe it was held at a Juftice-
Seat, that a Man may fell *Woods* in a Foreft for
the Fire or other neceffary Boots, by the View
of the Forefters or Verderors, but not to *fell*
without the Writ *Ad quod damnum* ; and that if
a Forefter takes any Thing for his Viewing,
'tis Extortion. *Whitlock's* Cafe, *W. Jones* 268,
277.

It was agreed at the faid Juftice-Seat, that
the Chief Warden of the Foreft could not grant
a Licence to fell *Trees* there ; nor the Chief
Juftice in Eyre, unlefs 'tis granted *fedente Curia*,
or after a Writ *Ad quod damnum. W. Jones's*
Rep. 277.

The Defendant was presented for felling *Timber-Trees* in *Windsor Forest*; and thereupon he at the Justice-Seat produced the King's Warrant in these Words, *(viz.)* *Whereas* Bagshot *Rails are in Decay, therefore he* (the Defendant) *should cause as much Timber to be felled, as would be convenient for the Repairs thereof*; and this was held to be no good Warrant, because the Decay of the Rails ought first to be *viewed*, and an Estimate to be made thereof; and then such a Warrant might be granted, but not before. Sir *Charles Howard*'s Case, *W. Jones*.

At the same Justice-Seat it was held, that a *Presentment* made by all the Officers of the Forest, that *Wood* and *Timber* was felled there, and by whom, is sufficient Evidence to convict the Offender. *W. Jones* 268.

The Inhabitants of *Egham*, and of all the Towns in *Surrey* within *Windsor Forest* joined in a Claim to cut down their *Coppices* at Pleasure; and *Noy* the Attorney General insisted at a Justice-Seat, that since the Charter of the Forest was made, a *Prescription* to cut down *Wood* there is not good; for by that Charter it was granted, that all Freeholders should have their *Woods* in Forests, as they had them at the Time of the *Coronation* of *H. 1.* which was above 120 Years before that Charter was granted; nay, a Prescription to cut down *Wood* by the View of the Foresters and Verderors is not good, for it must be *per Visum & allocationem, &c.* because if 'tis *per Visum* only, then if a Forester or Verderor is required

required to view it, and he refuseth, it may be cut down without View. *W. Jones* 275.

An *Under-Keeper* being presented at the said Juſtice-Seat for cutting *unlawful Brouſe-Wood*, ſaid in his Defence, that he cut it by the *King's Order to ſell*, and with the Money to buy *Hay* for the Deer in hard Weather. The Attorney General ſaid, that the King's Commands ought to be obeyed; but that there is a legal Way to put them in Execution. *Rowland Repley's* Caſe, *W. Jones* 279.

So where one was preſented for *felling and carrying away ſeven Timber-Trees*; he inſiſted at a Juſtice-Seat, that thoſe *Trees* were cut down to repair a *Bridge* which the King ought to repair, and that the Lops were ſold to pay the Workmen with the Money ariſing by ſuch Sale. And though the Verderors affirmed, that the *Timber* was imployed as aforeſaid, yet he was fined 5 s. for his undue Taking the *Trees*. *Clifton's* Caſe, *W. Jones* 279.

Though a Man may cut down his own *Woods* in a Foreſt for neceſſary Boots, without View of the Foreſters or Verderors; yet ſome Officer of the Foreſt ought to preſent it at the next *Court of Attachments*, and how much was felled, and that they had ſeen it, that it may appear on Record what Quantity was cut down. *W. Jones* 295. See the *Table*.

𝖂𝖔𝖔𝖉-𝖈𝖔𝖈𝖐, Is a Fowl of Warren. 1 *Inſt.* 233. *a.*

𝖂𝖔𝖔𝖉-𝕲𝖊𝖑𝖉, Is taken to be the Gathering or Cutting of Wood within the Foreſt; or it ſignifies to be free from Payment of Money for taking Wood

Wood in any Foreſt.' *Cromp. Juriſ.* 157. *Co. Lit.* 233.

Wood-mote, Is the old Name of that Court of the Foreſt, now called the *Court of Attachments.*

Wood-Plea-Court, A Court held twice a Year in the Foreſt of *Clun* in *Shropſhire,* for determining all Matters of Wood and Agiſtments. *Jac. Law Dict.* ſub Tit.

Woodward, Is an Officer of the Foreſt whoſe Charge is to look after the Woods and Verr there; his very Name denotes his Office; he muſt preſent all Offences within his Charge at the Court of *Attachments* or *Swainmote,* to the Chief Foreſters or Verderors; and if he ſee or know any Malefactors, or if he find any Deer killed or hurt, he muſt acquaint a Verderor therewith, and preſent the ſame at the next Court of the Foreſt, and in theſe Particulars his Oath doth conſiſt; but he cannot make any Attachments; and by the Law he muſt not walk with Bow and Arrows, but with a Foreſt-Bill or Hatchet. *Manwood* 389, 390, 409.

Sed. Q. If he may not attach Malefactors, for it may be impoſſible for him to preſent them to the Chief Foreſter, becauſe they may be gone before he finds the Foreſter. And indeed the 11th *Artic.* of the Aſſiſes of the Foreſt ſeems to clear this, for it is there ſaid, ' *Si quis viderit aliquos* ' *Malefactores infra Metas Foreſtæ aliquam feram* ' *capere vel aſportare, debet illos capere ſecundum* ' *poſſe ſuum;* ' which Words, ' *Si quis viderit* ' *Malefactores, &c.* being general, extend (as I apprehend)

apprehend) to *Woodwards* as well as all other Minifters of the Foreft.

The *Woodward* ought to appear at every Juftice-Seat, and when he is called he muft prefent his Hatchet to the Lord Chief Juftice in Eyre.

Where the King hath a Wood in his own Land in a Foreft, and *leafeth* the fame to another, the Leffee ought to provide a *Woodward*; and if he doth not appear at the Courts of the Foreft, the Wood fhall be feized, and alfo the Office of the *Woodward*; the Law is the fame where a Subjeft has a Wood in a Foreft. *W. Jones.* 278.

THE

THE

INDEX.

A.

The INDEX.

The

G.

N   A De-

The

N 2   𝕳eath.

I.

The INDEX.

N.

N 4   A

N 6.

Assises

6

27 *H.*

The INDEX.

F I N I S.

A P P E N D I X.

Since this Edition was printed off, the two following Acts have passed relating to the Game.

Doves.

[See Stat. 1 *Jac.* 1. *c.* 27. *p.* 213.]

BY Stat. 2 *Geo.* 3. *c.* 9. it is enacted, 'That if any Person after the 24th of 'June, 1762, shall shoot at, with an Intent 'to kill, or shall by any means whatsoever 'kill or take, with a wilful Intent to de- 'stroy, any House-Dove, or Pigeon, and 'shall be thereof convicted by Confession, or 'Oath of one Witness, before a Justice of the 'Peace of the County, or Place, wherein 'such Offence shall be committed, or the 'Offender apprehended, he shall for every 'Offence forfeit 20*s.* to the Prosecutor; and 'if not forthwith paid, he may be committed 'by such Justice to the common Goal of the 'County, or the House of Correction, in the 'Division or Place where he is convicted or 'apprehended, there to remain and be kept to 'hard-Labour for any Time not exceeding

" *three,*

' *three*, nor lefs than *one* Calendar Month, as
' fuch Juftice fhall order, unlefs the Forfei-
' ture be fooner paid.

   ' Provided, that nothing in this Act fhall
' be conftrued to hinder any Owner of a Dove-
' Cote, Pigeon-Houfe, or Pigeon-Chamber,
' or any other Place, built for the Preferva-
' tion or Breeding of Pigeons, from taking,
' killing, or deftroying, by himfelf or others,
' any Houfe-Dove, or Pigeon, in his own
' proper Dove-Cote, Pigeon-Houfe, &c.

   ' No Perfon convicted of any Offence a-
' gainft this Act, fhall be liable to be con-
' victed for any fuch Offence under any other
' Act; and Profecutions on this Act are to be
' commenced and carried on with Effect with-
' in two Calendar Months after the Offence;
' and where any Perfon fhall fuffer Imprifon-
' ment for Default of Payment of any Penalty
' impofed under this Act, he fhall not be lia-
' ble afterwards to Pay fuch penalty.'

Partridge, &c.

   By Stat. 2 *Geo.* 3. *c.* 19. ' For the better
' Prefervation of the Game', it is enacted,
' That *no Perfon* (*a*), after the firft of *June*,
' 1762, fhall, upon any Pretence whatfo-
' ever, take, kill, deftroy, carry, fell, buy,
' or have in his, her, or their Poffeffion
' or Ufe, any Partridge, (*b*) between the
' twelfth of *February* and firft of *September*, in

(*a*) That is, whether qualified to kill Game or not.
(*b*) See Tit Pheafant, p. 214.

          ' any

' any Year; or any Pheafant (c), between firft
' of *February*, and firft of *October*, in any
' Year; or any Heath Fowl (d), commonly
' called Black Game, between firft of *Ja-*
' *nuary*, and twentieth of *Auguft*, in any
' Year; or any Groufe (e), commonly called
' Red Game, between firft of *December* and
' twenty-fifth of *July*, in any Year.

' This Act not to extend to any Pheafant
' taken in the Seafon allowed by this Act, and
' kept in Mews or Breeding-places.

' This Act not to extend to *Scotland*.

' Perfons offending in any of the aforefaid
' Cafes, and convicted thereof by the Oath of
' one Witnefs, fhall forfeit for every Bird,
' five Pounds to the Profecutor, to be recover-
' ed with full Cofts, by Action of Debt, Bill,
' Plaint, or Information, in any of the Courts
' at *Weftminfter*; and no Effoin, Wager of
' Law, or more than one Imparlance fhall be
' allowed.

' The whole of the pecuniary Penalties, un-
' der the Act of 8 *Geo.* 1. (f) c. 19. may be fu-
' ed for and recovered, to the fole Ufe of the
' Profecutor, by Action of Debt, or on the
' Cafe, Bill, Plaint, or Information, in any
' of the Courts at *Weftminfter*, and no Effoin,

(c) Ibid.
(d) See p. 136, 137.
(e) Ibid.
(f) " For the better Recovery of the Penalties inflicted upon Perfons who deftroy the Game," See Tit
Game, p. 116.

' &c.

‘ &c. fhall be allowed; and if Plaintiff recovers,
‘ he fhall have double Cofts; and no Part of
‘ the Penalty recovered to go to the Ufe of
‘ the Poor of the Parifh, wherein the Of-
‘ fence fhall be committed.

‘ Profecutions to be within fix Months after
the Fact done.’

Breinigsville, PA USA
28 September 2009
224862BV00003B/109/A